AMONG
THE
HEROES

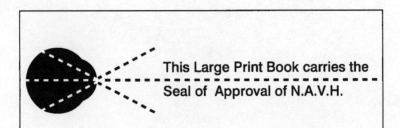

This Large Print Book carries the
Seal of Approval of N.A.V.H.

AMONG THE HEROES

United Flight 93 and the Passengers and Crew Who Fought Back

JERE LONGMAN

WHEELER PUBLISHING

Published in 2003 by arrangement with HarperCollins Publishers, Inc.

Wheeler Large Print Hardcover Series.

The text of this Large Print edition is unabridged. Other aspects of the book may vary from the original edition.

Set in 16 pt. Plantin by Elena Picard.

Printed in the United States on permanent paper.

Library of Congress Cataloging-in-Publication Data

Longman, Jere.
  Among the heroes : United Flight 93 and the passengers and crew who fought back / Jere Longman.
    p. cm.
  Originally published: New York : HarperCollins, 2002.
  ISBN 1-58724-360-1 (lg. print : hc : alk. paper)
  1. United Airlines Flight 93 Hijacking Incident, 2001.
2. September 11 Terrorist Attacks, 2001. 3. Hijacking of aircraft — United States. 4. Victims of terrorism — United States. 5. Aircraft accident victims — United States.
6. Heroes — United States. 7. Large type books. I. Title.
HV6432.7 .L65 2003
  974.8′79044—dc21   2002190763

In Memoriam

Captain Jason Dahl
First Officer LeRoy Homer Jr.

Flight Attendants

Lorraine Bay
Sandra Bradshaw

Wanda Green
CeeCee Lyles
Deborah Welsh

Passengers

Christian Adams
Todd Beamer
Alan Beaven
Mark Bingham
Deora Bodley
Marion Britton
Thomas Burnett Jr.
William Cashman
Georgine Corrigan
Patricia Cushing
Joseph DeLuca
Patrick Driscoll
Edward Felt
Jane Folger
Colleen Fraser
Andrew Garcia

Jeremy Glick
Kristin White Gould
Lauren Grandcolas
Donald Greene
Linda Gronlund
Richard Guadagno
Toshiya Kuge
Hilda Marcin
Waleska Martinez
Nicole Miller
Louis Nacke II
Donald Peterson
Jean Hoadley Peterson
Mark Rothenberg
Christine Snyder
John Talignani
Honor Elizabeth
    Wainio

ACKNOWLEDGMENTS

I am deeply indebted to the family members, friends and coworkers of those aboard Flight 93. In the midst of their grieving, they answered my questions with grace and patience far beyond what I had a right to expect. The same strength and dignity possessed by the passengers and crew are evident in their families. Without their assistance, this book could not have been written.

I would also like to thank Wallace Miller, the coroner of Somerset County, Pennsylvania. He gave me a tour of the crash site, always took my phone calls and provided invaluable guidance with his unflinching honesty. Joe Hopkins, a spokesman for United Airlines, and Bill Crowley, an agent and spokesman for the FBI in Pittsburgh, were helpful and always up-front about the questions they could answer, and those they could not.

At *The New York Times*, my editors Neil Amdur and Bill Brink were remarkably accommodating during the months it took to research and write this book. Sara Rimer and Jo Thomas, with whom I covered the crash of Flight 93, are superb reporters. I am also grateful to my *Times* colleagues Kevin Sack, Steven Erlanger, Matt Wald, Don Van Natta, David Johnston, Kate Zernicke, Steve Engelberg and Nick Fox for their direction.

I would like to thank my editor at HarperCollins, David Hirshey, for proposing the book and for his encouragement and frank advice. Jeff Kellogg at HarperCollins also juggled expertly many duties involving the manuscript and photographs. And I want to thank Lydia Weaver for her deft handling of last-minute changes. My agent Susan Reed was a constant source of support, especially during the early stages.

Finally, only with the great understanding and reassurance of my wife, Deborah Longman, and my daughter, Julie-Ann, could a project so unexpected and consuming as this one have been completed.

PREFACE

On September 11, 2001, passengers were not encouraged to assist the crew in the rare case of an airplane hijacking. They were actively discouraged. Passengers were to be mollified with food and drink, with vague information and nebulous assurance. That all changed with the brave insurrection of the passengers and crew members aboard United Flight 93, which was hijacked en route from Newark, New Jersey, to San Francisco. Having learned about the horrific unfolding of the morning's events from a series of telephone calls, and given time to act, those aboard the jetliner thwarted an attempt by the terrorists to crash the plane into a Washington landmark of government or security. As Americans, we believed we had control over our lives inside secure borders. On the day we lost that control, the forty passengers and crew members attempted to regain it. And thus, they won the first battle in the new war against terrorism.

"We believe those passengers on this jet

were absolute heroes," Robert S. Mueller III, director of the FBI, said at a memorial at the Flight 93 crash site outside of Shanksville, Pennsylvania. "And their actions during this flight were heroic."

Many crucial questions about the final minutes of the flight remain unanswered, but it is clear the passengers and crew acted with heroic defiance. They accomplished what security guards and military pilots and government officials could not — they impeded the terrorists, giving their lives and allowing hundreds or thousands of others to live.

"Flight 93 redefined sacrifice for me," President George W. Bush told *The Washington Post*. "And if a handful of people will drive an airplane into the ground to save either me, or the White House, or the Congress, you know others in our country will make the sacrifice to save us down the road."

I covered the crash of Flight 93 as a reporter for *The New York Times*, along with my colleagues Sara Rimer and Jo Thomas. When the idea of a book was proposed to me, I hesitated. There is no worse job for a journalist than having to speak with grieving families. Nothing you say can provide any solace. And in these disconsolate times, the last thing family members want is a notebook or camera thrust into their faces. Then I reconsidered. It seemed that someone ought to write about these remarkable people. Many years from now, their brave uprising will surely be remembered as a defining moment in American history.

This book was meant to accomplish three things — to recreate the actions aboard Flight 93 in as much detail as is known, to commemorate the forty passengers and crew members, and to attempt to understand how Ziad Jarrah, the hijacker pilot, became radicalized to the point of suicidal terrorism. It was important to write about all the pilots, flight attendants and passengers. While there is no doubt about the heroism of the four or five passengers who became well known from their phone calls, it would be reckless to assume they were the only ones who acted heroically.

"The term that keeps coming into my mind is esprit de corps," said Lisa Beamer, whose husband, Todd, was a passenger on Flight 93. "There were probably some people who hatched the plan and initiated it to other people, but I don't think there were people sitting back, going, 'Please don't jump on the hijackers, they might explode.' I've felt strongly all along that people did what they could do, whether it was pushing a cart down the aisle, or boiling water, or comforting others, or cheering them on."

For this book, I contacted the families of each passenger and crew member. All agreed to speak with me; in the end, only one did

11

not. I also contacted friends and coworkers of each passenger and crew member. And, after weeks of trying, I reached by phone, in Lebanon, the family of Jarrah, the hijacker pilot. Upon conducting more than three hundred interviews, I came to realize that the passengers and crew members aboard Flight 93 were not ordinary citizens placed in an extraordinary situation, as they have often been portrayed. As a group, these were people who were on top of their game, who kept score in their lives and who became successful precisely because they were assertive and knew how to make a plan and carry it out. The people aboard the plane had varied skills. Not everyone could rush the cockpit, but I am convinced that each person offered whatever resources he or she had available in the final moments of the flight. I heard tapes of a couple of the phone calls made from the plane and was struck by the absence of panic in the voices.

As could be expected with an early-morning flight, at least fifteen people were inadvertent travelers on Flight 93, having made travel plans at the last minute or having switched from another flight. One of the passengers, William Cashman, was an ironworker who helped build the World Trade Center. Another passenger, Donald Peterson, ran an electric company whose motors were used, according to his son, to operate the backup water-pressure system in the Trade Center. Kristin White Gould was a writer from New York and a descendant of one of the most influential Pilgrims on the *Mayflower.* Donald F. Greene, who had a pilot's license, was the son of a woman whose family founded Saks Fifth Avenue. His stepfather invented a device to warn against stalling, which is standard equipment on the world's aircraft.

There were connections, unknown on September 11, among a number of people aboard Flight 93. Of the passengers who made telephone calls, Todd Beamer and Mark Bingham both graduated from Los Gatos High School in northern California. Mark Bingham, Jeremy Glick and Tom Burnett were all presidents of their college fraternities. Cathy Stefani, the mother of passenger Nicole Miller, was a classmate of Captain Jason Dahl at Andrew Hill High School in San Jose, California. Jeremy Glick and Linda Gronlund both lived on Greenwood Lake that straddled the border between New York and New Jersey.

Richard Guadagno, who managed the Humboldt Bay National Wildlife Refuge in Eureka, California, was a federal agent who had been trained in close-quarter fighting. A handful of passengers had practiced martial arts. Several were emergency medical technicians. The lone married couple aboard Flight

93, Donald Peterson and Jean Hoadley Peterson, devoted their later lives to crisis counseling. While it is futile, even arrogant, to think that the existence of forty individuals can be wholly compressed into the pages of a book, I have attempted to get beyond the grim numbers of this tragedy and to portray the resolve and quiet dignity of human lives given so selflessly and heroically.

"Just the thought of people on an airplane saying, 'We're not going to let these guys get away with this,' makes you want to live your life better than you had been," said Ed Figura, a fifty-five-year-old salesman who visited the crash site a month after Flight 93 was hijacked.

Three days before Christmas, a British man named Richard C. Reid boarded American Flight 63 from Paris to Miami and attempted to ignite his shoe with a match. His shoes were packed with plastic explosives, authorities said. A flight attendant and passengers subdued the man, and doctors on board gave him a sedative. The plane was safely diverted to Boston. Given the bold lesson of United Flight 93, people knew exactly what to do. No longer would passengers and crew sit idly by while someone attempted to hijack or blow up a plane. No longer would passivity be an expected response to terrorism in the sky.

Author's Note

Flight 93 crashed, authorities said, with forty-four persons aboard: Two pilots, five flight attendants and thirty-seven passengers, including the four hijackers. However, there has been some discrepancy regarding the number of people aboard the plane before it left Newark. This is significant, given that the other three planes seized on September 11 had five hijackers, while Flight 93 had four. Originally, United and government officials said there were forty-five people aboard the plane. Later, authorities amended the figure to forty-four, saying that one passenger — apparently Marion Britton, in coach — had bought two tickets. In a call to her husband before boarding, flight attendant CeeCee Lyles said there were eleven passengers scheduled in first class and twenty-seven in coach. Authorities later said there were ten passengers in first class.

Terry Tyksinski, a longtime United flight attendant, said she was told six months after the crash, by a customer service supervisor who witnessed the incident, that two passengers left the plane when it was announced there would be a five-minute delay in pushing back from the gate. The first-class passengers were dark-complexioned, "kind of black, not black," the supervisor said, according to Tyksinski, a flight attendant for thirty-five years who is on disability leave and who was a close friend of Flight 93 attendant Lorraine Bay. The supervisor said she noted the names of the passengers and was subsequently twice interviewed by the FBI, Tyksinski said. This incident could not be independently confirmed.

In the interest of a coherent narrative, I have used the figures, provided by authorities, of ten passengers in first class, and twenty-seven in coach, when the plane took off from Newark.

1

The sky on September 11 dawned cerulean blue, one of those unblemished skies that often appeared in late summer after heavy rains or hurricanes — rinsed, cloudless, apparently cleansed of tumult. It was a week past Labor Day. The U.S. Open tennis tournament had just concluded, school was back in session, football season had begun, baseball had entered its stretch run. Casual fashion had faded to basic black. Autumn had arrived in the New York area, if not by calendar's decree, then by the urgent feel of resumption. Summer had been shaken away like sand from a beach towel.

Dressed in his navy blue uniform, the four gold stripes on the sleeves denoting his rank as captain, Jason Dahl entered United Airlines' flight operations center in a secure area of Terminal A at Newark International Airport. It was approximately seven a.m. on this Tuesday. Check-in occurred an hour before each domestic flight. The previous day, Jason had traveled to Newark from his home in the

Denver suburb of Littleton, Colorado. He would pilot Flight 93 to San Francisco, having traded a trip later in the month for this one. This was a long-awaited week. Jason would stop by and see his mother in San Jose, California, during his layover. In two days, he would return home to begin his plans for the weekend.

This would be the fifth wedding anniversary for Jason and his wife, Sandy. It was the second marriage for both, and Jason liked to do things in a big way. He had proposed to her on a cruise ship, hiring a plane to fly over with a banner that read SANDY, I LOVE YOU SO MUCH, WILL YOU MARRY ME? For their honeymoon, he told Sandy to pack for another cruise. They ended up in Tahiti. When he called on Monday night from Newark, Jason told Sandy that he had bought her a new Volvo. There would be more gifts. When it came to birthdays and anniversaries, Jason possessed the flamboyance of Monty Hall introducing a showcase on *Let's Make a Deal*. He and a family friend, Jewel Wellborn, had arranged for Sandy to receive a manicure, pedicure, facial and a massage on Friday afternoon. While she was distracted in her bedroom, deliverymen would arrive with a baby grand piano programmed with Jason and Sandy's wedding song. That night, Jason would cook a gourmet meal. On Saturday, he and Sandy would fly to London to celebrate their anniversary. "He was so thrilled, planning every intricate detail of surprise," Wellborn said.

In the United operations center, Jason signed onto a computer, verified his schedule, checked to see if there were any changes. From service representatives working in an open-window area, he received several printouts generated from company headquarters in Chicago. The paperwork told him of the general condition of the aircraft, whether there was a reading light out in first class, or a coffee maker on the blink in the rear galley. It gave him an update of maintenance service on the plane, a review of the weather, a manifest of the flight attendants, passenger load, an extensive flight plan, a reading of fuel levels, possible turbulence, runway data and estimated waiting times.

Flight 93 was scheduled to depart one minute after eight, but anyone who flew out of Newark regularly knew to expect delays. Planes could stack up like balloons in the Macy's Thanksgiving Day Parade. Given Newark's clogged taxiways and the crowded airspace above the three major airports in the New York City area, sometimes it seemed there was as much gridlock in the skies above Newark, LaGuardia and John F. Kennedy airports as there was on the streets below. After reviewing the paperwork, Jason signed a release for the plane, placing it in his control. Next to his name, he wrote "C-3," indicating that he was certified to perform landings in as little as three hundred feet visibility, the highest qualification that United offered.

In the operations center, Jason met LeRoy Homer Jr., the first officer on Flight 93. The two had never flown together, but they had one thing in common: they caught the flying bug early and this was the only job they ever really wanted.

Upon completing his paperwork, Captain Dahl boarded the plane and began his preflight checklist. This was performed in a precise order known as a flow, moving up one row of switches and gauges and down another. He did an overall check of the cockpit, making sure that life vests, fire ax and fire extinguisher were in place and in working order. If the plane was "cold," all systems still shut down before the early-morning flight, he brought the jetliner humming to life through an external power source or an onboard auxiliary power unit. From his seat, he reached up and flipped the switch on three laser gyroscopes. He checked the electrical system, the fuel system, the navigational system, the communications system. He ensured that the flight-data recorder and cockpit voicerecorder were functioning properly. He examined the engine instrument indicators, the fire detection system, the hydraulic system, the anti-skid brakes, the cabin-pressurization system. He programmed into the computerized flight management system his current position, his routing and his destination. Later, the first officer would double-check that the proper positioning and routing had been entered into the computer.

The 757 had a "glass cockpit," meaning that computer screens had reduced the number of dials found on older planes. The jet, manufactured by Boeing and fitted with two megaphone-shaped engines that protruded from beneath the wings, weighed a maximum of two hundred fifty-five thousand pounds, or one hundred twenty-seven tons, as much as a diesel locomotive. It was one hundred fifty-five feet three inches long and had a wing-span of one hundred twenty-four feet ten inches. The surface area of the wings was equivalent to the floor space of a three-bedroom house. This particular jet, delivered to United in 1996 and registered as N591UA, was known as a 757–200. It was fitted with two Pratt and Whitney engines and was built with thirty-four rows of seats. The jet seated twenty-four passengers in first class, one hundred fifty-eight passengers in coach. The freighter version of the 757 was voluminous enough to hold six million golf balls.

The 757 received generally good reviews from pilots, who liked its quiet, comfortable ride and its power. Even if it lost one of its two engines, the jet could still fly. It had a maximum cruising speed of six hundred miles per hour. With a fuel capacity of eleven thousand five hundred gallons and a range of three thousand nine hundred miles, it could travel cross-country with fuel to spare. Some pilots and flight attendants even found the plane cute, with its swooped bottle-nose that resembled a dolphin's.

Yet, the enthusiasm was not universally shared. The 757 was essentially a 727 stretched to accommodate the greatest number of passengers in the smallest amount of space. It was fitted with one narrow aisle, compared to the 767's two aisles. There were three seats on either side of the aisle in coach, with a GTE Airfone located in the center seats of each row. Phones were also located in the armrests of first-class seats. Some flight attendants were concerned that the jutting of passenger seats at row eight, the first row of coach, left insufficient space for the emergency exits. The jet's long narrow design also fostered concerns about the overall speed of evacuation in case of emergency. Bathrooms were located in the rear galley, which could be disruptive to flight attendants as they prepared to serve meals, snacks and beverages.

While Captain Dahl ran through his pre-flight checks, First Officer LeRoy Homer Jr., age thirty-six, inspected the underside of the plane, starting at the nose and walking in a counterclockwise direction. He looked for hydraulic leaks and possible damage from lightning strikes. He checked tire pressure gauges, tire conditions and brake-wear indicators. He looked for nicks in the engine's compressor fans and potential dents in the fuselage from collisions with catering trucks. LeRoy, who wore three stripes on his sleeves as a first officer, had flown with United for six years, often copiloting flights to London or to Los Angeles and San Francisco from John F. Kennedy Airport in Queens. Newark was more convenient than JFK, cutting in half his driving time from his home in South Jersey.

He had grown up in Hauppauge, New York, on Long Island, and from the time he was two or three, his parents had taken him to area airports to watch planes land and take off. "One more time, Daddy, one more time," he would plead, hoping to forestall the trip home. His bedroom grew cluttered with model airplanes and aviation posters, and it became a kind of museum to his youth when he left for college, his mother keeping everything in its childhood place.

Before the passengers boarded Flight 93, Captain Dahl met with Deborah Welsh, the flight attendant in charge, known as the purser. The job paid more and carried more responsibilities. She served as the liaison between the flight attendants and the pilots. It was also Welsh's job to assign duties to the other flight attendants. An hour before the flight, she had checked into what United flight attendants called the "domicile," an operations center located beneath baggage claim in Terminal A. Deborah initialed her name on a clipboard list and grabbed a briefing sheet bearing the flight number, type of aircraft, passenger load and names and seniority of her fellow flight attendants, names of the cockpit crew and special services that the passengers might need. She sat at a table with the four other flight attendants and gave the assignments for Flight 93. As the purser, she would work first class. Typically, in a briefing, a purser asked her colleagues, "Where do you want to sit and what do you want to do?" With fewer than forty passengers aboard a plane that held nearly two hundred, this promised to be a leisurely day.

For his briefing with the purser, Captain Dahl usually carried a checklist in his hand and spoke about the weather, any expected turbulence, when he wanted breakfast served, the audio entertainment and the scheduled movie, potential delays and requirements such as wheelchairs or oxygen for any of the passengers. He also spoke to the purser about security. Up to an altitude of ten thousand feet, the cockpit was to remain "sterile," which meant that no one could enter. Talk between the pilots was restricted to operations or safety. There would be no schmoozing about rounds of golf or the cute looks of a certain flight attendant. Dahl and Welsh also established the secret-knock sequence that she would use to enter the cockpit. The code was changed on every flight. United flight attendants did not carry cockpit keys, which were to be used for emergencies. One key was always located in the forward part of each aircraft, sometimes in the galley, but not always in the same place.

Although the cockpit door remained locked during flight, it provided only flimsy protection on September 11. The door was designed to withstand no more than one hundred fifty pounds of pressure, so that it could be forced open in emergencies, allowing pilots to escape outward or passengers to escape inward to climb out of a cockpit window. A heavy shoulder would dislodge the door. Flight attendants carrying meal trays into the cockpit sometimes worried that it would open when they gave it a hard kick. They told a story, perhaps apocryphal, that upon the landing of a 727 on one United flight, a metal meal cart came loose from the rear of the plane, rolled down the aisle and crashed through the door into the cockpit. It was not unheard of to see the door swing open during takeoff or remain open and un-guarded for a few moments during meal service.

In the event of a hijacking, flight attendants were to phone the cockpit and mention the word "trip." Something along the lines of "We have something to discuss with you about this trip." Both pilots and flight attendants had been taught passive compliance: Take the hijackers where they want to go. Get the plane down safely. Disable the plane, if you can, on the ground. Take care of the passengers and crew. Cooperate the best you can. Protect yourself, stay calm, be non-threatening. The United flight attendant's manual offered this advice: "Be persuasive to stay alive. Be released or escape. Delay. Engage in comfortable behavior. Be yourself. Maintain a professional role. Do not become an accomplice. Trust the law. Control other passengers. Deter aggression. Keep passengers occupied. Provide food and nonalcoholic beverages. Let the hijackers select a liaison. Do not challenge their power. Use eye contact to calm and reduce anxiety. Provide body space. Use friendly, non-threatening social and direct conversation. Inform them before making a movement. Learn and confirm the kind of weapon. Gather information; be a good listener. Communicate openly rather than covertly. Report demands verbatim [to ground personnel]. Do not be a negotiator.

Keep the passengers informed with non-strategic information. After the hijacking, avoid the media. Make no comments. Debrief with authorized United personnel."

This advice was based on old familiar rules that would soon cease to apply. Rules that were mortally inadequate. They discouraged assistance from passengers and suggested appeasement for a scenario in which demands would be met, exchanges would be made, lives would be spared. They did not anticipate the use of planes as suicide missiles. Flight attendants were trained to evacuate a plane in ninety seconds, sometimes even while blindfolded, but they were in no way trained to fight murderers at thirty-five thousand feet. Such a confrontation would be a sick game, not a fair fight. Advice to remain calm and non-threatening would not work against a knife at the throat and an intent at martyrdom.

2

In a taxi on the way to the Newark airport, Tom Burnett left a voice-mail message for his boss. He had changed his plans. There was room on United Flight 93 to San Francisco. He would be leaving at eight a.m. instead of taking Flight 91 that was scheduled for nine-twenty. He would get home an hour early to see his wife, Deena, and their three young daughters in San Ramon, California. Most of the last six weeks had been spent on the road. Tom was chief operating officer of Thoratec Corporation, which was headquartered in Pleasanton, California. This was an urgent, opportunistic time for the company, a leading manufacturer of heart pumps for patients awaiting transplants. Thoratec was seeking approval to use the pumps as permanent implants. That morning, D. Keith Grossman, the company's president and chief executive officer, was scheduled to ring the opening bell at the Nasdaq stock exchange.

Tom had been traveling frequently, bringing investors and reporters up to speed about the company's plans. The previous Friday, he arrived home at four p.m. from Los Angeles, spent a few hours with his family, then flew out again to Minneapolis. He had grown up in the suburb of Bloomington, Minnesota. He met his father at the Minneapolis airport, and they drove to a farm that Tom owned in Wisconsin. They spent Saturday building a tree stand for an upcoming Thanksgiving deer hunt. On Sunday, September 9, Tom was scheduled to fly to Newark for Monday meetings at Thoratec's eastern subsidiary in Edison, New Jersey. Before his flight, he realized that he had lost his cellular phone. So many numbers were programmed into the phone, it would have been a terrible inconvenience not to retrieve it. He realized that the phone may have fallen out of his pocket at a local sporting goods store. He returned to the store, and, using his mother's phone, dialed his own number, heard the ring and located the missing cell phone, which had fallen behind a display. He walked out of the store smiling, giving his father a thumbs-up sign. They drove to the airport in just enough time to catch his flight to Newark.

For the fourth or fifth time already this morning, CeeCee Lyles, a flight attendant, called her husband, Lorne. He was working the overnight shift as a patrolman for the police department in Fort Myers, Florida. It

29

had been a slow night, so he had time to talk from his patrol car. They spoke often when she was gone, up to two dozen times a day. CeeCee called when she awakened at five a.m. She called again when she boarded the flight attendant's shuttle to the airport, telling Lorne which bills to pay, what chores to complete while she was traveling. She called a third time from the airport to say that her flight, United 93, was a light load.

"I've got an easy day," she said.

Georgine Corrigan placed her roller bag on an X-ray machine conveyor belt. She had long ago learned to pack her jewelry in clear plastic bags so the baubles could easily be identified by security personnel. An antiques dealer from Honolulu, Hawaii, she had arrived on the East Coast with two suitcases and was leaving with four, including a carry-on full of jewelry. Georgine spent a month or more each year on the mainland. She had grown up in the small farm town of Woodville, Ohio. Kids worked on the high school prom in her basement, and things seemed to accumulate around the spacious yard, leading her father to say that the family owned everything made since 1930, "and four of them."

When Georgine went to Bowling Green University, one of her roommates owned a model-T Ford, which her brother Robert

Marisay bought for five hundred fifty dollars. He later collected several antique cars, as well as flare guns from airplanes and ships, one of which he donated to the USS *Arizona* memorial at Pearl Harbor. For ten bucks, the family also bought a turn-of-the-century pool table out of a chicken coop and restored it. Georgine soon learned her way around the business end of a pool cue. In college, she took a billiards course and so impressed the instructor that he let her help teach the class. "She got credit for the course, of course," her brother Kevin Marisay said.

After college, Georgine worked in the banking business in Toledo, Ohio, until, following a chance transaction, she was offered a job with an import-export company in Honolulu. It was 1976, and she was a single mom with a young daughter. She took the job, Kevin Marisay said, only to discover within a week that the company was bankrupt. "When they come to take over, tell them you're the bookkeeper," her boss told her and walked out the door. Georgine then went to work for the Bank of Hawaii, and later worked as a graphic-design artist, managed a beauty salon and baby-sat at a Hilton Hotel for the children of stars such as Tony Danza and Olivia Newton-John. She did craft work, drawing silhouettes and painting designs on Christmas ornaments, stemware, vases, glasses. She also operated as a broker for a supply business that delivered radios, cell phones, computers, nonperishable foods and furniture to South Sea islands.

"She was involved in so many things that she couldn't master one of them," said Georgine's daughter, Laura Brough. "There was always something to distract her from making that one thing blossom."

About seven years earlier, Georgine got into the antiques business. She was not the kind of person to sit behind a desk or a computer. She loved going to markets and sales, meeting people, telling stories. "If there are six million people on Oahu, she had three million on her speed-dial," said her brother Kevin, also an antiques dealer. "She was talented talking to customers, sometimes too talented. She'd lean across the counter and block her inventory. I'd say, 'Move to the side, so your jewelry can be seen. If you hide your inventory, you'll go out of business.' "

Although Georgine had an interest in the future, with a love of *Star Trek* and science fiction, her business was rooted in the past. She traveled the world in search of exotic items, always returning from some place like New Zealand with a four-foot-high wine-bottle opener, an English hunting horn, a gorgeous opal ring. She lived with her daughter, Laura, and the two were as close as sisters. When Laura was younger, Georgine went trick-or-treating with her, dressed as a witch, relishing her delicious cackle. "For some reason, they gave me candy and they gave my mother beer," Laura laughed. "I'd get candy and she'd get a six-pack."

Finally, it seemed that, at age fifty-five, Georgine was on the verge of a breakthrough in her business career. She had built a reputation for painting tropical flowers on Christmas ornaments, decorating them with hibiscus, plumeria, anthurium, pikaki and poinsettias. Her work had caught the attention of the largest importer of silk flowers and plants in Hawaii. She was negotiating to have her prints mass-produced on Christmas balls in China and sold around the world. Georgine had also cast her first piece in a line of jewelry she had created, an orchid pendant.

"She was the eternal optimist," Laura Brough said of her mother. "When others would give up and say, 'This is too hard,' she would laugh and go on. She was on the verge of having things marketed for her instead of having to do it herself. She had struggled so long and now things were going to blossom."

There had been some cautionary news lately. Georgine had received an abnormal result on a mammogram test four months earlier. She had been participating in a ten-year research program. Her mother had suffered from breast cancer, so it was a concern, but

Georgine did not return for a follow-up exam. Still, she did not seem overly alarmed. She was as thin as she had been in a long time, and she had looked forward to visiting a friend in Salt Lake City on this current trip to the mainland. Her brother Kevin asked her to travel east to assist him at an antiques show in Brimfield, Massachusetts, which featured more than two thousand vendors. After the show, they returned to her brother's home in Teaneck, New Jersey. Georgine did not do as well as she wanted at the show, but she had picked up some items she liked — china cups and saucers, sugar bowls and creamers, cake plates. And when Georgine checked in for her flight home to Hawaii, there was good news. Her trip had been scheduled to make two stops before she arrived in San Francisco, but United Flight 93 was available and it was non-stop.

"See you in November," her brother told her as they said good-bye. Georgine was due back for a holiday antiques show in lower Manhattan. It was a yearly event held on a pedestrian bridge that connected the World Trade Center with the World Financial Center.

At seven-twenty, forty minutes before scheduled takeoff, a United agent at Gate 17 made the first boarding call for Flight 93. The gate ran like a spoke from a central

34

waiting area, where passengers bought coffee and bagels and muffins for a quick breakfast and selected newspapers, magazines and books to occupy themselves on the six-hour flight. First-class passengers and those in coach who traveled frequently on United were allowed to board first.

Lauren Grandcolas called her husband, Jack, in San Rafael, California. Given the three-hour time difference, he was still in bed. She left a message. She had been scheduled for United 91, but her car service had arrived at the airport early. "Hey, I just want to let you know I'm on the eight o'clock instead of the nine-twenty," Lauren said. She would get to San Francisco about eleven-fifteen. In a watery state of half-sleep, Jack Grandcolas vaguely heard the message left on the answering machine downstairs in the kitchen.

Lauren, who was thirty-eight, had flown to New Jersey to attend her grandmother's funeral, and had stayed with her sister, Vaughn Lohec, in Chatham, New Jersey. The night before, always organized, she packed her bag and left it by the front door. Before she went to bed, she set out a spoon, sugar and a mug for her coffee. From the airport, Lauren called her sister and told her, too, about the rescheduled flight. Lauren did not have time to grab a bagel, but she would get breakfast on the plane. She was looking forward to getting home an hour early. Her grandmother's funeral aside, this was an exhilarating time for Lauren. She and Jack had been married ten years, and after suffering a previous miscarriage, Lauren was pregnant again. A marketing expert, she was also researching a book that would provide guidance for women in the areas of finance, health and self-esteem as they navigated their careers. A publisher had expressed interest, and Lauren was searching for a ghostwriter.

Donald Peterson and Jean Hoadley Peterson of Spring Lake, New Jersey, had also been scheduled for a later flight. They would be the lone married couple aboard Flight 93. They were headed to Yosemite National Park for an annual family trip. Both were retired. Don, sixty-six, had been president of Continental Electric Company in Newark, a firm his grandfather had founded in 1922. The company's motors were used to provide backup water-pressure in the World Trade Center. Jean, fifty-five, was a registered nurse. Born-again Christians, they had devoted their lives to volunteer work in the church and the community. Humble, self-effacing, they did not trumpet their own deeds or achievements. Those who knew them in the church were surprised to learn that Don had earned a degree in electrical engineering from the Massachusetts Institute of Technology, an

MBA from Rutgers and had taken an executive education program at Harvard Business School. He had also served on the New Jersey Board of Higher Education. Jean was the daughter of Walter Hoadley, who had been the chief economist and senior vice president of the Bank of America. She had received her undergraduate degree in nursing from Rochester University and a master's degree in education from Columbia University.

"I had no idea they helped as many people as they did," said the Reverend Jim Loveland, pastor of the Community Baptist Church in Neptune, New Jersey, where Don and Jean worshipped for several years. "They kept it quiet. They used their financial means to help a lot of people, but never showed they had means. They drove an average car, lived in a modest house for their town."

Don and Jean married in 1984, both having been previously divorced. The blended family consisted of Don's three sons and Jean's three daughters. Her mother's divorce had put her on a more urgent spiritual path, said Jennifer Price, Jean's eldest daughter. "She had been raised in a religious home, and the church is where she found comfort and solace," Price said.

Jean taught nursing and later became an emergency medical technician, riding with an ambulance service in Madison, New Jersey. She loved helping people, getting another chance to use her nursing skills and learning the advancing technology of the medical field. "She enjoyed being on call, the beeper going off, and having to run out the door," Jennifer Price said. "Mom was the kind of person who always drove fifty-five on the highway. She loved to get behind an ambulance; it was a rush for her. She was so conservative in her life, this was a fun outlet for her."

She met Don through her eldest daughter's kindergarten teacher. "Don showed up at the door one day and kind of never left," Price said. One of his passions was America's Keswick, a Christian retreat center and an addiction recovery ministry located in Whiting, New Jersey. Don counseled men in the residential colony who were struggling with drug and alcohol dependencies, keeping in touch with a number of the residents after they had left the center.

"He quietly helped some couples who needed a start with their mortgage," Loveland said. "He would loan money and never charge interest."

Don had been born into affluence and had lived a life of privilege in Short Hills, New Jersey, belonging to exclusive and restricted clubs up and down the East Coast, playing tennis several times a week with governors and other members of the power elite. But he later came to feel uncomfortable in that world, leaving the Short Hills life behind, along with the Episcopal Church and his golf- and tennis-club memberships. He once joked that his epitaph would read: RESIGNED FROM THE MOST CLUBS EVER. "There was an inner hunger not being met," said Don's son, David Peterson.

Divorce had brought about a painful life crisis for Don in the late 1970s and early 1980s, his son said. In Jean Hoadley he seemed to find a kindred spirit. "I kind of wondered what was going on," Dave Peterson said of his father's religious conversion. "Not everyone agreed with what they were doing, but they did it in a way that was respectful of others. What impressed me was that they stood by what they said."

Don and Jean helped those in need in a variety of ways. They counseled couples with troubled marriages, gave financial assistance, provided character references in court. Don was famous for taking people to breakfast. Jean cooked, baby-sat, took people to doctors' visits.

Jean became affiliated with the Helping Hand Pregnancy Care Center in Shrewsbury, New Jersey, a pro-life organization that counseled women with crisis pregnancies, encouraging them to keep their babies. As a volunteer, Jean was in charge of donations of clothing and diapers for the center. She took donated clothing home and washed it to prepare the items for needy mothers and their newborns.

In the summer of 1999, Jean and her daughter Grace spent three weeks on a medical mission in Ecuador, assisting American doctors in distributing vitamins and performing health checkups and surgery for such things as cleft palates and tubal ligations. "People would travel for days and line up the night before," Grace Price said. "My mom got to use her nursing skills. It was an incredible experience."

Don and Jean also led Bible study groups and traveled to Saint Lucia in the Caribbean to help with a mission at a sister church. They later opened their home to five women who made a reciprocal visit to the Community Baptist Church in Neptune. Dressed in their windbreakers, Don and Jean took daily walks on the boardwalk in Spring Lake. Don, who had a replacement hip, could not walk long distances, but he pruned the shrubs and bushes at his church. Recently, he had cleaned up and taken care of the trash after a rehearsal dinner for the marriage of Reverend Loveland's daughter.

"These were compassionate and loving people," Loveland said. "They were quick to pick up the towel and the wash cloth, not the microphone."

Jean was the kind of person who sent care packages, showed up with a cake on birthdays and mailed a flurry of cards for birth-days and holidays. She also joined an investment club called the Wise Women, al-though the members' ardor apparently ex-ceeded their acumen. "They absolutely lost their shirts," Jennifer Price laughed. "If you looked at their portfolio, I'm not sure you'd think they were wise."

Jean's first grandchild had been born two and a half weeks earlier to her eldest daugh-ter, Jennifer. She had knitted an afghan for the baby and had spent a week visiting with her three daughters and granddaughter in Boston. On this trip to Yosemite, Jean was to join her own parents and her brother. She was looking forward to hiking in the majestic park and to visiting with her family. Eager to get across the country, Don and Jean arrived at the airport early for United Flight 91. Space was available on the eight o'clock flight, so they switched to Flight 93.

Assigned to 18F, a window seat, John Talignani prepared for a somber trip. The re-tired bartender at the Palm restaurants in Manhattan was traveling to collect the re-mains of his stepson, who had died in an auto accident while on his honeymoon. The car in which Alan Zykofsky and his wife were riding had collided with a gravel truck on a winding road in the redwood hills near Se-quoia National Park. Alan's two brothers had flown out to California on September 10. John had to take his sister to the doctor that day, so he booked a flight for the 11th. Only two weeks earlier, John had celebrated his seventy-fourth birthday. A former owner of a pizzeria, he still made three pies each Thanksgiving, along with a turkey. He was a burly man, with glasses and a shock of white hair, but he had a bartender's practiced calm and willingness to listen. Nothing seemed to rattle him. He had aunts more than a hundred years old, and no one could ever remember him being sick or visiting a doctor. In his days at the Palm, and the Palm Too, John had run across celebrities like George C. Scott, Arnold Schwarzenegger, Donald Trump and the pitcher David Cone, but he preferred to talk about his regular customers, mostly guys in the advertising business. He worked the day shift, standing behind the bar with his arms crossed, and if anybody was too drunk when the night bartender arrived, John would speak in unruffled code: "These guys are nice, but they're crazy."

His three stepsons considered him a father, not a stepfather. "I was ten or eleven and we were living in a three-room apartment, one bedroom, and he asked if it was okay if he married my mother," Glenn Zykofsky said. "All of a sudden, we were in a house, eating proper food. In my eyes, he took us from the gutter to a mansion. That's a hero."

Alan became a stockbroker, Glenn ran a recreation center, Mitchell was a sergeant in the New York Police Department. Glenn played baseball at St. Francis College and had tryouts with a number of major-league teams. Once, John drove home all the way from Florida to get Glenn to a tryout with the Seattle Mariners on Long Island. A Mets fan, he even went to watch Glenn try out at dreaded Yankee Stadium. John had grown up in Brooklyn with the Dodgers, and he owned a scale model of Ebbets Field, where he had gone as a kid with his own father, dressed in his Sunday best.

John purchased the scale model off of the Internet. He couldn't resist these online purchases. His apartment in Staten Island became cluttered with hedge clippers, chain saws, rug-cleaning machines, model cars, a BB gun, dough-making machines, a framed ticket to the original Woodstock. Once, he became so exuberant with the clippers that he cut down all of his sister's hedges for a reason that no one could explain. "We teased him and he'd say, 'This is important stuff,' " Mitchell Zykofsky said. "He'd say, 'I really need this cavalry sword.' "

At seven thirty-three, as he waited in the boarding area, Todd Beamer received a call on his cellular phone. It was his boss, Jonathan Oomrigar, calling from California. Todd was a top account manager for Oracle software. He had generated thirty-three million dollars worth of business for Oracle in the previous fiscal year, blowing out all the numbers. Six months earlier, he had put together Oracle's largest deal ever with Sony's semiconductor division, according to Oomrigar, an Oracle vice president. The two men and their wives had returned the day before from a trip to Rome and Florence, a company reward for their hard work. They had agreed not to discuss business while in Italy, but they had an important meeting this morning at Oracle's headquarters in Redwood Shores, California, in the Bay Area. His body clock still on European time, Oomrigar awakened at four in the morning. A half-hour later, he was on the phone to Todd, who had driven forty-five minutes to Newark from his home in Cranbury, New Jersey.

Usually, Todd flew Continental, but he had chosen United on this trip to save his company money. He spoke to his boss for about fifteen minutes.

"Is that the final call yet?" Todd asked one of the gate agents about boarding the plane. He had been assigned a seat in Row 10, near the front of coach.

No, the agent replied, and the two colleagues continued to talk.

A top Sony executive was flying in from Japan for the meeting. As they spoke, Todd and his boss made a bold decision. They would put all their other accounts on the back burner and concentrate on Sony. If they remained patient, in eighteen months they might pull off a deal worth fifty million to one hundred million dollars.

That was one of Todd's virtues. Patience. The ability and willingness to think long-term when the nature of the business was short-term, when the inclination was to take the money and run. He was Type A; they all were at Oracle. He had played baseball and basketball at Wheaton College in Illinois, and sales, like sports, provided an unambiguous way to measure himself. But Todd did not act rashly. His wife, Lisa, had been surprised when he bought her a diamond tennis bracelet in Italy. He never made impulsive decisions. He thought things through, acted deliberately. After careful research, he and his brother-in-law had bought identical vans and lawn mowers. They were both starting the same diet, Todd having wanted to shed twenty pounds from his six-foot, two-hundred-pound frame, seeking to return to his college playing weight. Organized and meticulous as always, he had removed a tray of M&Ms from his home office, put together a cookbook of allowed diet foods and drawn up the required exercise schedule.

In meetings, Oomrigar never had to ask if Todd was taking notes. He always was. When it was time to work, it was time to work. Todd disliked what he called "Barney meetings" — back-patting affairs where the conversation was, "I love you, you love me," and little got done. He preferred to dress casually at home, a ball cap always covering his dark, wavy hair, but at work he carried a sense of professional urgency. "Time to step up to the plate," he liked to say.

When things were going well with an account, when he was on the verge of a major deal, Todd did an elaborate baseball pantomime, stepping up to a fanciful plate, settling into his stance, swinging easily and making that reassuring hollow sound of a ball connecting with a bat. He would point to an imaginary fence and say, "We just hit a home run." This Sony deal, if it worked out, would be a grand slam.

The last place Jeremy Glick wanted to travel was California. Each trip seemed worse than the previous one. At six foot one, two hundred twenty pounds, so broad-chested and slim-hipped that he had to have his suits custom-tailored, the former collegiate judo champion did not fit comfortably into a coach seat. And he did not want to be away from his infant daughter, Emerson. Jeremy and his wife, Lyzbeth, had tried for such a long time to have a baby, and Emerson had been born prematurely only twelve weeks earlier. Her sucking reflex had not been fully developed, so Jeremy would awaken at night to feed her milk through a tube taped to his pinkie finger. He became so attached to his daughter and this method of feeding that when Lyz wanted to begin using a bottle, she felt it necessary to ask Jeremy, "Are you okay with it?" He had to think about it before saying yes.

Already, he had been to California once since the baby was born. Emerson was five weeks old at the time, and when Jeremy came home, he said forlornly, "I've missed a fifth of her life." He was a sales manager for Vividence, a Web management company, but he had been quietly looking for another job, one that would not require him to travel cross-country. At one point, he thought of concocting some medical excuse to avoid the trip, but Lyz insisted that he go. It was his job and he couldn't phone in sick, especially not at a time when the economy was slowing and Vividence was laying people off.

He had been scheduled to fly out the day before, but he had called to say there was a fire at Newark Airport and his flight had been canceled. The next available flight would not put him in San Francisco until the middle of the night. He decided to go home to Hewitt, New Jersey, and try again this morning. Lyz Glick felt secretly pleased. The previous weekend, when Jeremy mentioned his travel plans, a wave of fear overcame her. They were standing in the kitchen, and when Jeremy told her of his Monday flight, she became anxious. She didn't worry when he flew, but she had a bad feeling about this one. She felt almost sick. A college roommate had died in the crash of a small family plane. Quickly, Lyz tried to put the thought out of her head. *Don't be so silly,* she told herself. *These things don't happen. Lightning doesn't strike twice in the same place.* She did not tell Jeremy of her feelings, and when his plans changed, she felt relieved.

Just before he boarded Flight 93 to take his seat in Row 11, Jeremy called Lyz to say good morning. Because he was going to be away, Lyz had gone to the Catskill Mountains to stay with her parents in Windham, New York. Jeremy reached Jo Anne Makely, his mother-in-law, who said that Lyz was still sleeping. She had been up most of the night with the baby.

"Tell Lyzzie I'm boarding the plane and I love her and I'll call when I get to San Francisco," Jeremy said.

3

Flight attendants Lorraine Bay and Wanda Green stood inside the doorway at Row 8, greeting passengers as they boarded. Travelers did not enter a 757 at the front as they did many other jets. Instead, they came aboard in the area that separated first class from coach. The ten passengers traveling in first class were guided down the aisle to their left. The twenty-seven traveling in coach were ushered down the aisle to the right.

Transcontinental flights, or transcons, were popular with senior flight attendants. They could avoid the up-and-down nature of shorter flights. Instead of flying a handful of legs in a day, they could fly one leg, avoiding the repeated changing of passengers and the repetition of duties. There was a joke that flight attendants sometimes told: "What animal has five legs and sucks? This trip."

At this stage of her career, Lorraine Bay left first class, with its pay perks and more demanding passengers, to the younger flight attendants. She would work coach. Each month, flight attendants and pilots bid on their schedules for the following month, and their routes were determined by seniority. With thirty-seven years on the job, Lorraine Bay ranked fourth in seniority among the seven hundred flight attendants based in Newark. The airport elicited strong opinions from those who worked there. Many called it the pits, "Manureark," for dreary facilities that seemed outdated and flights that were subjected to frequent, long delays. Others, though, appreciated Newark's convenience, the opportunity to avoid New York traffic and a sense of camaraderie that built up among the senior flight attendants. Lorraine was one of those who fostered this esprit de corps. She was known by some as the "Card Lady," someone who would always send a card or a gift at birthdays, holidays, any special occasion. To Mary Bush, a fellow flight attendant, she had sent knee pads for tiling a kitchen floor, and a parking sign that said RESERVED FOR IRISH GRANDMOTHERS ONLY. ALL OTHERS WILL BE TOWED. Always, Lorraine spent a moment to brighten someone's day.

She had no children or siblings, and her friends and their relatives became her extended family. Each April 1, Terry Tyksinski, another friend and flight attendant, would receive a call from her mother in London.

"I've received a birthday card from Lorraine."

"That's nice," she would reply.

"But I didn't get one from you," her mother would say.

"That's because your birthday is not until the twenty-ninth."

At fifty-eight, Lorraine flew for the joy of it, for the travel and the encounters with people, not the money. The previous year, on a layover in Oklahoma City, she had jumped in a cab and visited the memorial to those who died when Timothy McVeigh bombed the Murrah Federal Building. She said she felt the need to pay tribute. "You have to go," she told her friend, Mary Bush. "You will be awed."

The previous February, Erich Bay, Lorraine's husband, had sold his tool-making company. He cut his work schedule back from seven days a week to four, so that he and his wife could spend more time together. They were not big travelers. Lorraine had lived out of a suitcase long enough. But she loved to shop for belts and shirts and ties for him, and, in three days, they would have their weekly Friday night dinner at their favorite restaurant. This week's dinner would be special. Erich's birthday was coming up, and he had scheduled a trip to Germany.

As usual, Lorraine was up at two-thirty a.m. on September 11, sending e-mails, writing cards to her friends. When Erich awakened at four-thirty, Lorraine was putting on her makeup. Her back hurt, and her stomach bothered her, she said. "I feel like calling in and saying I can't make it," she told her husband. He did not encourage her. Erich had run his own business, and he knew that companies needed their employees. At five, Lorraine kissed him and headed out the door from the couple's home in East Windsor, New Jersey, for the hour-long trip to Newark.

"See you tomorrow," she said.

Wanda Green had worked for United since 1973. She had grown up in Oakland, California, with a twin sister named Sandra. They played the usual tricks that twins played, switching identities at parties, or when boyfriends came to visit. Even later, when Wanda became a flight attendant, friends encouraged Sandra to impersonate her sister on a plane, but the twins always declined.

"No way," said Sandra, whose married name is Jamerson. "I'd be so nervous if there was an accident and I'd have to help passengers off the plane."

Theirs was a working-class family, and education was stressed as a way out of the despair of the inner city. Eventually, the Greens and their relatives built careers in law, politics, teaching, communications. Wanda did some modeling and joined United for the reason that many flight attendants did — to see the world and meet interesting people.

She had turned forty-nine on August 22, and was looking to retire in another two years, to sell real estate full-time. With thirty years of service at United, her union retirement package would reach its peak benefit. She had been scheduled to fly on September 13, but she moved her trip ahead by two days. She thought she might have a closing on a house that she was brokering. One day, she wanted to open her own real estate firm. Wanda Green and Company, she would call it. She had been known to lend people money if they came up short on closing costs. She even let one of her customers store his belongings in her garage after he sold his town house and a deal on a new one fell through.

"There was a quality about her," said Sandra Jamerson, Wanda's twin sister. "People latched onto her. I don't know if it was her smile or what. She was always there for people when they needed it."

The day before she was to fly on Flight 93, Wanda had expressed reservations about traveling, said Donita Judge, her best friend and a fellow United flight attendant. Wanda had spent the day registering a car belonging to her eighteen-year-old son, Joe, and she was tired. Her days always seemed to be full. She was a flight attendant, a real estate broker, a deacon at the Linden Presbyterian Church in

Linden, New Jersey, a member of a book club, a single mother raising two children. Her daughter, Jennifer, was twenty-one. Always practical, Wanda bought both of her children new pajamas every Christmas. She could always be relied on to baby-sit if one of her friends got stuck in a jam, and she had a certain character that led the teenage daughters of her friends to confide in her. Those who knew her joked that Wanda was often late, but she spent her days running from place to place as if her life were a permanent scavenger hunt. "She's as close to a person you'd want to emulate as anyone I've met in my life," Judge said. "You had to be a better person just to be around her."

A week earlier, Wanda had become unnerved on a flight scheduled from Newark to Los Angeles. The A320 Airbus developed engine trouble and made an unscheduled landing at Dulles International Airport outside of Washington, DC, according to Judge. It was the first time in many years, maybe the first time ever, that Wanda had experienced such an alarming trip. "She talked about it for an hour," Judge said. "She knew something was seriously wrong and she went to first class to ask the purser what was going on." When Wanda told her friend she didn't want to work on the eleventh, Judge wondered whether she was feeling anxious from her previous trip. Donita's phone rang at ten-thirty on the night of the tenth. It was Wanda. Donita knew she could call her back in the morning. When she did, though, Wanda had already left for the airport.

"Wanda did mention that other trip — it shook her up a little," her sister, Sandra, said. "She said it was eerie. But she kind of felt with flying that if her time was up, her time was up. You could only take so much precaution."

First class on Flight 93 consisted of six rows, four seats in each row. Fewer than half of the seats would be occupied. Deborah Welsh, the purser, made her way through the forward cabin, offering juice and asking if she could hang up any suit coats and jackets. Four Middle Eastern men were among those in first class. Ziad Jarrah took seat 1B, first-row aisle, the nearest seat to the cockpit. Ahmed Alhaznawi, Saeed Alghamdi and Ahmed Alnami sat in 3C, 3D and 6B, the last row of first class.

Deborah Welsh had not been scheduled for Flight 93. Another flight attendant sent her an e-mail, saying she needed the time off. Could Debby switch trips? "Sure, I'll take it," she said. She loved her job.

Having worked as a flight attendant for Eastern, Kiwi and United since 1972, she had often traveled alone, embracing the cultures, languages and foods of the countries she visited. She had hiked the high-altitude Inca trail to Machu Picchu in Peru, taking pictures of the sky beneath her feet, and she had survived a near-fatal episode of pneumonia in Bali. She called her mother to marvel at the northern lights she had seen while crossing the polar region, and another time, she phoned and put her mother's favorite actor, Andre Braugher, on the line. Once, she had met the comedian Henny Youngman, and he had given her his coat of arms — a business card featuring a coat and seven arms.

Six feet tall, Debby could be assertive. Once, she overpowered an inebriated passenger and shoved him back into his seat. Around her neighborhood in Hell's Kitchen in New York City, she had become an activist for pedestrian rights after a neighbor's mother had been struck by a bicyclist and died of complications from a broken hip. Whenever she saw someone riding a bike or an electric scooter on the sidewalk, Debby would yell, "It's a side-*walk,* not a side-*ride,* you idiot." She remained controlled in times of crisis, calling 911 whenever there was an accident at the intersection where she and her husband lived in a walk-up apartment. She would run downstairs, trying to provide assistance until the ambulance and police arrived. She was also known to take leftovers out of her refrigerator to feed the homeless.

Sometimes, after a trip, she kept dishes of uneaten airline food, handing them out to the needy as she walked to her apartment from the Port Authority bus terminal.

"She never gave much thought to reaching out, she just naturally did it," said Patrick Welsh, an actor and her husband of ten years. "She would be out walking the dog and the next thing she'd come back in and say, 'There's a man outside and it's freezing cold, where are your old gloves?' She'd take gloves, a scarf, an old sweater. That was a truly amazing thing about her."

At age forty-nine, blond, blue-eyed and fair-skinned, Debby had suffered three bouts of melanoma cancer, and every six months she underwent screening for the disease. This was troubling — her father had died of lung cancer — but Debby managed to keep a mirthful outlook, wearing a series of frivolous hats and doing silly umbrella dances on the beach during summers at the Jersey Shore. She loved Indian food and cigars, played the piano by ear, had a bit part in the cult movie *Liquid Sky*, and was teaching herself a guitar number by Led Zeppelin called "Baby, I'm Going to Leave You." She also had a flair for changing her hairstyle and wearing dramatic clothing. She and Patrick had a Dalmatian named Dylan, and Debby had found a kind of Dalmatian coat in a thrift store, white raglan with large black splotches that gave her a signature look in the neighborhood. Once, she dressed as Cruella de Vil for Halloween, Patrick said, "and we had fifty drag queens running behind us, thinking she was a guy in a wig."

He teased her about the hat she wore with her United uniform, a kind of pillbox hat that reminded him of a sailor's hat. He said she reminded him of the figure on a box of Cracker Jacks, though he thought Debby was one of the few who could pull off the look.

They had met fifteen years earlier at a bar in New York. Debby waited tables when Eastern employees went on strike and Patrick was hired as a bartender the next day. "It was a Sam and Diane relationship," Patrick said, evoking the characters from *Cheers*. "We used to drive each other absolutely crazy. After the first date, we said, 'We might as well stick together,' and we never looked back."

Her own world travels had been partly a spiritual journey. The eldest of six children, she was raised Catholic in the Philadelphia suburbs. On Christmas Eve, when she was nine, Debby gathered her younger siblings and converted the living room into a living manger scene, placing her six-month-old sister, Eileen, in a doll's crib as the Baby Jesus. "You can imagine what good that did to a mother's heart," said Lillian Jacobs, Debby's mother. However, Debby later began to question her faith, and explored Eastern religions, visiting an ashram in the Bahamas several times, her sister said. Eventually, she returned to her Catholic roots, and began singing in the choir at St. Paul the Apostle Church in Manhattan. "She was always searching, trying to find the answer," Eileen Brady, her sister, said.

She also had a funny side. When Eileen gave birth, Debby accompanied her to the delivery room and told the doctor, "You look like you're sewing up a turkey." The night of September 10, Patrick and Debby went to see a friend perform at a comedy club and returned home at ten or eleven. She awakened at five and dressed. Her suitcase felt heavy as always, and as Patrick carried it downstairs, he made his familiar joke that she seemed to be lugging a couple of bowling balls. They kissed and Debby began to walk toward the bus station. Usually she gave Patrick her flight information, but this trip had been scheduled at the last minute. He forgot to ask.

About seven forty-five, only fifteen minutes prior to Flight 93's scheduled departure, a Chevy Beretta pulled up to the curb at the United terminal. The two men inside hugged quickly. Mark Bingham grabbed his blue canvas bag — it still had his name on the side from his championship rugby days at the

University of California at Berkeley — and slung it over his six-foot-four-inch frame. He ran through the automatic door of Terminal A and disappeared into the labyrinth of the airport.

Mark and Matt Hall, the driver, were formerly casual friends who had begun dating several weeks earlier. They had spent the night at Hall's town house in Denville, New Jersey, forty-five minutes from the airport. Mark set his alarm for six a.m., but switched it off when it rang. When he woke up again, it was six thirty-one. "We've got to get going," Hall told him. "We're going to be late."

Mark had considered flying a day earlier, but he had celebrated the birthday of his roommate in Manhattan and had awakened with a hangover. The man loved his shots of Jagermeister and his Cosmopolitans. He ran a public relations firm with an office in San Francisco and another in New York, where he worked out of his apartment. He had to fly to the West Coast for a business meeting and a weekend wedding, where he was to serve as an usher for a fraternity brother of Egyptian and Muslim descent. Mark was flying on a reduced-fare ticket known as a companion pass. It was made available because his mother and his aunt were United flight attendants. There were seats available on two early-morning flights, he was told in a call to the airline late the previous night. If he made the seven o'clock flight, fine. If not, he would catch the eight o'clock. But now he was about to miss the later flight, too.

Leaving his house, Hall began taking short-cuts to the Newark Airport, getting frustrated at the traffic backups on the interstate, complaining about Jersey drivers not knowing how to merge. As they approached the airport, they could see the Manhattan skyline, and Mark said, "There's the Twin Towers." The sun had not yet illuminated the World Trade Center, and the towers appeared to Hall to be all cold, blue, dark steel. After they arrived at the airport, Mark cleared security, found the gate for Flight 93, and, with no time to spare, was the last passenger to board the plane. He sat in seat 4D, across the aisle from Tom Burnett, who was in 4B and headed home to see his family.

Flying made Mark nervous, said Paul Holm, his former partner. He would grow tense. Mark liked being in control and, in the air, he felt he lacked authority. This apprehension, however, did not keep him from flying frequently between the coasts. As Hall drove away from the airport, his cell phone rang. It was Mark. "Thanks for driving," he said. "I made the plane. I'm in first class, drinking a glass of orange juice."

A curious vision popped into Hall's head. Mark was sitting in his first-class seat, smiling at him, the sun coming through the window over his shoulder. Clear as a bell Matt could see him, as if he, too, were across the aisle in first class. How odd. What did it mean? *Is this the last time I'm going to see him?* The thought appeared and evaporated in an instant. "Give me a call when you get there," Hall said.

4

With all passengers aboard Flight 93, the door at Row 8 was closed and sealed. Another busy air-travel morning was underway around the country. Eventually, more than four thousand five hundred flights would be airborne, their speed and direction and altitude intricately spaced and choreographed by the nation's air traffic controllers.

Only thirty-seven seats were occupied on Flight 93, which had a capacity of one hundred eighty-two. This left passengers ample room to spread out for reading, working or sleeping. With such a small load, the five flight attendants would have an easy time serving a hot breakfast of omelets and waffles, pushing the metal drink cart down the long aisle first, then the food cart. Later, a movie called *A Knight's Tale* was scheduled to be shown.

Toshiya Kuge, a twenty-year-old college student, was returning to school in Japan. He had taken an English-language immersion course at the University of Utah in March to improve his speaking and writing skills. When a teacher's assistant, Eiji Yamamoto, took students to a supermarket in Salt Lake City, Toshiya said he preferred to go alone. He often went shopping and to the movies by himself. "I want to act independently, because I want to use English practically," he said. Toshiya returned to North America in late August to go whale watching, rafting and horseback riding. He also visited Niagara Falls, met a friend in New York and inspected colleges. A sophomore in the School of Science and Engineering at Waseda University in Tokyo, he was considering obtaining his master's degree in Canada or the United States.

"He longed to come to America," said Toshiya's mother, Yachiyo Kuge. "Perhaps he liked the freedom. He loved the language and the music. And sports. He wanted to play sports there."

He loved challenges and was disciplined and dynamic in his efforts to achieve them. Toshiya had shaved his hair in a buzz cut as a sign of his determined youth. He was an engineering student, but he eagerly attended English courses at the university's Institute of Language Teaching. A leader in the class, he often assisted others on difficult questions about the language and the American culture. "Because his engineering classes were held far away from the building that our classes were in, he bought a bicycle so that he wouldn't be late for class," said Eleanor Kelly, an American who taught Toshiya at Waseda. "There were a few weeks when Toshiya had injured his leg, and it was in a cast, and he had to use crutches, but even then, he came to class as quickly as possible on foot."

Toshiya had been a soccer goalkeeper in high school, and, wearing number ninety-five on his maroon jersey, he had played American football as a linebacker in his freshman year at Waseda University. A passionate fan of the National Football League, he sometimes stayed awake in the middle of the night to watch games delivered by satellite. He had a poster of the San Francisco 49ers on his bedroom wall, but his favorite team was the Pittsburgh Steelers. He had a Steelers' jersey and took it with him on his trip.

"He had a very strong sense of what the right course in life was," his mother said.

Deora Bodley also was headed back to school for her junior year at Santa Clara University. She was majoring in psychology, with a minor in French. Even though she attended school in northern California, she dressed as if she were still in her hometown of San Diego — in blue jeans and a tank top. She wore her dark hair pulled back, and, at twenty, had the fortunate metabolism to remain thin despite a taste for sweets. Some of her friends called her Buddha, riffing on her last name, and she sometimes carried little Buddha statues with her, or handed them out for good luck. Her teachers found her to be a young woman of unusual introspection. At age eleven, she wrote: "People ask how, what, where, when and why. I ask peace." Deora seemed to thirst for solutions to antagonism and discord, perhaps, in part, because her own parents had divorced when she was young. "I don't think she necessarily suffered as a child of divorced parents, but she did look for answers to problems having to do with life, some of them revolving around blended families," said Deora's father, Derrill Bodley. An inveterate reader, she favored science fiction and fantasy, books where war and poverty and famine could be eradicated by simply dreaming, where good prevailed over evil in mighty struggles.

"She had a fierce inward eye, always looking at herself, questioning," said Chris Schuck, chairman of the English department at La Jolla Country Day School, an exclusive school near San Diego that Deora attended.

Her senior year, Deora was captain of the basketball team. During the season, Schuck said, she faced the dilemma of keeping quiet or alerting school authorities to the fact that one of her younger teammates had been pouring vodka in a water bottle and drinking before practices and scrimmages. It was a wrenching adolescent struggle. Should she turn the teammate in and risk being called a snitch, or keep quiet?

"She decided that, in her role as captain, she needed to look out for the well-being of the team and the health of a fourteen- or fifteen-year-old kid, so Deora let the coach know," Schuck said. "She did it knowing she would likely incur the wrath of other players and students, looking like someone who had turned someone else in. She was the kind of person who faced these internal struggles and was always trying to do what was right, what had to be done."

Deora also participated in a peer program at the school, in which students educated others about the scourge of AIDS. She served as a volunteer at a local animal shelter, and struck employees as one of the few teenagers who never seemed to be standing around waiting to be picked up by their parents. "When her mother picked her up, she had to go to the kennels to find Deora," said John Van Zante, a spokesman for the Helen Woodward Animal Center. "As long as she was here, she was going to be with the animals."

As part of a work-study program at Santa Clara, Deora participated in America Reads, spending two hours a day, four days a week, tutoring third- and fourth-graders at a local elementary school. She read to kids, helped them with their writing, assisted them in putting on puppet shows. For a pair of Vietnamese twins who had come to the school from Toronto, she translated stories from English to French. "Deora made the sun shine brighter," one of the students wrote, expressing what many felt about her eager smile and open personality. "She spread her light and all of us have a piece of her," said her mother, Deborah Borza.

"Deora was one of those individuals who was born to work with kids," said Kathy Almazol, the principal at St. Clare Elementary School. "She didn't have to work at it. It was easy for her."

She had spent the summer at the school as an aide to second-graders, and after traveling east to visit a friend, she was due back to begin work during the fall semester. "I'm coming back early so I can get started," Deora told Almazol before she left.

Patricia Cushing and Jane Folger were traveling to San Francisco on vacation. They were sisters-in-law who lived in Bayonne, New Jersey, and who sat together in Row 19. Both women were retired after working hard to support large families in the absence of their husbands. Patricia, sixty-nine, was a widow. Jane, seventy-three, was divorced. Their personalities meshed as pieces of a jigsaw, Patricia being a soothing influence on her more trenchant sister-in-law. A nervous flier, Patricia longed to visit San Francisco, but she had been grounded by her late husband's even greater reluctance to board a plane. Thirteen years after he died, Patricia would finally get to see the Golden Gate Bridge in person. She could ride a cable car and shop and feel the pampered, clean-scrubbed energy of a city bathed in fog and pale light.

If there were any sales to be found in San Francisco, Jane would locate them the way a divining rod located water. She had a disciplined shopper's stamina and patience, a retired bank officer's precision with numbers. She walked three miles a day, keeping fit for her forays into New York City, which she visited at least once a week by bus, shopping alone or with her sister-in-law, eating lunch at Lord & Taylor, mastering the art of buying expensive clothes at bargain prices.

"She knew the mark-down racks like she knew her own house," said Kathleen Kulik, Jane's daughter.

The dissolution of a contentious marriage had been complicated for Jane by the deaths of two of her six children. One son, John, had been killed in Vietnam in 1969 and another son, Terence, had died of AIDS in 1994 after a blood transfusion, which numbed their mother's vitality. "I think she

69

lost her spirit for living," her daughter said. Where Jane had once been timid, her emotions suppressed, they now surfaced in a voice that could be outspoken and caustic. It was her grandchildren, and the energy of New York City, that seemed to reinvigorate her. She had six grandchildren and she took them frequently to Manhattan, a scout leader and her troop of cultural explorers. The previous spring, Jane and two of her granddaughters were photographed atop the World Trade Center. With her grandkids, with her sister-in-law, or alone, she visited the city on walking tours, attended concerts, shopped, patronized the theater and museums. She would write down everything she did and save it for her weekly chats with her daughter.

"She wanted to get out and be independent; she never was when she was married," Kulik said.

The trip to San Francisco had been a gift from Kulik, who figured that her aunt would be the perfect traveling companion for her mother. Patricia never seemed to get rattled or have a bad word to say. She loved movies, the opera, ballet, and she always found a pearl of encouragement in life's gritty irritations. When her husband died of a heart attack in 1988, she remained calm, persevering, returning to her job as a service representative for New Jersey Bell to raise her five children. When one of her sons suffered a diving injury, she made dinner for him every day for two months, taking it to the hospital across the river in New York, pushing him to regain his mobility.

"She would come home so exhausted, but she never missed a day," said Patricia's daughter, Pegeen Cushing. Later, when they found out about Flight 93, her children reminded themselves to remain as composed and upbeat as their mother always had been.

Her children jokingly chided Patricia about her fastidious nature, about how she made them sit ramrod straight at the table and kept the living room off-limits so that it would be spotless for visitors. Her whole life seemed to be organized in her daily planner. She played mahjong once a week and was learning to use a computer. She had a cell phone, but used it only in the car, for emergencies, and did not bring it on the trip. Just before she left, Patricia worried whether the lettuce in her refrigerator would keep for a week while she was gone. "A week later, the lettuce was still good," Pegeen Cushing said later with a rueful laugh. "She would have been so happy to come home to that damn lettuce."

In the days before they left for San Francisco, Patricia and Jane moved up the time of their flight, Pegeen Cushing said. They also had one of Jane's sons call a friend in California to ask when earthquake season was, as if earthquakes occurred with the timeliness of crops and migrating whales.

"Ma, what are the chances of an earthquake?" Pegeen Cushing asked.

The women were taking no chances. They would tell the front desk at the hotel that they wanted to stay on the ground floor.

"If there's an earthquake, we want to get out," Patricia Cushing said.

As Flight 93 prepared to roll away from Gate 17, Captain Jason Dahl began the standard call-and-response conversation with the ground crew.

"Cockpit, this is ground crew. Our pre-departure checks are complete. Standing by for pushback clearance."

"Roger, stand by for pushback clearance."

Captain Dahl likely had First Officer LeRoy Homer Jr. call Ground Control on his VHF radio and ask for authorization to depart the gate. Authorization was granted, with directions to point the tail of the plane to the north or south. Captain Dahl then pushed another button on his radio console and called the ground crew again.

"Clear to push. The brakes are still set."

"Roger, clear to push. Release brakes."

"Brakes released."

After the plane was pushed away from the gate by a tug, the ground crew instructed

Captain Dahl to reset the brakes. The conversation was identical and methodical on every flight, each instruction repeated to ensure no one on the ground was crushed by a plane weighing more than one hundred twenty tons.

"Roger, brakes set," Captain Dahl replied. If all went well, he was to respond, "Pressure normal."

The ground crew then alerted the cockpit that the tow bar had been disconnected and a pin had been removed from the landing gear. "Am I clear to disconnect headset?" the ground-crew member asked.

"Roger, clear to disconnect headset. I will look for your salute."

The ground-crew member pulled the tug away from the 757, got out and saluted Captain Dahl, who flashed his taxi lights in response. By this time, the engines were likely started. First Officer Homer having spooled the turbofans to a certain speed, drawing in compressed air and delivering fuel for ignition.

"I have salute, release from guidance, taxi clearance," Captain Dahl said, readying his audio panel to speak to air traffic control.

With Flight 93 still on the ground in Newark at eight a.m., American Flight 11 departed from Boston's Logan Airport for a cross-country flight to Los Angeles. The

Boeing 767 was instructed to climb to thirty-five thousand feet, but the instructions were ignored. The plane climbed only to twenty-nine thousand feet and then halted radio contact. It had been hijacked.

At eight twenty-four, a voice thought to be that of the terrorist Mohamed Atta was overheard. He apparently believed that he was speaking to the passengers. Instead, he reached the air traffic controllers: "We have some planes. Just stay quiet and you will be okay. We are returning to the airport. Nobody move, everything will be okay. If you try to make any moves, you'll endanger yourself and the airplane. Just stay quiet."

At eight twenty-five, the Boston air control tower alerted several air traffic centers that Flight 11 had been hijacked. Four minutes later, the Boeing 767 made a turn that took the shape of a shark's fin and headed almost due south toward Manhattan.

At eight thirty-four, one of the hijackers again spoke on the air traffic frequency: "Nobody move please, we are going back to the airport. Don't try to make any stupid moves."

The pilots, flight attendants and passengers aboard Flight 93 were unaware of the trouble aboard American Flight 11. The pre-flight routine continued as normal. Unknown to the forty other people aboard, the four

Middle Eastern men seated in first class were confederates of Mohamed Atta's. The men — Ziad Jarrah, Ahmed Alhaznawi, Saeed Alghamdi and Ahmed Alnami — had been advised to pray as they sat on the plane.

On an undated videotape, made perhaps six months earlier, a man identified as Alhaznawi said, "We left our families to send a message that has the color of blood. This message says, 'Oh, Allah, take from our blood today until you are satisfied.' The message says, 'The time of humiliation and subjugation are over.' It is time to kill Americans in their own homeland, among their sons, and near their forces and intelligence."

Wearing a scraggly beard, a camouflage vest and a checked head scarf on the videotape, Alhaznawi read from a spiral-bound notebook titled "The Last Will of the New York and Washington Battle Martyrs." The notebook bore an Islamic date equivalent to March 6, 2001.

"The United States is nothing but propaganda and a huge mass of false statements and exaggeration," Alhaznawi said on the videotape. "However, the truth is what you saw. We killed them outside their land, praise be Allah. Today, we kill them in the middle of their home."

By now, the morning of September 11, the four Islamic men in first class were to have made an oath to die, showered, shaved the excess hair on their bodies and splashed themselves with cologne. They had been given detailed handwritten instructions on how to prepare for their final hours on earth. The author of the four-page document was unknown. Perhaps it was Atta, the suspected ringleader of the four September 11 hijackings. The letter was to have been read the previous night. It was a spiritual and practical guide on how the terrorists should fortify against self-doubt and infighting, on how they should prepare to enter paradise by killing their victims and themselves. They were to know their plan well and to expect a response from the passengers, from the enemy. The letter read:

"Remind your soul to listen and obey and remember that you will face decisive situations that might prevent you from one hundred percent obedience, so tame your soul, purify it, convince it, make it understand and incite it. God said, 'Obey God and His Messenger and do not fight amongst yourselves or else you will fail. And be patient, for God is with the patient.' "

Their souls should have been purified of all unclean things.

"Completely forget something called 'this world.' The time for play is over and the serious time is upon us. How much time have we wasted in our lives? Shouldn't we take advantage of these last hours to offer good deeds and obedience? You should feel complete tranquility because the time between you and your marriage [in heaven] is very short. Afterwards begins the happy life, where God is satisfied with you, and eternal bliss in the company of the prophets, the companions, the martyrs, the good people, who are all good company."

They should have blessed their bodies by reading the Koran. By a rubbing of the hands, they should have also blessed their luggage, clothes, knives, IDs, passports, papers.

"Check your weapon before you leave and long before you leave. You must make your knife sharp and must not discomfort your animal during the slaughter."

They should have tightened their clothes before the battle. They should have secured their shoes and worn socks to make sure their feet would stay in their shoes. They should have said a morning prayer in a group, and prayed again in the car or the taxi to the airport, and they should have smiled and remained calm, for God was with the faithful.

They should have prayed: "Oh Lord, take your anger out on [the enemy] and we ask you to protect us from their evils." And: "Oh Lord, protect me from them as you wish." And: "Oh Lord, block their vision from in front of them, so that they may not see."

Before they entered the plane, they were to have prayed and remembered "that this is a battle for the sake of God." When the plane took off, they were to pray for victory over the infidels and say, "Give us victory and may the ground shake under their feet."

They were to pray for themselves and their brothers and ask God to grant them martyrdom facing the enemy, not running away from him. When the confrontation began, they were to clench their teeth and "strike like champions who do not want to go back to this world." They were to shout, "Allahu Akbar," (*God is Great*), "because this strikes fear in the hearts of the infidels."

"God said, 'Strike above the neck and strike at all their extremities.' Know that the gardens of paradise are waiting for you in all their beauty and the women of paradise are waiting, calling out, 'Come hither, friend of God.' They have dressed in their most beautiful clothing.

"If God decrees that any of you are to slaughter, dedicate the slaughter to your fathers, because you have obligations toward them. Do not disagree, and obey. If you slaughter, do not cause the discomfort of those you are killing, because this is one of the practices of the Prophet, peace be upon him."

They were not to distract or confuse each other and they were not to act out of revenge. "Strike for God's sake," the letter read, adding, "Take prisoners and kill them. As Almighty God said, 'No prophet should have prisoners until he has soaked the land with blood.'"

They were to welcome death when the "hour of reality" approached, and they were to welcome death for God, praying in the seconds before the target was reached or saying, "There is no God but God, and Mohammed is His prophet."

God willing, they would all meet in heaven.

It had been so easy to this point for the hijackers. American intelligence officials had failed to stitch together threads of information that warned of a possible major terrorist attack. The FBI had known for several years that Osama bin Laden and his Al Qaeda terrorist network had sent pilots to be trained in the United States, and that a hijacked plane might be flown, as a suicide mission, into CIA headquarters or another federal building in Washington, according to *The New York Times*. A 1999 report made for the National Intelligence Council, an adjunct of the CIA, warned that terrorists linked to bin Laden might hijack a plane and fly it into the Pentagon, White House or CIA headquarters in McLean, Virginia, the *Washington Post* reported. However, information gathered bit by bit was not shared comprehensively among intelligence officials. On July 5, an FBI agent in Phoenix warned his superiors that bin Laden might be using the cover of American flight schools to train terrorists. He urged an investigation of Middle Eastern flight students. The information was not acted upon by the FBI in Washington, and was not passed along to agents in Minneapolis, who had grown concerned about a Frenchman named Zacarias Moussaoui. He had raised suspicions at a flight school in August when he asked to train on a Boeing 747 simulator despite little experience as a pilot. FBI agents in Minneapolis were also turned down by Washington when they requested permission to open a criminal investigation of Moussaoui after he was arrested on a visa violation on August 17. He would later be charged as a co-conspirator in the September 11 attacks.

President George W. Bush was warned on August 6 that bin Laden might be plotting a hijacking, but the president would later say that he had not been presented with the scenario that planes would be used as missiles.

"Had I known that the enemy was going to use airplanes to kill, I would have done everything in my power to protect the American people," the president would say eight months later.

Remarks by the administration, however, would anger some Flight 93 families, who believed the government had acted insufficiently to prevent the unfolding catastrophe.

"You've got to expect the unexpected; we got caught with our pants down," said Jack Grandcolas, the husband of Lauren Grandcolas. "How long has it been, thirty years, since that movie, *Three Days of the Condor*, where the CIA and the FBI were being paid to play what-if games? That's their job, to expect the worst-case scenarios. You have an obligation to alert the FAA and the airlines to be on the lookout for these individuals. And you've got to have an exit strategy, which any third-grade class can figure out: As soon as planes are being hijacked, land the others immediately. Put the planes on the ground. It haunts me to think this could have been prevented."

The prospect of four Middle Eastern men occupying first-class seats on Flight 93 with one-way tickets apparently had raised no alarm at the ticket counter. And, at American airports, the screening of passengers and carry-on baggage was hardly foolproof. The security company operating at Newark International Airport, Argenbright, had come under heavy criticism for lapses that included hiring screeners with criminal records in Philadelphia and allowing the skipping of training sessions. The screeners had a high turnover rate. They were poorly paid, and, in many instances, poorly educated and poorly motivated. But American complacency went beyond the people who manned the X-ray machines and magnetometers. United Airlines and airport officials said they were unaware of any security breach in Newark on September 11. There was hardly any need for one. Knives under four inches in length were legal to carry on a plane. There was no uniform rule against box cutters. Cockpit doors offered little resistance. Self-defense training for pilots and flight attendants did not prepare them for hijackers who wanted to use the planes as missiles instead of bargaining chips. While the unsuspecting passengers went about their pre-flight routines, the terrorists intending to hijack four flights this morning had done their homework. They had studied the flights for months, taken rehearsal trips, armed themselves with low-tech weapons that would not be detected or confiscated. The hijackers aboard Flight 93 were armed with at least one box cutter that appeared to have been store-bought and another cutting device that seemed to be homemade, a piece of metal wrapped in tape.

The Monday rush of businessmen and tourists was over. Tuesday was a light travel day, fewer passengers to confront, maximum fuel to detonate on a scheduled cross-country flight.

Tuesday, September 11.
9/11.
911.
National Emergency Day.

Mark Rothenberg, known to his friends and family as Mickey, flew United so often that he had been invited to company head-quarters in Chicago as a consultant for passenger services. He had flown more than a million lifetime miles. "You could wallpaper a room with all of his upgrade coupons," said his wife, Meredith. The trick was, Mickey used to say, half the time the coupons were never collected, and he could fly a whole year on the same six upgrade certificates. United always bumped him up to first class. On this trip, in seat 5B, he was headed to Taiwan for business. He liked the eight a.m. United flight because he would have a long layover in San Francisco, and he could work the phones for a couple of hours instead of wasting a whole day. He was a one-man business, MDR Global Resources, serving as a middleman between American importers and producers of housewares in Taiwan, Hong Kong and mainland China. He brokered deals for everything from cookware to ice buckets to mouse pads. Whatever people needed, he could get it made. Sometimes he designed patterns for glassware, a business he and his father had previously owned in Brooklyn, New York. Mickey traveled to China as often as ten times a year. He was always working. At Madison High School in Brooklyn, he played golf and bridge, and he told friends that one of his bridge partners had been Charles Schumer, who became a United States senator. Now, Mickey liked to watch sports on television and drive his BMW convertible in Scotch Plains, New Jersey, but all he really had time for was his work and his family. He was the father of two daughters — Rachel, twenty-seven, and Sara, twenty-three.

"He was a complete workaholic," his wife said. "He wanted to be very successful."

Because of the time difference between the East Coast and Asia, Mickey worked upside-down hours, sleeping from four in the morning until nine. He had a bad back, and smoked a pack a day, but he was a human Rolodex with phone numbers and he had a salesman's passionate optimism and casual ebullience. On flights, he always seemed to find himself seated next to interesting people. Richard Branson, the chairman of Virgin Atlantic Airways. The political commentator Arianna Huffington. A handful of celebrities. Always he introduced himself. "If he saw a celebrity, he met a celebrity," Meredith said.

Once, Mickey ran into the comedian Jackie Mason at a restaurant in Los Angeles, and their identical black Mercedes-Benzes got switched in valet parking. Mickey drove back to his hotel and later that night he got a call from Mason, who said, "I don't know if I stole your Mercedes or you stole my Mercedes," and they had a laugh and exchanged cars. He ran into Mason one more time in L.A. and told him, "Remember me, I'm the guy who stole your car."

Mickey could pack for a trip in ten minutes, grabbing clothes out of his closet, not bothering to count the number of shirts and slacks. He always wore the same thing, a black cashmere sweater and slacks. Sometimes he'd come home with product samples in his luggage and Meredith would find broken glass among his clothes. At other times, he was far more particular. With food especially. Once he went to lunch in Lake Placid, New York, ordered a cheeseburger and sent it back, not one time, or twice, but eight times.

"He was used to his own way and he usually got it," his wife said.

At the same time, he was outgoing, trusting of others. At college at Franklin and Marshall in the late 1960s, he would tape a nickel to his windshield every night, assuming that the meter maids would stick it into the parking meter in the morning. When he flew and met someone from another country, he would invariably say, "Welcome to the United States." He had become so close to one of his business associates in China that he was named godparent to two of his partner's children. On United Flight 93, though, four of the other men in first class were not businessmen but terrorists. Meredith Rothenberg later wondered if her husband had been sitting near one of these men or what happened if he had tried to speak with them. Did they make an example of him? She became convinced that he was killed early.

"He was a salesman, a negotiator, that's what he did for a living," Meredith said. "He would have said, 'Guys, take it easy, we can work this out.'"

After Flight 93 pushed back from the gate, it fell into a line of twelve to fifteen planes that were taxiing toward the runway. This was typical in Newark. But the airlines had in recent years built delay time into their schedules. Depending on headwinds, Flight 93 might still make an on-time landing in San Francisco at eleven-fifteen a.m.

When he had made his way to the front of the line for takeoff, Captain Dahl was given the standard instructions from the Newark control tower: "United 93, you are cleared to position, hold on runway four left."

"Roger, position hold, four left."

And finally, "United 93, you're cleared for takeoff, runway four left."

"Roger, cleared for takeoff, runway four left."

The flight attendants were now seated for takeoff. Deborah Welsh sat in a jump seat in first class, while Lorraine Bay and Wanda Green took the jump seats at the door between first class and coach. CeeCee Lyles and Sandra Bradshaw sat in the rear galley.

With the guttural, thirty-six-thousand-pound thrust of its twin Pratt and Whitney engines, Flight 93 roared down the runway, lumbering inertia giving way to inexorable speed, the nose wheels lifting and the rest of the plane leaving the ground with a kind of swooping weightlessness. It was eight forty-two a.m. Following standard procedure, Flight 93 took off to the northeast, on a forty-degree heading, turned another twenty degrees to the right and followed this path for four miles toward Manhattan. It held to an altitude of two thousand five hundred feet because of approaching traffic at higher altitudes, and then banked westward at a heading of two hundred ninety degrees — nearly due west. Jetliners seemed to hover as they approached these graceful, teardrop turns. Off to the right, the towers of the World Trade Center, rising one hundred ten stories, were visible in the metallic shimmer of early morning.

The previous day, Alan and Kimi Beaven had celebrated their eighth wedding anniversary. Both were recovering from illness, and they celebrated by staying home and having a wonderful, quiet time together. Alan had a long drive to Newark International Airport on the eleventh. He was up and gone by four-thirty, giving himself plenty of time for the two-hour trip. Since mid-August, Alan, Kimi and their five-year-old daughter, Sonali, had been living in an ashram in South Fallsburg, New York. The ashram was affiliated with the SYDA Foundation, a meditation and philanthropic organization. SYDA was the acronym for the Siddha Yoga Dham of America. During the summer, the ashram was a popular destination for thousands of people daily. As it billed itself, Siddha Yoga was dedicated to the "upliftment of humanity and the end of human suffering" through meditation, contemplation and selfless service.

An attorney, Alan practiced environmental law. While at the ashram, he had been rising at five each morning, meditating for an hour, preparing for a pending case in California, then doing legal work for the SYDA Foundation. He was scheduled to become its general counsel. Alan was headed to San Francisco to dispose of a Clean Water Act case so that he might soon begin a year's sabbatical. His plans were not firmly set, but he was considering traveling to India to do environmental work in a valley region outside of Bombay. He had hiked in the region the previous year and had grown concerned about India's severe problems of pollution and deforestation.

"He got really impassioned and inspired to see what he could do," Kimi Beaven said. "There was this beautiful countryside, but it was horribly contaminated, and it was clear that in a very short time it would be lost."

At forty-eight, Alan had passed the bar exam in his native New Zealand, England, New York and California. Previously, he had served as a prosecutor for Scotland Yard and as a securities and antitrust attorney. Alan wore khakis and flannel shirts to work and declined to be hard-wired to the modern technological conveniences of computers, dictaphones and cell phones. Nor did he display his diplomas in his San Francisco office. He wrote his briefs in longhand, often completing them weeks before they were due, and he stored his files in accordion folders that were kept on the floor in his office.

"I bought him a new computer once and the next day his monitor was covered with Post-it notes," laughed Joe Tabacco, a law partner of Beaven's. "I wouldn't say he didn't know how to use a computer. He just used it as a bulletin board."

In the beginning, Alan knew little about environmental law except that it would make him a lot less money than securities law did. Still, it appealed to him on several levels. He had grown up amid the isolated beauty of

New Zealand and had later dived and surfed in southern California. And he felt that private environmental litigation could accomplish more substantive results than suits filed by nonprofit organizations such as the Sierra Club.

"I don't know if he was ever a tree hugger," Tabacco said. "He was grounded and pragmatic. I think he enjoyed the intellectual challenge of the Clean Water Act. He felt he could have fun and do some good."

In court, his style was not to try to dominate a case, but to let his opponent dig a trench for himself. He was of the opinion that a person never learned anything when his mouth was open. Still, he thrived on winning, and his courtroom manner was succinct and clever to the point of audacity. Once, while he was practicing in England, his client was accused of stealing a large cut of meat from a supermarket. The man also happened to be a magician. In court, Alan asked his client to make the hunk of meat disappear, which he did, into a large pocket. Why, Alan asked the jury, would his client leave a store with a roast that was visible to security guards when he could have easily hidden it and made a furtive escape? Although the judge later admonished Alan not to try such theatrics again, his client was found not guilty.

Upon arriving in England from New Zealand, according to a friend, Alan showed up at Oxford University and asked for a teaching job in the law department. Appalled at his brazenness, university officials sent him away. Undeterred, Alan next went to Cambridge. This time, the friend said, he impressed a professor with his confidence and persistence, and was put in touch with King's College in London, where he did gain a position teaching law.

"Alan just went for things," said the long-time friend, Dr. Richard Gillett, a psychiatrist. "He knew courage was very necessary for a life to be fully lived."

In his first environmental case, Alan took on Mobil Oil. Alone. "He got creamed," his wife said. "Later, he won a case against Shell in California."

While assisting his partner, Joe Tabacco, in a civil suit in 1994, Alan showed up in court dressed in a lime-green suit, skinny tie and slicked-back hair to read the deposition of an absentee defendant in a stock-fraud case. Later the defendant settled out of court after agreeing to pay thirty-five million dollars. "Alan looked like the sleaziest guy you'd ever meet," Tabacco said. "Afterward, when we talked to the jurors about what they were thinking, they said that the testimony of the defendant was terrible. He wasn't even there."

His competitiveness carried over to the tennis court, where at six foot three, two hundred five pounds, he developed a ferocious serve and a reliable slice on his ground strokes. He played in a determined way, not accepting defeat easily. "He always worked his ass off to win," said Gillett, who played tennis with Alan for two decades. Meditation seemed to help him deal with his inner frustrations, Tabacco said. "Ninety percent of the time, he was a sleeping volcano," he said. "When that ten percent erupted, you didn't want to be around. He would go after you with a vengeance, in a clipped, controlled way. You could see it in the way he played tennis, running everything down."

But he had a gentler, inspiring side, especially with children. Alan taught children to swim, to climb rocks, to lose their fear. His daughter, Sonali, would climb to the high branches of a tree, close her eyes and drop, trusting completely that her father would catch her. Every morning, before he went to work, Alan read to Sonali. "I'll never say no to a book," Alan said. This morning, however, he left for Newark long before the sun came up. He returned his rental car and checked in at seven a.m. He expected that his case in California would be settled in a few days. He phoned his wife, Kimi, said he loved her and that he hoped to be home by the weekend.

Seated in seat 17C, Hilda Marcin was

92

headed cross-country to live with her daughter in Danville, California. At seventy-nine, she had retired as an instructional aide at an elementary school in Mount Olive, New Jersey, where she worked with special-education children, many of whom had come from families that were abusive or riven by drugs and alcohol. She had been a popular and dependable member of the staff, always remembering birthdays with a card and a pound cake or a box of doughnuts, serving as a substitute secretary, sitting with her message pad at the ready, pen uncapped, her hand near the phone so that she could answer it the moment it rang. "She was wonderful, never a harsh word," said Danielle Fredrickson, the vice principal at the Tinc Road School. "She had high morals. Her standards were very high."

Born Hildegarde Zill in the German village of Schwedelbach, Hilda had grown up on a farm where she kept a pet goose in a tub and wrapped her piglets in blankets and brought them to sleep inside on cold winter nights. She told the stories of her childhood to her two daughters, and they wrote them down: Hilda's father was a musician in the renowned Circus Krone, and when he traveled, the family rented out a room to make extra money. One of the rooms had been rented to a Jewish woman, a seamstress. Nazi enforcers — policemen or perhaps storm troopers — showed up at the farm one day in 1929, demanding half of everything produced on the farm. Hilda's mother cut the head off a chicken and said defiantly, "Here's your half." The men also told the family not to rent rooms to Jews anymore and took the woman boarder away "to live with others like her."

Living in Germany had become untenable. Leaving the farm only with what could be packed in a few trunks, the family immigrated to the United States, passing through Ellis Island and settling in Hoboken, New Jersey, then Newark and, finally, Irvington. Hilda was eight at the time, fluent in German and French, but she did not speak English, and she was held back several times in grammar school. But her mother would not allow French and German publications in the house, and soon Hilda learned sufficient English to graduate from high school with other kids her age. Later, she would grow impatient with those who kept their foreign accents long after they had entered the United States. And she would never return to Germany after she had been unnerved by the tall, threatening men at the door.

Her father operated a pushcart vegetable business to make a living during the Depression, and when he broke his ankle, Hilda helped her mother scrub floors for neighbors on Saturdays to pay the mortgage. In

Irvington, the family lived next to an amusement park, which provided free admission to those who were subjected to the constant rackety din and unison screams of the rollercoaster. The park also had a band shell, where Hilda's father worked as bandleader. When she later married, Hilda loved to go dancing at the park, and roller-skating at an indoor rink.

The shock of the Japanese attack on Pearl Harbor on December 7, 1941, stayed with her through the years. "We weren't in the war yet, things like that didn't happen," said her daughter Elizabeth Kemmerer. "It was devastating, all those people killed." During World War II, Hilda was hired as a bookkeeper at the shipyards in Kearny, New Jersey. She worked seven days a week, so many hours that she did not even have time to buy her own nylons. She used to joke that she could have christened the ships by reaching out of her office window. On February 13, 1943, she married Edward Marcin, who was a welder in a defense factory and later became a police officer. They met on a blind date and married three months later. There was no time for a honeymoon, however, and the next day, Valentine's Day, Hilda went back to work.

She was a vibrant woman who could still do an elegant cartwheel in her fifties. After her husband died, she learned to drive at age sixty-four. "I come back from vacation and my mother's tooling around in a station wagon," her daughter Elizabeth said. "My heart was in my throat." She was of a generation that learned frugality from the Depression and possessed an immigrant's zeal for exactitude. She never threw food away, and saved the buttons from old shirts, saying, "It's hard to get buttons that good." Hilda's years as a bookkeeper had made her precise with numbers and meticulous in her record-keeping. For two decades, she handled the pension fund for Waiters and Waitresses Local 109, and, according to her daughter Carole O'Hare, she once testified against a union official in a fraud-and-extortion case.

"My mother was writing checks," Carole said. "She knew the money was not going where it was supposed to be." Hilda was just as fastidious about her own personal transactions. As a young girl, she had once lost the monthly mortgage money on a bus ride to school, and her father had punished her by making her scrub floors. She would never be so careless again; she saved coupons, noted every bank deposit and withdrawal, kept income tax and credit card receipts all the way back to the 1970s. Her records filled lawn-and-leaf bags.

She remained an independent woman who could take care of herself. The only thing she seemed to fear in life were bicycles. She had never ridden one. Bikes intimidated her. Most things didn't. Once, while she was working at Local 109 and taking the bus home from Newark, a man approached her at a bus stop to ask for directions, while his partner attempted to swipe her purse. "I know your game," she said and whacked the thief over the head with her umbrella. Three times her house in Irvington had been robbed. She chased one burglar away with a billy club that had belonged to her late husband, and, recognizing the man as someone who lived in the neighborhood, she apologized to his parents but said she had to identify him to the police for his own good. Fifteen years ago, when someone stole all her Christmas presents and ate the bananas and oranges she had in her kitchen, she moved out of Irvington to Budd Lake, New Jersey, near her daughter Elizabeth. It was not uncommon for Elizabeth to awaken in the morning to find that her mother had come over to make coffee, or to arrive home to discover that Hilda had cooked a meat loaf for dinner. When she was baking or watching her favorite television program — she loved British comedies — it was difficult to reach her because she often took the phone off the hook.

She was getting older, and the winters were not easy on her arthritis, so Hilda decided to move to California to be with her other daughter, Carole, when she retired from her school job. She usually visited Carole in the summers, traveling west in July. This time Hilda had stayed in New Jersey until after Labor Day, caring for family pets while her daughter Elizabeth and her granddaughter attended a wedding. Carole had not been able to travel to New Jersey for her mother's retirement party, and she spent the summer with an odd, displaced feeling. *Am I going to see her again?* On September 11, Carole woke up with excited anticipation. She had not seen her mother in more than a year. As usual, Hilda had been frugal in her ways, promising Carole that she would walk around with a flashlight at her daughter's home so as not to use too much electricity. The weather would be nice in California, Hilda could putter around in the yard. Her eightieth birthday was approaching in December, and there would be a nice party. She always asked that no one throw her a party, then loved it when they did. Before she flew to her new life outside of San Francisco, she packed four suitcases and all of her jewelry, and made copies of her personal papers for her daughters. She even wrote her own obituary so the newspapers would get it right.

5

Five minutes after Flight 93 took off, American Flight 11 rammed into the north tower of the World Trade Center at nearly five hundred miles an hour. As a third flight, Northwest 1543, began to ascend upon leaving Newark, Mary Steiner heard a gasp in first class. She was seated on the left side of the plane. "Did you see that?" someone across the aisle said. According to Steiner, some passengers had seen the American plane crash into the tower a quarter of the way from the top. Steiner remembered no fire from her vantage point, only smoke. "It was a beautiful morning, and then this," she said. "It was stunning." There was no screaming on her flight, just urgent whispering, she said.

Northwest Flight 1543 was due to depart for Minneapolis at eight a.m., a minute before United Flight 93, but passengers found themselves stuck in the same sclerotic taxi lines. The plane eventually left a few minutes later. Steiner had taken the Northwest flight to build up her frequent flier miles, while her co-worker Christine Snyder chose United 93 for the same reason. They were flying home to Honolulu, Hawaii, after attending the National Urban Forestry Conference in Washington, DC. Christine, who was thirty-two and a newlywed, had never before traveled to the East Coast. Steiner was a native of New Jersey and had decided to give her friend the grand tour of New York City before they departed. Steiner was the chief executive officer of The Outdoor Circle, Hawaii's oldest non-profit environmental organization, whose mission was to keep the five major islands clean, green and beautiful. The Outdoor Circle had lobbied for underground utility wires and, since 1927, had been successful in the banning of billboards in the state.

Christine, who held a degree in political science from the University of Hawaii, served as the environmental group's project manager for landscaping and planting, coordinating a group of volunteers in The Outdoor Circle's eleven branch offices. Tall and blond, she had joined The Outdoor Circle six years earlier as a receptionist and had taken training to become a certified arborist. Once, she had told Steiner, "I could never get emotional over a tree," but her passion soon grew deep roots. She coined the term "tree hater," and she worked diligently to get those who operated schools, shopping centers, military installations and state highways to come around to her way of thinking on preservation issues.

Once, angry that a shopping center had cut all the green off of a stand of trees in order to make the center's sign more visible, she wrote a letter to the editor and gave interviews to express her displeasure. "Management admitted they made a mistake and that the trees wouldn't be topped again," Steiner said.

Christine spent time with maintenance workers at Honolulu schools, explaining proper tree-trimming techniques. Homeowners sometimes called her for advice. She did not hesitate to get out of her car and ask strangers to stop crude pruning with their chain saws. At a development of high-end stores in Waikiki, she succeeded in saving two large banyan trees. Recently, she had planted seventy-five milo, beach heliotrope and coconut palm trees in a Honolulu park, and had completed another planting of fifty trees in conjunction with the opening of an upscale clothing store.

"She had such a keen sense of what was right," Steiner said. "It was black or white, there was no gray with Chris. That was one of the things that was really cool about her. And sometimes it made it difficult from my perspective as her manager. Part of what I do is in the gray area."

While they were in Washington for the forestry conference, Steiner insisted that Christine see New York City. They stayed with friends, and for three days, Steiner served as a tour guide, taking Christine to Chelsea Piers, Times Square, a Broadway show, the Museum of Natural History, the New York Stock Exchange and the World Trade Center. On September 10, they had a drink at Windows on the World on the one hundred sixth floor of the World Trade Center. Christine took rolls and rolls of film, but she was particularly absorbed by a visit to Central Park, an arborist's dream. "It was a mob scene, a beautiful Sunday afternoon, and Chris was blown away by the numbers of people using the park," Steiner said.

Three times Christine changed her return flight, finally settling on Flight 93, which would get her home in time to recover for work in Honolulu on September 12. She and Steiner shared a car service to Newark Airport, then Christine hopped out at the United entrance at Terminal A, saying, "I'll see you tomorrow, have a good trip." Steiner continued on to the Northwest departure area. Christine would connect in San Francisco, Steiner in Minneapolis. In the morning, they would compare their arrival times in a friendly game of who got home first.

From his coach seat on Northwest Flight

1543, Ryan Brown could also see smoke streaming from the punctured World Trade Center. His mother sat in a row behind him. They were on the left side of the plane and could hear murmuring from those on the right side of the aisle. *Why is smoke coming out of the Trade Towers? There must have been an accident.* Maybe a commuter plane had gone astray. Perhaps it was a construction mishap.

"Nobody thought it was terrorists," Brown said.

Then he began to get worried. Nicole Miller, who had been his longtime girlfriend, was also flying that day, aboard United Flight 93. Nicole tried to get home to northern California the day before on a US Airways flight. She sat on her plane in a thunderstorm, waiting for it to pass, but the flight was delayed, ruining her connection. Back in the terminal, she was given an option to reschedule her return flight. She called her mother in San Jose, California, to say that she could fly out later the night of the tenth or wait until the morning of the eleventh. "It's probably safer to fly in the morning," her mother, Cathy Stefani, told her. Nicole called back later to say that she had switched to United 93.

She had flown east to spend time with Brown and his family. They had dated for five and a half years, and had talked of marriage, but their relationship had been contentious. Nicole had begun dating another man, her father and sister said, although she still had feelings for Brown. They had been together since high school.

"They were friends who still cared about each other, but not as fiancés, or boyfriend and girlfriend," said Tiffney Miller, Nicole's sister. Brown's mother saw it differently. "They were still an item," she said.

Nicole was twenty-one, a student in junior college, and her mother thought she could not afford to miss school or work to fly to New Jersey.

"He'll think you're committed to him again," her mother told her.

"I'm going as a friend," Nicole replied.

She flew out on September 6, her father's birthday. David Miller said he tried to talk his daughter out of traveling east. Nicole said that she was twenty-one, an adult, and was going as a friend.

Brown's family had paid for her ticket. Nicole was looking forward to a good time. She had never been to New York. She thought of herself as glamorous, and what city had more allure than the Big Apple? Anyway, Brown wanted her there. He had not been to New Jersey in seven years. It had been too painful. On his last trip, his mother's sister had died in an automobile accident two days before Christmas. Nicole's company would make the trip bearable. A month earlier, Brown said, he had been laid off from his job in software sales. She would cheer him up. He rented a Ford Mustang and picked her up at Newark Airport. They traveled hundreds of miles in three days, down to an aunt's beach house in Wildwood, New Jersey, with the teenage swarm on its boardwalk, up to Atlantic City and the casinos, both of them twenty-one, finally legal but naïve. Nicole blew through forty dollars in one unpracticed rush at the slot machines at Caesar's. They drove through Times Square and down to the skyscraper canyons around the World Trade Center. Nicole seemed to be laughing the whole time. On the Ferris wheel at Wildwood, the wind blowing in her hair. On the streets of mid-town Manhattan as she rushed around one corner, then another, hot-wired to the city's energy. She had bronze skin and a fresh, approachable beauty. In restaurants, strangers came up to her and told her how much they liked her smile. She and Brown used all the film in two disposable cameras and loaded up on souvenirs, the touristy gifts of first-timers, shot glasses decorated with the Manhattan skyline.

Nicole seemed to have a gear that was shifted permanently into overdrive. She took classes in business communication at West Valley College, taught corporate exercise and weight-training classes, ran five or six miles a day, worked at a Chili's restaurant. At Pioneer High in San Jose, she swam on a championship team and played centerfield on the softball team. At five foot four inches, one hundred fifteen pounds, Nicole was small, but her muscular definition was pronounced from rigorous workouts. Two years earlier, Nicole had given up red meat, preferring salads with vegetables and chicken, topping them with salsa and mustard. The Mustard Queen, Brown called her. Her health kick, however, did allow for Starbucks coffee.

"That was her life, working out and staying healthy," her mother said. "She could go and go and go. Probably all that coffee."

When she was younger, Nicole took karate lessons, and she and her sister, Tiffney, rode in horse-show competitions. As a pre-teen, she once jumped off a horse in full gallop to come to the assistance of her sister, who had slipped off an English saddle. "That was typical Nicole," Tiffney Miller said. "She didn't care about herself. She jumped off in full run to see if her sister was okay." At her father's home in Chico, California, she could relax, go hiking, step off the daily treadmill of her life. The baby, her father and stepmother called her. Sometimes she just needed to be hugged. Nicole could be feisty, but she also had a quality that made other people feel at ease. Even animals seemed to grow calm around her. A three-hundred-pound pot-bellied pig that rooted around her father's neighborhood would lay at rest like a pet dog in her presence.

After their intended flights were rescheduled for September 11, Nicole and Brown returned to his grandparents' home near Trenton to spend the night. Nicole was a little nervous about flying alone. Brown bought her a teddy bear and told her to put it in the seat next to her. He told her she was lucky to be on Flight 93. It was non-stop, while he would have to connect to the West Coast. "Flying's safer than driving, especially the way you drive," he joked with her.

They awakened at six for the drive to Newark. Nicole had tried to switch onto Brown's Northwest flight, but was told there were no seats available. He then tried to get on her flight. Brown stopped at Terminal A, walked Nicole to the check-in line and asked whether the United flight was full. No, the ticket agent said. Brown tried to switch to her flight but got nowhere.

What did United care? Brown asked. The flight was almost empty.

They had different destinations, the ticket agent pointed out, Nicole to San Francisco, Brown to San Jose.

He could change his ticket, but it would be expensive. So, Brown stuck with Northwest.

He would connect in Minneapolis, then fly home to San Jose. Nicole would arrive ahead of him in San Francisco and get a ride home. The eleventh had been a special anniversary day for them. They had begun dating five years, eight months ago. When Nicole got home, Brown said, she planned to get her nails done, and they would see each other for dinner, maybe a movie.

"It wasn't like we went just as friends," Brown said. "We were as close as could be."

Brown thanked Nicole for coming on the trip — "You saved me" — and began to walk out of the terminal toward his car. He turned around and looked at her, and Nicole said, "I love you."

"I love you," Brown said.

They had talked again of marriage on the trip, and had made plans to return East to ski in the winter, said Brown's mother, Muriel, who accompanied them. Nicole meant everything to Brown. "ilovenicole" was even the password on his e-mail address.

Later, Nicole left a message on his cell phone. She had bought him a gift in the airport and was looking forward to dinner. "I can't wait to get home," she said.

While Brown's Northwest flight waited on the taxiway, he could see Nicole's United jetliner parallel to his, so close that he pressed his face to the window to see if he could recognize her aboard the gray-and-blue 757.

★ ★ ★

The Northwest flight would not reach its intended destination of Minneapolis. At eight forty-one, the cockpit of another plane, United Flight 175, reported hearing a suspicious transmission — presumably from American Flight 11 — on its departure from Boston to Los Angeles. Then the cockpit went silent on United 175. Air traffic controllers also lost the radar track and became concerned about a second hijacking. The Boeing 767 made a fishhook turn toward Manhattan and descended through eighteen thousand feet at more than five hundred miles an hour. At three minutes after nine, United 175 sliced into the south tower of the World Trade Center, a deadly scythe, and sent up a mushrooming explosion. It did not seem real to people who saw the collision on the ground or watched it on television. Over and over, they said, it seemed like a movie. But it was clear now that the ramming of the towers had not been an accident.

According to Mary Steiner, the captain of her Northwest flight informed the passengers that both towers of the World Trade Center had been hit by hijackers and that all flights were being grounded. Northwest 1543 was being diverted to Toronto instead of Minneapolis. "People were pretty upset," Steiner said. "We had people on our flight who worked at the World Trade Center." She tried to call Christine Snyder on her cell phone to see if she was safe aboard United Flight 93. There was no answer.

Ryan Brown did not remember the captain saying anything about the World Trade Center, only that there had been a tragedy and two hijackings, and that the plane had been ordered to land immediately. *Nicole,* he thought. *Is she all right?* He began to get a sick feeling. He turned to his mother, Muriel Brown, who was seated behind him, and said, "Mom, it's Nicole. Nicole's gone."

Frantically, he began to make phone calls. Eventually, his cell phone would go dead, and he would use the air phone at his seat. By the end of the day, he said, his bill would reach four hundred dollars. Before the plane landed in Toronto, he called Nicole's cell phone. "I'm worried, please call me. I want to hear from you."

He called his roommate, he spoke with Nicole's sister, and later he talked with Cathy Stefani, Nicole's mother.

"Cathy," he said. "What the hell's going on? They're not telling us anything."

"Where are you?" Cathy wanted to know. "What flight is Nicole on?"

Their words were spoken in worry-panic.

"Oh my God, where's Nicole?"

As the flight was being diverted to Toronto, people were talking on their cell phones, and Brown could not sit still. He was a reservist in the Marine infantry, trained in close-quarter combat, all five foot nine inches and one hundred ninety-five pounds of him worried and coiled. He walked the aisle and looked for potential hijackers, not knowing exactly what he was searching for, a suspicious face, furtive danger that could be prevented. Then he sat down and his flight landed in Toronto and taxied to the gate. For more than seven hours, the passengers would not be allowed to leave the plane.

6

At home in the Chicago suburbs, Hank Krakowski shaved his face as he prepared for work. As director of flight operations at United's system control center near O'Hare Airport, he oversaw the dispatch system that monitored one hundred fifty United flights airborne in the early morning. As he listened to National Public Radio, Krakowski heard that a light plane had hit the World Trade Center. He turned on CNN and saw a second plane slam into the south tower at three minutes after nine. This was no general aviation aircraft. It had been traveling nearly six hundred miles an hour. He could tell that it was a 767, and the plane appeared to be dark in color, perhaps a United aircraft, but he could not see any distinctive markings.

"Right then I knew we were in trouble," he said. "Something big and bad was happening."

He called United's control center, located ten miles northwest of O'Hare in Elk Grove, Illinois. At that time of day, O'Hare's domestic operations were in full swing. International flights were inbound over Alaska from Hong Kong and Tokyo, and European flights were headed stateside over the Atlantic.

"Are all of our planes accounted for?" Krakowski asked Mike Barber, the dispatch manager.

"No," Barber responded. United Flight 175 from Boston to Los Angeles was "nordo," meaning there was no radio contact.

Krakowski began to get a sinking feeling. Within a few minutes, he realized how likely it was that Flight 175 had hammered into the World Trade Center.

After dropping her sister, Colleen Fraser, at Newark Airport to catch United Flight 93, Christine Fraser made the ten-minute drive back home to Elizabeth, New Jersey. Recently, Christine had hurt her back. This was her first day out of the house in a while, so she drove to a nearby park and sat in her Honda Civic, drinking coffee and eating a bagel. It was such a beautiful morning.

Colleen was headed to Reno, Nevada, for a grant-writing seminar. Two months earlier, she had been elected vice chairwoman of the New Jersey Developmental Disabilities Council. Born with rickets, a nutritional deficiency that can cause deformity of the bones, Colleen underwent numerous surgeries and stood only four feet six inches tall. When she gave speeches, she sometimes stood on a box at the podium, ensuring that her feisty voice became loudly heard as an advocate for the disabled. She served as executive director of the Progressive Center for Independent Living in Ewing Township, New Jersey, and believed strongly that the disabled should be able to live independently rather than in institutions. She detested the patronizing of what she called "head patters" and campaigned vigorously and ostentatiously for the disabled to be able to speak for themselves, rather than having others speak for them.

"You better not pat her on the head," said Ethan Ellis, executive director of the New Jersey Developmental Disabilities Council. "Anyone who made that mistake got at least a long lecture, if not a heel mashed on their toes."

Street theater was a tactic Colleen often employed. At fifty-one, she wore her hair in red spikes and often wore a button on her vest that said IF YOU'RE NOT PART OF THE SOLUTION, YOU'RE PART OF THE PROBLEM. She carried a miniature copy of the Bill of Rights with her, and she whipped it out of her wallet when she felt aggrieved, saying to the offending person, "You can't argue with the Constitution." Sometimes she also handed out imitation parking tickets, sticking them under the windshield wipers of cars, letting people know that parking ille-

114

gally in spaces for the handicapped would not be tolerated. When she became truly animated, she had even been known to wave around her favorite cane, since lost, which bore the carved head of the champion horse Seabiscuit.

During a Congressional hearing in September of 1988 to consider passage of the Americans with Disabilities Act, Senator Tom Harkin, the Iowa Democrat and one of the bill's authors, said he had just been handed a note stating that sixty-four people were in attendance from New Jersey. "Hell, no, there are one hundred and fifty of us," Colleen shouted. Later, she commandeered a para–transit bus and rode with a dozen activists to Washington, pressuring New Jersey Senators Bill Bradley and Frank Lautenberg to endorse the bill. It passed in July of 1990, and Colleen was invited to the White House when the ADA was signed into law by President George Bush, protecting the civil rights of millions of Americans with physical and mental disabilities.

"She was enormously impatient with the progress in establishing rights for the disabled," Ellis said. "She recognized that getting a law passed was not good enough. It didn't lead to Nirvana. There was still a lot of convincing to do."

Colleen and her sister Christine were a year apart, both disabled, roommates, as close as twins. Their mother had left them when they were seven, Christine said, and their father, a taxi driver, had raised them, with much encouragement, in public housing. Each summer, Colleen and Christine spent three weeks at a camp with others who suffered from disabilities. At the camp, they were unrestrained, unself-conscious. "It taught us independence," Christine said. "We were free. We couldn't run, but we were just as fast as all the others."

It was at this camp that Colleen realized that her disability did not have to exclude her from the American mainstream. At Rutgers University, Colleen lived on campus. At nineteen, she went to Woodstock. "She had a cast on her foot and they were in the mud and she absolutely loved it," Christine said. Later, Colleen became an accomplished wood carver and painter, devoured movies and books, patiently listening to *Gone With the Wind* and *Harry Potter* on tape in her car. She and her sister remained in Elizabeth, Colleen demanding that they stay in the city instead of moving to a rural community. She was willing to drive forty miles to work each day. "I don't know how people live out here," she would say when she got to the country. "There are no road signs to tell you where you are."

Before leaving for Reno, Colleen cooked several meals for her sister to eat while she was away. For months, she had been looking forward to the trip and to writing more grants. "With a little training, I might be dangerous," she joked with Christine. As the sisters arrived at Newark Airport, they were listening to REM's "Losing My Religion" on the radio, a song they both loved. Colleen grew quiet and Christine tapped her on the arm. "You okay?"

"I was until I saw that [airport] sign," Colleen said.

When she flew for the first time, on a trip to Disney World years earlier, her sister rehearsed the boarding process with her, coaching Colleen to take deep breaths to overcome her fear of flying. Colleen breathed deeply on this morning, too, and she seemed fine. She got out of the car, sat on her motorized scooter and began to check in for Flight 93. She would be in Row 19, she told her sister, who had noticed an eerie calm at the airport. Later, as Christine Fraser sat in her car at a park in Elizabeth, she heard on the radio that a plane had hit the World Trade Center. In the pit of her stomach, she knew her sister was going to die.

At Langley Air Force Base in Hampton, Virginia, a captain in the North Dakota Air National Guard, whose code name was Honey, spoke on the phone with his girlfriend. A plane had crashed into the World

Trade Center, she told him. It was the first he had heard of it.

Honey and two other pilots from the Guard's 119th Fighter Wing, known as the Happy Hooligans, were on duty. Honey, on military leave from his job as a pilot for United Express, was based full-time at Langley. At twenty-nine, he was the operations officer in charge this morning. Two other pilots had rotated in from North Dakota for a week. Protecting American airspace from attack was not a demanding job before September 11. The idea that hijacked planes would be used as suicide bombs seemed so unlikely that only fourteen National Guard jets in the entire country were on standby. A week at Langley was a time to relax, watch television, work out, spend time on the computer, catch up on business. Like firemen, the pilots sat and waited for something to happen. When it did, they were usually scrambled to escort Navy jets with transponder problems to their home bases. Or to find doctors lost over the ocean in their Beechcraft Bonanzas. Or, occasionally, to sniff out drug runners. It was a sleepy job. Dozing for dollars, they called it.

As he hung up with his girlfriend, Honey got another call — this one from the fighter wing's home base in Fargo, North Dakota. "Did you hear what happened?" an intelligence officer asked.

"Some plane slammed into the World Trade Center," Honey replied.

"Be ready," the officer said. "There might be something up with that."

Within a minute or so, a Klaxon horn sounded a "battle stations" alert.

The pilots were to climb into their F-16s and await further instructions. There were four hangars at Langley, two on each side of a central building that housed maintenance and sleeping quarters. Inside each hangar was a stoplight. During battle stations, the light showed yellow.

It was nine twenty-four a.m., thirty-seven minutes after the first plane hit the World Trade Center. A National Guard major with the code name Lou removed his glasses and put on his contact lenses before climbing into his F-16. On television, he saw a bulletin on CNN about a second plane hitting the World Trade Center. Then he joined the lead pilot, who in his regular job flew for Northwest Airlines. They were still in the dark about the gravity of the moment. Honey, their supervisor, walked seventy-five yards from the administrative office and told the pilots, "This is just a precaution, I'm sure."

He didn't think anything of it.

Five or ten minutes later, a phone rang in the hangars. This time it was the North East Air Defense Sector, a regional division of the North American Aerospace Defense Command, or NORAD. An urgent voice spoke on the other end.

"How many planes can you send?"

"We have two ready," Honey said.

"That's not what I asked," came the curt reply. "How many can you get airborne?"

"With me, three," Honey said. He hustled to his living quarters and grabbed his flight gear.

The Klaxon horn sounded again, the lights flashed green in the hangars and the F-16s, laden with missiles, roared into the sky. It was nine-thirty now. The pilots were sent east over the Atlantic Ocean, and then north up the coast. They likely reached six hundred miles an hour in a couple of minutes. Flying at twenty-five thousand feet in a straight-line formation, each jet flying two miles behind the other, the pilots assumed they were being scrambled toward New York.

After turning westward, United Flight 93 climbed past seventeen thousand feet, then above twenty-three thousand feet as it was shuttled from local to regional air traffic control. The 757 reached its cruising altitude of thirty-five thousand feet in about twenty minutes, its flight path to San Francisco appearing as a magenta line on a cockpit computer screen below the artificial horizon. Captain Jason Dahl trimmed the plane, making it stable along all three axes, and turned on the autopilot. At this point, said those who flew the latest generation of aircraft, they felt more like managers than pilots until they started to descend for landing.

Captain Dahl, who was forty-three, carried with him on every flight a small box of rocks, a present his teenage son, Matthew, made for him when he was a young boy. It had become a kind of good-luck charm. His own love of flying had consumed him for as long as he could remember. Jason still had a flight magazine he had taken from a plane when he was young. He built model planes and rockets as a kid, and he wrote an article about his love of flying when he was fifteen, winning a scholarship for free flying lessons. The day of his first solo, his father had to drive him to a suburban airport in San Jose, California. While Jason was now qualified to operate a plane, he did not yet have a license to operate a car. Later, he studied aviation at San Jose State University. He wrote that he chose flying over his other hobby, photography, because it afforded "the pleasure of getting paid to do what I enjoy."

He had been hired by United on June 18, 1985. Dave Dosch met Jason that same morning at the airline's Denver training center. Dave showed up a half-hour early for an indoctrination class, hoping to get a front row–center seat, only to find Jason sitting there already. The two would become fast friends. Both rose steadily from flight engineer to copilot to pilot. Jason's seniority number was now two thousand fifty-six among United's ten thousand pilots, and Dave's was two thousand fifty-seven. Both were certified to fly the 757 and the 767 jets, which had common cockpit designs. Jason was a standards captain, which meant he spent about half of each year training and evaluating other pilots and the other half flying. This allowed him to spend more time with his family. Once, when his son, Matthew, had taken a class trip to Washington, DC, Jason had flown the plane himself. He had done the same thing for Jennifer, his stepdaughter. He was also as resourceful with a hammer and a screwdriver as he was with the controls of an airplane. He had spent considerable time the past two years remodeling his home in Littleton, Colorado, which afforded a stunning view of both Denver and the Rocky Mountains. He bunked with his wife, Sandy, in sleeping bags, as he extended the master bedroom and the kitchen. He put in a pond so extravagant — with two waterfalls — that people called it Lake Sandy. Jason could handle the plumbing, the electric and the woodwork, and he was popular with the neighbors for his acts of kindness, lending his tools, cleaning gutters for those who had come to borrow his ladder, stapling loose shingles in place during rainstorms, helping crane operators deliver hot tubs to backyards.

"He didn't know a lot of these people," Sandy Dahl said. "He was just neighborly, willing to help."

Within four years, Jason likely would have become qualified to captain a 777 jet, and eventually a 747, the largest in the fleet. When he retired at sixty, he would have a projected seniority ranking among the top one hundred United pilots. In his profession, seniority meant everything, from the type of aircraft flown to preferred routes to days off for playing golf or attending a child's Cub Scout meetings. He was known for being unfailingly personable, fun and professional as a pilot. At a modest five foot eight, Jason would sometimes jump up to appear taller than his pilot friends when they were having their photographs taken. And he could carry out intricate pranks. Once, he invited Dosch and his wife to an elaborate picnic in Yosemite National Park, complete with wine and cheese. Just when Dosch said he was nearly brought to tears of gratitude by a friend he had known only a few months, Jason asked with a straight face, "Dave, have you ever heard of Amway?"

"I almost had a heart attack," Dosch said. "I thought he was going to give me a thirty-minute presentation on selling door-to-door."

On the job, Jason possessed a sense of responsibility and seriousness that came from shouldering obligations from a young age. When he was thirteen, his older brother, Kenneth, became ill in Vietnam and later died. Before his brother left for his tour of duty, he told Jason, "You have to be the man of the house and take care of the folks when I'm gone." Several years later, his father suffered a heart attack, and Jason helped to run the family dairy business, rising at three-thirty in the morning before his high school classes and driving a truck full of milk and ice cream to school districts in the San Jose area. Occasionally, he continued to drive a truck even after he was hired by United, supplementing a beginning annual salary that was less than twenty-five thousand dollars.

"He was fun, but on the job he was definitely a captain," Dosch said. "He's one of the best, if not the best, I've flown with. In the military, they call it having good hands. Jason had great hands. Flying is a thinking-man's game. It's more than hands and feet. You have to stay ahead, anticipate what you would do if you had engine failure, hydraulic problems, structural problems and how you would keep it flying safely. He could do that. He spent countless hours in that simulator."

Once it became evident that Flight 175 had been hijacked, the United flight operations center began alerting all of its flights. Each United dispatcher monitored ten to thirty flights during a shift; at any given time, a few flights to two dozen were being handled at once. The dispatchers began firing off messages: "Beware cockpit intrusion." And: "Confirm operations are normal." The alert was sent to United Flight 93 via a cockpit computer device called ACARS, the Aircraft Communications and Reporting System. ACARS was often used for transmitting flight plans and weather updates. But this warning was far more urgent. It arrived either via the on-board printer or as a kind of e-mail, making a chiming sound and appearing as green text on a black screen.

"Confirmed," United 93 answered, the one-word response having been typed on a keypad.

Later, Sandy Dahl, the wife of Captain Jason Dahl, would wonder why a more detailed message was not sent, why Flight 93 had not been contacted directly by radio, and whether voice communication might have saved the aircraft from being hijacked. "They should have told them exactly what was going on," Sandy Dahl said. "There should have been a warning, 'We have terrorists and we need to get everyone out of the sky, do not let anyone in the cockpit.' There should have been something in place when all hell broke loose, and there wasn't."

Each United dispatcher sent what he felt was an appropriate message, Hank Krakowski said through a spokesman. The situation was very fluid and was evolving quickly without a lot of reliable information, he said. Voice communication would have taken much longer, and might have been impossible, given the amount of traffic in the air. The ACARS message, on the other hand, was nearly instantaneous.

As Flight 93 approached the Cleveland "en route" center, a regional air traffic center that guided long-range, high-altitude flights, one of the pilots reported with a chipper "Good morning." The plane was flying at thirty-five thousand feet, experiencing intermittent light choppy air. While other pilots asked in a puzzled way about vague problems in New York, Flight 93 did not. The Cleveland center alerted the 757 to another flight off to its right, twelve miles away, at thirty-seven thousand feet.

And then came an interruption, an indeterminate rush in the cockpit, a screaming of "Hey" and violent non-words, high-pitched and muffled exertion, the rustling of surprise and ominous resolve. An air traffic controller was startled and confused by what he heard: "Did somebody call Cleveland?"

Silence followed for half a minute, then either Captain Jason Dahl or First Officer

LeRoy Homer Jr. had the presence of mind to key a button on the audio panel. The cockpit scuffle played desperately over the air traffic control frequency. More yelling, an American voice in blood scream: "Get out of here!" then the same scream again, this time sounding wounded and pleading and in slow motion, and then "Get out of here!" a third time, an angry unheeded order.

The controller at Cleveland center sounded alarmed and asked Flight 93 to verify its altitude at thirty-five thousand feet. No reply. Another call to verify, more silence, the plane heading westward into a threatening unknown.

"United 93, Cleveland," the controller said, raising his voice, concerned and irritated at being ignored. "United 93, Cleveland."

"United 93, if you hear Cleveland center, ident please."

The center called to another United aircraft in the area, Flight 1523: "Did you hear some interference on the frequency here a couple of minutes ago, screaming?"

"Yes, I did," the pilot replied. "And we couldn't tell what it was either."

"Okay," Cleveland center said. "United 93, Cleveland, if you hear the center, ident."

American Flight 1060: "Ditto on the other transmission."

Cleveland: "American 1060, you heard that also?"

"Yes, sir, twice."

"Roger, we heard that also, thanks," Cleveland said. "I just wanted to confirm it wasn't some interference."

Executive Jet Flight 956: "We did hear that yelling, too."

"Okay, thanks," Cleveland said. "We're just trying to figure out what's going on."

It was nine thirty-two a.m.

The hijackers had control of the plane now, out of breath from subduing the pilots.

"Ladies and gentlemen here, it's the captain," one of the terrorists said, believing he was speaking to the passengers but broadcasting over the air traffic control frequency instead. "Please sit down. Keep remaining sitting. We have a bomb aboard."

7

Although her fifth-floor apartment sat directly across the Hudson River from Seventy-second Street in Manhattan, and the kitchen, bedroom and living room offered an unimpeded view of the damaged and teetering World Trade Center, Margaret Cashman had no idea of the day's events unfolding. She was in a spare room, painting, and the television was turned off.

Her husband, William, had jumped into a cab in West New York, New Jersey, at ten after six. Manhattan had just been awakening across the Hudson. Margaret forgot to ask him what flight he was taking. She did not like traveling. Airplanes scared her. She had flown only once in her life, thirty-one years earlier, on her honeymoon to Puerto Rico.

William Cashman, sixty, and Patrick Joseph Driscoll, seventy, were headed on an annual hiking trip to Yosemite National Park. Another friend, John Linner, was already there, with his son. Linner planned to complete his day's hike, get the beer and wine iced, and await their arrival from Fresno that after-noon. All three men had grown up in New York City. Bill Cashman and John Linner were ironworkers and had been paratroopers. Linner grew up in the same neighborhood with Joe Driscoll, as everyone called him, a retired executive director of software develop-ment for Bell Communications Research. Some people liked to walk around malls when they became senior citizens. These men from the cramped city preferred the vast shoulder-room of the wilderness. They could hike for hours, making each other laugh with the silly intimacy of long friendships.

"Hey bear, here we come," Joe Driscoll would say loudly, using his street smarts to scare any predators off the trails. He would joke with his friends that they should always travel with one slow guy. "I won't have to outrun the bear," he would say. "I'll just have to outrun you."

Bill Cashman was tall and wiry, quiet, but he could zing a one-liner, too. Linner thought he was like Jack Benny. Just by looking at you the right way, he could make you laugh. Bill grew up in Hell's Kitchen on Manhattan's West Side, and had helped in-stall iron support structures for the interior ceilings of the World Trade Center. He also taught welding at Metal Lathers Local 46 in New York. He awakened at four-thirty each morning, went to early Mass. He was a blue-collar guy, and he loved sports, but he was curious about many things. He went to the theater, visited downtown art shows to see his nephew's work and was considering acting classes to improve his public speaking, so that he could become a union delegate. Years before, Bill had taken lessons in martial arts and had learned to break a board with his hand. Five years earlier, he had undergone surgery when his intestines burst, and the last rites had been administered. After that, he changed his diet and his life, stayed healthy, went on frequent walks in local parks, took a big hiking trip each year. At six feet, one hundred forty-five pounds, Bill was supple enough that, when hiking, he could pull his foot nearly to eye level and rest it on a tree to tie his boots.

"He loved the idea of being in nature, the fact that you feel so small and insignificant before something that is so large, the sky and the plains and the mountains," said Daniel Belardinelli, a New Jersey attorney and artist who was Bill's nephew. "It was very tranquil for him. He was a monkish-type person in that way."

Seven or eight years earlier, Bill had bought a plot of land in the Pocono Mountains of Pennsylvania. He never built on the land, his nephew said, because he was a man who paid cash for everything and did not want to tap into his pension. He was conservative that way. He didn't drive over fifty-five, and when he flew, he liked to sit by the wing, where he thought it was safer. He had been known to lend two, three thousand dollars to relatives in need, even to the sensei at his martial arts dojo, but he never built his place in the Poconos. "Next year," he would say. Always, next year.

Joe Driscoll had been a hardscrabble kid in the Yorkville section of Manhattan, playing stickball and making footballs out of newspaper and tape. He became a high school swimming champion who later worked as a lifeguard at Coney Island. A superb baseball player, he was scouted by the New York Giants. In his prime, he played in five softball tavern leagues at the same time. Even in his late sixties, he'd go back to play in a yearly old-timers' game. For a period, he competed as a race-walker. The whole family was athletic. Two of Joe's sons, Stephen and Patrick, played college basketball; a third son, Chris, played rugby; and his daughter, Pam, ran track.

The son of poor Irish immigrants, Joe put cardboard in his tattered shoes as a kid, ate Thanksgiving dinners at a charity house and seemed destined for a career in the fire department until the Navy steered him toward college. After the Korean War, he entered engineering school at New York University, and later earned a master's degree in computer science from Rutgers. He was intensely driven to succeed as an engineer and an athlete, and, at age fifty-five, Joe was still racing friends on the beach in the summer at the Jersey Shore. He was tough and quick-tempered, and he had become impatient with what he perceived as foreigners who came to the United States, taking advantage of educational and job opportunities and yet resenting the American way of life.

His personality had mellowed in recent years when Joe's body, always so muscular and reliable, began to fail him. He underwent triple heart bypass surgery in 1993, and had a hip replaced in 1998. He seemed to soften, to be more willing to express his emotions and his approval of his children. At age seventy, Joe was an altar boy, serving at eight a.m. Mass each day at Our Lady of Mercy Catholic Church in Englishtown, New Jersey. He would come home from church and greet Maureen, his wife of forty-two years, and say, "Hi, pretty lady." He always called her that, pretty lady, and she always called him her hero. She loved the way he looked at her, as if she were still the prettiest girl at the party. Every evening they took walks, holding hands.

"He grew up such a typical hardworking father, very successful, not in the picture so much," said Joe's daughter, Pam Gould. "His heart went bad, and his whole world changed. His interest in the outdoors flourished. He put his priorities in order. He realized that sports and work were not everything. He put so much pressure on my brothers, but he grew so much later on. He became more godly, more sensitive and emotional. He kept saying, 'I'm sorry I wasn't there.' All he needed to do was realize that. He changed it. I'm so glad. So much good came out of it."

Joe had rugged good looks, and even now, at seventy, recovered from his health problems, he kept himself in terrific shape, hiking, doing push-ups, watching his diet. After he retired in 1992, he did consulting work, and when his business took him out West, he would stay for a few extra days, driving into the mountains, backpacking and sleeping in a tent. He snow-shoed in Bryce Canyon in Utah, snowmobiled in Yellowstone Park, kept detailed journals of his trips, took a yearly visit to Ireland, made a shrine in his family room with panoramic photographs of Yosemite National Park. His wife, Maureen, who sometimes accompanied him, used to joke, "Vacationing with you is like being on the Burma March."

New York offered crowded vistas of concrete and steel. Out West, Bill Cashman and Joe Driscoll and John Linner could hike a trail all day long and run into one or two people, or one or two bears. They could start the morning in a valley floor in Yosemite and hike nearly five thousand feet up to the cracked granite of Half Dome, using cables to pull themselves the final steps along the steep trail. Or they could cross the Continental Divide in Glacier National Park and swim in cold mountain lakes. "Joe would jump into anything," John Linner said. For Joe, hiking was a spiritual quest as much as a fitness endeavor. He would stand in a valley, surrounded by sheer mountains, and proclaim that he felt nearer to God. "This is the greatest cathedral in the world," he would say. "It makes St. Patrick's look small."

Joe and his wife, Maureen, awakened early on September 11 for the hour-long drive to Newark. They had just sold their home in Manalapan, New Jersey, and taken a winter rental in Point Pleasant, down the Shore. They arrived at the airport at six-thirty, an hour and a half before Flight 93 was scheduled to depart for San Francisco. Maureen drove home and went back to bed. She assumed her husband probably took an earlier flight. Many times Joe had ushered her quickly through the airport to catch the first available plane.

Unlike Maureen Driscoll, Margaret Cashman never flew with her husband. "Billy, leave me alone," she'd tell him. "I'm too afraid. I'd ruin your trip." She asked for Bill's return flight before he left, but he couldn't remember. He said he would call from California and let her know. This morning, Margaret was painting in the solitude of her spare room when her niece arrived and said, "I want to watch this from here."

Margaret misunderstood.

"You're not watching me paint," she said.

"Don't you know?" her niece said. "Two planes went into the World Trade Center."

Margaret walked to her kitchen window and saw terrible smoke pouring from the towers. She began shaking.

As they swept over the Atlantic and up the East Coast from Langley Air Force Base, the Air National Guard pilots, Captain Honey and Major Lou, did not know that a third suicide plane had just hit the Pentagon. At eight-twenty, American Flight 77 had departed from Dulles International Airport outside of Washington for a non-stop flight to Los Angeles. Forty minutes later, having ceased radio contact, the Boeing 757 turned back toward Washington, then made a looping turn south of the Pentagon. At nine thirty-eight, it crashed into the southwest side of the building. Off to the west, about thirty or forty miles, the National Guard pilots could see a black column smudging the perfect sky. "Holy smoke, that's why we're here," the thirty-four-year-old Lou said over his radio. He had not been to Washington since kindergarten, and he did not immediately recognize the Pentagon, thinking the F-16s were still headed for New York. Then the lead pilot was asked on his radio to verify whether the Pentagon was burning. He was not familiar with the area either. "Anybody know?" he asked.

"That's affirmative," Honey said.

"That's what we just learned," came the response from the North East Air Defense Sector.

The National Guard pilots said it did not occur to them that a commercial plane had caused the damage.

"It seemed like some type of fire or explosion, we didn't know what," Lou said. "I figured it was a truck bomb."

At nine-forty, the Federal Aviation Administration began ordering all flights to land. The North Dakota pilots said they set up a defensive perimeter over Washington, flying combat air patrol at six miles a minute, escorting Attorney General John Ashcroft's plane to Reagan International Airport and flashing their wings at a four-passenger aircraft, signaling it to land immediately.

In the jumble of radio communications, the lead Air National Guard pilot received a garbled message on an air traffic frequency that Honey and Lou did not hear. The message seemed to convey that the White House was an important asset to protect. "Something like, 'Be aware of where it is, and it could be a target,' " Honey said.

"He said, 'I think the Secret Service told me this,' " Lou said.

Hank Krakowski, director of flight operations for United, dressed quickly and drove to work at the airline's system control center near O'Hare Airport. While he was in the car, he heard that the Pentagon had also been hit.

"The gravity of what was going on was very clear," he said.

Upon arriving at the operations center, Krakowski spoke again with Mike Barber, the dispatch manager.

"Where are we?" Krakowski asked.

United's operations center was a rectangular room as long as a football field. The center did not look so different from a trading room at a Wall Street firm, three hundred people sitting at computer terminals, controllers and dispatchers tracking flights and pulling up crew schedules, maps, text messages, weather graphics.

Barber had disconcerting news. As with Flight 175, the operations center had also lost radio contact with Flight 93. The Boeing 757 had made a series of erratic maneuvers as it neared Cleveland, climbing without authorization to thirty-six thousand nine hundred feet, then to forty thousand seven hundred feet.

By this time, flight attendants from Flight 93 had called United's maintenance center in San Francisco and reported that the plane had been hijacked. The airline's customer service staff also received information that passengers were making calls from the plane's GTE Airfones. Senior management began to gather in the airline's crisis center, a terraced, theater-like room that resembled NASA's Mission Control. Andy Studdert, United's chief operating officer, was in the room. On a screen that was six feet long and four feet high, United's flights were displayed. Other flights were filtered out and Flight 93 was highlighted. Its track appeared red on a black background. At nine thirty-six, near Cleveland, the plane had made an ominous turn to the southeast.

Flight 93's transponder also had been turned off. The transponder is a receiver/transmitter that gives air traffic control a plane's identity, speed, direction and altitude. On the screen in the crisis center, the flight could still be tracked, but United officials could no longer tell how high it was flying. The jetliner's speed began to vary wildly, indicating that the hijacker-pilots, who apparently had no real experience flying commercial aircraft, struggled to control the 757. The plane slowed from five hundred six to four hundred miles per hour, then accelerated to five hundred eighty-five miles per hour before eventually slowing to four hundred eighteen, as Flight 93 sliced across southwestern Pennsylvania toward Washington. Its intended destination was reprogrammed from San Francisco to Washington's Reagan National Airport for an arrival at ten twenty-eight.

"The plane had a similar pattern as Flight 175," Krakowski said. "The transponder was out. It reversed course. We knew what was going on. We could see the airplane headed toward the capital. We were wondering whether the military was going to intervene or not."

For the first time in its history, United began grounding its entire fleet, as instructed by the FAA. Planes landed in Alaska and Gander, Newfoundland, and Yellowknife in Canada's Northern Territories, putting down all over the United States, except for Flight 93, which kept ignoring all attempts at contact.

"About the time we sent messages to ground the fleet, I think 93 was already in trouble," Krakowski said.

At her home in Marlton, New Jersey, Melodie Homer had also watched on television as a second plane rammed into the World Trade Center. *What's going on?* she wondered. *Should I be worried?* Her husband, LeRoy Homer Jr., was the first officer aboard

Flight 93. He had been scheduled to take off more than an hour earlier. His flight was headed to San Francisco. Surely, he would be nowhere near New York. But two planes flying into identical towers a few minutes apart did not seem like a coincidence. Melodie decided to check with United, just to be certain that everything was fine. She called the airline's operations center in New York and asked to have a message sent to her husband in the cockpit: "Your wife just wants to make sure you're okay."

Flying was the only job her husband had ever wanted. LeRoy Homer Jr.'s father died when he was twelve, and by the time LeRoy was fourteen, he worked thirty-plus hours a week, cleaning medical buildings on Long Island to save money for flying lessons. At fifteen, he took a solo flight to Boston, and at sixteen, he earned his license to pilot small planes. He received an appointment to West Point, but wanting to be a commercial pilot, he preferred the Air Force Academy, from which he graduated in 1987. A year later, he entered the military and, during the Persian Gulf War, he flew C-141 Starlifter cargo planes. After joining United, LeRoy went into the military reserves, but after American troops became involved in the war in Kosovo, his wife became fearful that he would be activated, and he became a recruiting liaison for the Air Force Academy.

"I was very concerned about him being activated," Melodie Homer said. "It scared me."

LeRoy's friends and relatives invariably described him as even-tempered and modest yet determined. Martin Hnatov, one of a group of five Air Force buddies who later became United pilots, said he had known LeRoy for fourteen years and had never seen him raise his voice or get angry, even on long days in the military that stretched twenty-four to twenty-six hours. "We've all blown up because we've been tired, but that wasn't part of him, which was why he was a great leader," Hnatov said. Other friends said LeRoy possessed a wily persuasiveness developed from growing up with seven sisters.

"He had a way of putting people at ease from the moment you saw him," said Joe Maksimczyk, who served with him in the 18th Military Airlift Squadron at McGuire Air Force Base in New Jersey. "LeRoy could get you to tell him all your deepest, darkest secrets by just asking, 'How are you?'"

As a young boy, LeRoy marveled at the physics of flying and seemed in awe that something so large and heavy as a plane could stay aloft. At nineteen, he flew to Hawaii and developed a passion for travel that never subsided. He even met his wife for the first time in an airport, shortly after he was hired by United in 1995. After being introduced through a mutual friend and speaking on the phone for several weeks, LeRoy traveled cross-country to visit from New Jersey. Melodie, who is a nurse, met him at Los Angeles International Airport. "How will I know what you look like?" she asked beforehand. "I'll be wearing my United uniform," he said. She met him at the gate and was struck by how kind and warm his eyes looked. They were married three years later.

He was the romantic sort, becoming engaged to Melodie on Valentine's Day and making special plans for their birthdays, which were only two days apart in late August. He even polished his wife's shoes when he polished his own. When he left for trips, LeRoy would write notes and leave them for Melodie when she awakened: "Great dinner last night. I miss you already." When their only child, Laurel, was born ten months earlier, LeRoy gave Melodie a bouquet of roses and saved the petals so they could be tossed at their daughter's own wedding. "He always thought of sweet things," Melodie said. "He was very charming. He had a good way with people. He could talk to anyone. My mom loved him instantly."

LeRoy took Melodie to the South Pacific on their honeymoon, vacationed with her in the Greek islands, took his in-laws on a getaway trip to London, brought home bath soaps and lotions for his mother, took photographs of sunsets in Tahiti and the Greek islands that were framed in the hallway of his home. Melodie traveled with her husband when she could, even when she was eight months pregnant, telling her father, "If anything happens, LeRoy is in the cockpit; he'll land somewhere." He flew to Argentina, Brazil, India, sometimes bringing his in-line skates to exercise, making the most of his layovers by visiting museums and restaurants, building a career on the forces of lift and aerodynamics that he always found intriguing and longed to understand as a boy. "How was my landing?" he would always ask his wife when they traveled together. "You made a great landing," she would reply.

"LeRoy loved the vastness of the skies," said Colonel Brian Binn of the Air Force Academy. "He would have gone anywhere to fulfill his dream."

In 1996, LeRoy took his mother, Ilse Homer, back to Germany, where she lived as a girl during World War II. After both of her parents died during the war, Ilse lived with an aunt and uncle and, later, with strangers in eastern Germany. In the beginning of 1945, she and her aunt walked for three months back toward their family home in western Germany, near Dusseldorf and Cologne, traveling at night to avoid the plundering advance of Russian soldiers. Later, upon receiving a degree in business administration, she went to work for the United States Army in Berlin, and met an Army officer, LeRoy Homer, whom she married. LeRoy Jr. would later become conversant in German, as well as in French. From his mother, he developed a passion for classical music and theater, and from both parents — one black, the other blond and blue-eyed — he received lessons in racial tolerance and harmony. In his own travels, he had been insatiable in his attempts to experience as many cultures as possible.

"He was proud of his heritage," Ilse Homer said. "He understood the white and the black race; he liked to go in-between. He thought people were basically the same, some were more ambitious, had bigger hearts, were more generous. He never put anyone down. We taught him, 'You can't throw stones, they might be thrown back at you.'"

LeRoy and Melodie lived in Marlton, New Jersey, a Philadelphia suburb, and he was up at four forty-five this morning for his ninety-minute commute up the Jersey Turnpike to Newark. As was his ritual, he laid out his uniform the night before he left, hanging his shirt from a knob on the armoire, attaching the wings and epaulets, placing his ID in the pocket. He showered and dressed quietly in the bathroom and kissed Melodie on the forehead before he left. In the two days that he was to be gone, he was sure to call and want to know all the details of his daughter's day, what time Laurel had eaten, how she had played, what time she went to bed.

"He loved being a dad," Melodie said. "He was hands-on from day one, changing diapers, giving her a bath. I told him he was not allowed to clip her nails — he had big fingers — but he said, 'Anything you can do for her, I can do.'"

As Melodie Homer waited on the phone, her message was sent to the cockpit of Flight 93 from the United operations center at JFK Airport in New York.

"If you want to hang on, we'll get a message back in a couple of minutes," the center told Melodie. She said she would.

A second message was sent. Still nothing came back. Perhaps it was just too hectic at the moment. LeRoy might be too busy to respond right away. Or perhaps the weather was interfering with the transmission of the message, she thought. These things happened. Not until two weeks later was Melodie Homer told that the message had been received. No response ever came.

8

The hijacker's voice had carried a panting formality, an odd pleasantness, over the air-traffic frequency. "Ladies and gentlemen," the Flight 93 passengers were called, as if being asked to take their seats in a theater. "Please sit down," the man said again. This was believed to be the voice of Ziad Jarrah, a twenty-six-year-old from Lebanon. No, his family said later, resisting the idea that he could have been a murderer who felt no sanctity for his own life or the lives of others. Perhaps someone stole his identity. If he was aboard the plane, it must have been as a passenger, not a terrorist.

Those who had come to know Jarrah in the United States were also stunned. Acquaintances suggested that he could not have made a conscious turn toward extremism, that he must have been forced or brainwashed. They described him as unfailingly polite, if distant. He did not have the cold, dead eyes of Mohamed Atta, the suspected ringleader among the September 11 hijackers.

Instead, Jarrah had appeared studious, even owlish in his round-frame glasses. He wore casual catalogue fashion — a white T-shirt underneath a short-sleeved polo shirt — and he laughed with a jovial chuckle.

"The type of guy you bring home to Mom," said Roxanne Caputo, who worked at a martial arts center in South Florida, where Jarrah had trained.

This is what made his plan so successful and chilling. It was as if he had followed to the letter the handbook of Osama bin Laden's Al Qaeda terrorist network, skillfully exploiting a culture that he despised. Blend in with the locals, the handbook instructed. Act as they do, dress as they do. "Avoid seclusion and isolation from the population," the handbook said, adding, "Have a general appearance that does not indicate Islamic orientation."

Jarrah entered the United States in June of 2000 and immersed himself into transient, touristy, racially diverse South Florida so thoroughly that he seemed no more out of place than the humidity. His accent was a confluence of German and Middle Eastern, and his skin was so light, his appearance so blandly handsome, that some thought him European instead of Arabic. Later, people would not even agree on how tall he was, or how heavy he was, whether he stood five foot eight or five foot eleven, whether he weighed one hundred seventy pounds or one hundred ninety. He felt so confidently protected in his imitation life — and in the unsuspecting nature of those he encountered — that he signed for apartments in his own name and rented a red sports car. Even some clumsy mistakes did not foil his plan. At least twice Jarrah was stopped by authorities — once in the Middle East, a second time for speeding by a Maryland state trooper two days before the hijackings — but he was cooperative and soon on his way, disappearing like smoke up a chimney.

"You have to tip your hat to them," said an FBI agent who spoke on the condition of anonymity. "It was a brilliant plan — amoral, but brilliant."

If there was any retrospect giveaway in Jarrah's face, it was in his halted smile, neither a smirk nor a grin of graciousness or delight, but a resolve of unforeseen circumstance. It resembled the patsy-murderer look that Lee Harvey Oswald had in his pursed lips of history altered. And despite the disbelieving statements of Jarrah's family, investigative strands formed a convincing web. According to the United States Justice Department, Jarrah, Atta and others formed and maintained an Al Qaeda terrorist cell in Germany, beginning in 1998. In the port city of Hamburg, the Justice Department said, Jarrah roomed for a time with Atta and with Marwann al-

Shehhi, who flew the two planes into the World Trade Center. Later, officials said instead that he frequently visited the two men.

The spring before the hijackings, Jarrah lived near Atta in Hollywood, Florida, and they received Florida drivers' licenses on the same day, May 2. In the weeks preceding September 11, Jarrah lived in Florida with Ahmed Alhaznawi, identified as another terrorist aboard United Flight 93. Earlier in the summer, all four of the hijackers on that flight opened a Florida SunTrust Bank account with a cash deposit. As did other terrorists on the four suicidal flights, Jarrah traveled to Las Vegas over the summer, and practiced self-defense. He lived near other hijackers in South Florida, training at nearby flight schools, but because Al Qaeda cells operated with planned murkiness, purposeful separation, the overlapping contact was flimsy and difficult to detect. A tape later released by bin Laden said that the hijackers had been kept apart intentionally to avoid detection. While the terrorists knew they were participating in a "martyrdom mission," they did not know its precise nature until shortly before they boarded the planes, according to the tape.

Fifteen of the nineteen hijackers on September 11 were from Saudi Arabia. Jarrah grew up in Beirut and in the Bekaa Valley in Lebanon, fertile soil for the cultivation of terrorism in a desperate, war-ravaged country. Yet, his was a prominent middle-class family in the village of al-Marj that said it did not involve itself stringently in politics or religion. It was an extended family of bankers, customs officers, schoolteachers, social security officials. Though he was a Sunni Muslim, Jarrah attended Catholic schools of French instruction, drank alcohol, went to parties, dated girls, was indulged as an only son in a family with two daughters. He played basketball and took disabled kids camping and volunteered in an anti-drug program. This was not a terrorist, his family insisted.

"Ziad was never far from his family, and we never knew him to be engaged with such terrorist parties, or such beliefs," said his uncle, Jamal Jarrah, a banker. "He had no cause to be a radical. He never talked about politics. He had a very happy life, he did well in university, he had a girlfriend, he liked to go to parties. He liked the United States very much. He thought it was very civilized, modern. There were so many things to make you believe he can't be connected to terrorists."

A darker side later emerged, according to the Justice Department, and a resentful zealotry overtook his genial social nature. He belonged to a new generation of Islamic extremists, one that had appeared in the last fifteen or twenty years. The stereotype of the poor, uneducated, unworldly radical, his rancorous determination as unrestrained as his beard, no longer applied. The new extremism had a shaved face and bristled coarsely inside. It danced, drank liquor, entered sexual relationships before marriage, wove itself into the complacent fabric of the West. That was the brilliant treachery of Al Qaeda, whose handbook asserted: "Necessity permits the forbidden." Its foot soldiers were reminded to remain guarded around even the closest relatives: "It was said in the proverbs — the hearts of freemen are the tombs of secrets."

Jarrah and a cousin left Lebanon for Germany in April of 1996, traveling first to the city of Greifswald to become proficient in the German language. It was there that he also met a Turkish medical student named Aysel Senguen, who became his girlfriend. In 1997, Jarrah moved to Hamburg and studied flight training and aeronautics for eight semesters at the University of Applied Sciences. He also apparently received a pilot's license. When his girlfriend moved to the distant industrial city of Bochum, he visited on weekends. He was considered a likable but unexceptional student. Michael Gotzmann, a classmate and friend, described Jarrah as devoutly Muslim but not rabid about politics, a man who prayed five times a day but was open in his views and wanted to continue his studies in the United States, when he abruptly left the school in the fall of 1999. "That's what he said when he left, and I never heard from him again," Gotzmann said. "He broke off contact."

While Jarrah spoke of a debilitated Lebanon and how the Israelis had cut off the water supply to his native country, according to Gotzmann, "He never said anything bad about the United States." This was consistent with what other acquaintances said about Jarrah, and with the Al Qaeda training manual, which instructed its members to avoid provocative religious or political remarks.

It was in Germany that his views seemed to harden into a kernel of hatred that would germinate in terrorism and suicidal martyrdom. How could Jarrah have stepped out of his old friendly self into a new menacing self, as if changing a pair of pants? His family would not be able to come to terms with this. Even months later, it seemed impossible to consider. The family would release a videotape of Jarrah smiling and dancing at a wedding, as if to assure that he celebrated life, not destroyed it. Islamic experts saw a more familiar archetype of radicalism that emerged in him.

Jarrah was born in 1975, the same year that Lebanon was fractured by civil war between leftist Muslims and right-wing Christians. Israel and Syria would both intervene militarily during his boyhood, and tens of thousands of people, many civilians, would die during sixteen years of fighting. The term "suicide bomber" was first used in a 1981 Associated Press story from rubbled Beirut, where a car loaded with explosives drove into the Iraqi embassy. In 1982, hundreds of Palestinians were massacred at two refugee camps outside Beirut during the Israeli occupation; Ariel Sharon, who later became the Israeli prime minister, lost his job as defense minister after an inquiry found him indirectly responsible for the slaughter. In 1983, when Jarrah was eight, two hundred forty-one United States Marines were killed by a truck bomb at their barracks in Beirut. Recruited suicide promised maximum horror for the victims and martyred redemption for the perpetrators in the embrace of seventy-two black-eyed virgins.

Even a middle-class family that spirited Jarrah out of Beirut in the summers, and sheltered him in a green valley between mountain ranges, could not have closed the doors completely, pulled the blinds entirely, on the baleful light of war. The family lived next to a mosque in al-Marj, but proximity to a place of worship could not exorcise war's collateral evils of killing, corruption, nepotism, unemployment, inflation, the destruction of buildings, foreign investment and tourism, the sense of helplessness over being invaded by neighbors.

"He did not grow up in a politically stable situation," said Nizar Hamzeh, an associate professor of political science and an expert on Islamic movements at the American University of Beirut. "The atmosphere was pessimistic. The perception was that there was some sort of deadlock, no way out. People were killing each other, alienation was at a high level, you had the external influences of Israel and Syria. This feeling of a lack of fairness, equity and justice influenced his generation."

His disaffection became apparent to others in Germany. No one could say with any certainty what changed Jarrah. There were suspicious connections, relationships under investigation, possibly furtive travel, but the facts were elusive, specifics were unconfirmed. He met a student cleric named Abdul Rahman al-Makhadi in Greifswald, and perhaps he grew sensitive when the cleric called him weak because he lacked religious devotion and lived with a woman to whom he was not married. (Al-Makhadi denied in an interview with MSNBC that he had radicalized Jarrah or that he had forced strict Islamic behavior on local women.) Perhaps Jarrah developed an identity crisis and began to feel inferior and remote in a new country with a new language. Perhaps he struggled in school and became detached when his girlfriend moved to another city, and he could see her only on weekends. Perhaps, after he moved to Hamburg, he became disillusioned with Western values and culture and this alienation found sympathetic voices in an Atta-led university prayer group, in fervid discussions in Atta's second-story apartment at 54 Marien Street, in radical exhortations at the Al Quds mosque. The connections to Atta in Hamburg would be staticky, faint, tenuous. They did not attend the same university, and their primary residences were more than a half hour apart by train. Jarrah's girlfriend insisted he had never mentioned Atta's name. German authorities told *The Los Angeles Times* that the only connection established between Atta, al-Shehhi and Jarrah was "the FBI's assertion that there is a connection."

Even if they were once parallel, the three lives met at a deadly intersection on September 11.

It would not have been immediate, Jarrah growing inflamed by smoldering resentment toward the United States. It would not have been overnight that he came to mortally reject American policies in the Middle East, to abhor the export of American values, muscle, customs, movies, music, fashion, which seemed to leave the Islamic world threatened and marginalized. "They did not come to Jarrah saying, 'Okay, we want you to join the Holy War,'" Professor Hamzeh said. It did not work like that. It began with a weakness in a person's immune system, and grew, with words and rituals and small tests of faith and ideology, into an affliction of zealotry.

"You begin to feel you've bonded on an ideological level, or there is some financial incentive, or you feel an acceptance," Hamzeh said. "You feel secure; you are not left alone on your own. The recruitment process might take a year. He would have been tested on a faith level, on his political views, on his closeness or remoteness from issues, on leaders he supported or stood against. He might be asked to do minor, to become major, missions. He has to prove himself. Joining is not automatic."

Jarrah's landlady came to recognize small changes in her tenant in Hamburg. He wore a beard, brought a prayer rug to his apartment, gave her a Koran for Christmas. His girlfriend, Aysel Senguen, also told the German newspaper *Bild* that she had come to detect a harsher attitude in him toward Western influences. They were fighting a lot. He wanted her to wear a head scarf. She was dissuaded from listening to Western music and going to parties. "All of a sudden, he wanted me to live strictly according to Islam," Senguen told the newspaper.

The coincidences linking Atta and Jarrah formed a distinctive, troubling pattern, like whorls on a criminal fingerprint. Jarrah's landlady, Rosemarie Canel, said that he occasionally spent the night with an unnamed friend in the working-class Harburg section of Hamburg, which is where Atta lived. In 1999, Jarrah, Atta and al-Shehhi, all future hijackers, reported their passports stolen at roughly the same time in Bavaria and received new ones. German officials theorized that they may have wanted to purge any evidence of travel to Afghanistan, Pakistan, Iraq or other places associated with terrorism, so it would be easier to obtain visas to travel to the United States.

Also in 1999, Jarrah was photographed at the wedding of Said Bahaji, a German of Moroccan ancestry who had been a roommate of Atta's in Hamburg and would become one of the suspected plotters of September 11. *The Sunday Times* of London reported that Bahaji had a strong religious influence on Jarrah, who returned once to Lebanon with a beard, infuriating his father, and who wrote in a journal: "Tomorrow will come. The victors will come. We vow to vanquish you. The ground beneath your feet will tremble."

In June of 2000, several weeks after Atta arrived in the United States, Jarrah followed, according to the Justice Department. However, a person named Ziad Jarrah and fitting the hijacker's description, rented an apartment in a three-family house on East Third Street in Brooklyn, New York, from March of 1995 until February 1996. He would have been twenty at the time. Another man named Ihassan Jarrah lived with Ziad, drove a livery cab and paid the eight-hundred-dollar monthly rent. The men were quiet, well-mannered, said hello and good-bye. Ziad Jarrah carried a camera and told his landlords that he was a photographer. He would disappear for a few days on occasion, then return. Sometimes a woman who appeared to be a prostitute arrived with one of the men. "Me and my brother used to crack jokes that they were terrorists," said Jason Matos, a construction worker who lived in a basement apartment there, and whose mother owned the house. When the two men left, Matos said, what remained were signs of a spare existence. Mattresses on the floor. A bathtub filled with plaster and sheet rock. Open cans of food and a stove that did not appear to have been used for cooking. A computer monitor. A small tape recorder and tapes in Arabic. Jarrah's family would later dispute this, saying Ziad was in Lebanon at the time, not New York.

Whether it was his first trip to the United States or not, Jarrah arrived in Atlanta on June 27, 2000, on a Delta flight from Munich. His face was chubbier than it would later appear in the lineup of photos that newspapers would arrange in a kind of hijacker's yearbook. He entered on a valid visa that had been issued on May 25, 2000, in Berlin.

Atta and al-Shehhi, topplers of the World Trade Center, made their way to Venice, on Florida's Gulf Coast, to train at Huffman Aviation School. Many international pilots trained in South Florida. The weather was good, the flat land was absent the threat of mountains, and the fees were less expensive than in Europe. Jarrah also moved to Venice, but went to a different flight academy, the Florida Flight Training Center, where he was enrolled from June of 2000 to January 15, 2001, according to the center's owner, Arne Kruithof.

All told, Jarrah spent sixteen thousand dollars in training, and the money was wired from his parents, Kruithof said. When Jarrah arrived, "We had to do more to get him ready than others," Kruithof said, adding, "His flight skills seemed to be a little bit out there." Eventually, Jarrah received his private license and instrument rating, and flew required hours toward a commercial license, but never received it while at the training center, Kruithof said. Jarrah became an "average" pilot, Kruithof said, adding that after two hundred hours of flying, "he was a guy who needed some more."

In August of 2000, Jarrah attempted to enroll Ramzi Binalshibh of Yemen into the flight school, the Justice Department said. Four times Binalshibh applied for a travel visa to the United States, but each time he

160

was denied. After September 11, Binalshibh would become an international fugitive, wanted in connection with the planning and carrying out of the hijackings. At one point, American investigators believed, he was supposed to be the twentieth hijacker.

While training in Venice, Jarrah flew small planes such as Pipers and Cessnas, and roomed with three others, including a twenty-three-year-old German flight student, Thorsten Biermann. "He was friendly but reserved, introverted, a loner, he kept his distance," Biermann recalled. While Jarrah studied for his commercial license, and talked about flying, Biermann said, "When it came to what we wanted to do, and what airline we wanted to join, he didn't talk much about that."

He occasionally left town on unexplained trips. His visa showed that he made a trip to, or through, the Bahamas on November 24, 2000. Jarrah could be helpful and often cooked spaghetti dinners, but he avoided pork and did not drink, even the few times he and Biermann went to bars together. His girlfriend called on occasion, and Jarrah talked some about Lebanon, speaking in German with almost no accent. Biermann thought two things curious about his roommate. One, Jarrah kept another apartment in Venice but did not sleep in it. Two, Jarrah seemed to have an unnerving need to be in control when he flew. On one trip, the two flew across the state to Fort Lauderdale, and Jarrah was set to pilot the plane on the return leg. He handled both the radio and the controls and twice ignored Biermann's request to refuel as a safety precaution in bad weather. The plane landed in Venice with little fuel, and Biermann was shaken. "I decided I did not want to fly with him anymore," Biermann said. "Everyone I knew who flew with him felt the same way."

Mostly, Jarrah remained behind when Biermann and two other roommates went to dinner or a movie. But once, when he did come along, he insisted on eating first, and the four men missed the movie. Jarrah was driving his car, so the others could not complain, Biermann said, "but he had this attitude. He decided things on his own."

Still, Kruithof said, Jarrah was likable, always on time, prompt in paying his bills. "Not just nice, but he had qualities you look for in a dear friend, someone you trust," Kruithof said. Jarrah always looked him in the eye and offered a firm handshake and a friendly smile. He would have a beer or two, "but not three," and he made seemingly benign jokes about how fat and lazy Americans were. He remained vague about which airline he preferred to work for, but he was a serious student who did not seem to be wasting his parents' money. "If you go by the airline hiring checklist, he must have studied well before he came over here," Kruithof said. "He fooled us."

In mid-January of 2001, Jarrah left the flight school, saying he was returning to Germany. He said he would come back to Venice later to complete his training for a commercial license, but Kruithof never saw him again. By April 23, 2001, Jarrah had returned to Florida's Atlantic coast. He showed up that day at the rental office of the Bernard Apartments in Hollywood, located south of Fort Lauderdale International Airport. It was a tidy place landscaped with palm and banana trees, catering to French Canadians and featuring stucco apartments the color of butterscotch. Signs warned in English that the security deposit could not be used to pay the rent. In French, renters were cautioned not to walk on the front sidewalk because they might scuff the shuffleboard court. Jarrah presented a German passport and signed a rental application in his looping handwriting. He listed his previous address as a hotel, saying he was a pilot, and leaving a German phone number that purportedly belonged to his grandmother. He did not take one of the stucco apartments, but rather a white one-bedroom clapboard bungalow with a full kitchen. The apartment was in the rear of the complex and faced onto another street. The Al Qaeda handbook advocated that its agents take ground-floor apartments to facilitate escape. Jarrah, however, did ignore instructions to rent apartments using a false name.

Dressed neatly in jeans and a nice shirt, Jarrah stayed until June 22, always paying his weekly rent of one hundred sixty-five dollars on time, appearing at four or five in the afternoon at the window of the rental office. He did not use the apartment pool or shuffleboard court and was not one to make conversation, according to Carol Noel, the apartment manager, but he smiled pleasantly and said "Have a nice day" when he paid the rent. Upon checkout, his apartment was clean. He offered to pay for a broken coffee cup, and Noel said she laughed before returning the security deposit of one hundred fifty dollars. "Most people break all of the dishes and cups and don't offer to pay for anything," she said.

On May 7, just a mile north of the Bernard Apartments on Highway One in Dania, Florida, Jarrah walked into the U.S. 1 Fitness Club. He paid one hundred sixty-one dollars for four months of a basic membership, but he appeared less interested in strength and cardiovascular workouts than in self-defense. The bottom floor of the fitness center was cluttered with familiar weight-lifting machines, but Jarrah preferred private sessions upstairs, with its boxing ring and three heavy bags. A poster autographed by Eric Lee, a relative of the late martial arts champion and actor Bruce Lee, hung in the stairway and exhorted: "Whatever you conceive, take it beyond your most wildest dreams and we will surpass those who do not dare."

He wanted lessons in martial arts, Jarrah told the center's owner, Bert Rodriguez. He said he was from Saudi Arabia. He had come to the States to vacation and train to be a pilot. A frequent traveler, he wanted to learn to defend himself. He had been to a few other centers, but he did not want to learn formal disciplines. He wanted to learn to protect himself in a street fight. This was the right place. Rodriguez held eight black belts in various martial arts. He trained police officers, corrections officials and drug enforcement agents in close-quarter combat, and he trained champion boxers and kickboxers. Essentially, the lessons he taught were those of physics and leverage. The body was a strong instrument, and a weak one. Holds could be applied to pressure points, vulnerable spots could be hit or kicked, and a person could be knocked down, subdued or killed in a matter of seconds.

From the beginning, Jarrah appeared to be in excellent shape. He said he played soccer and kept a strict diet. The first private lesson cost seventy-five dollars, the remaining nine lessons in the set cost fifty dollars apiece.

Jarrah paid for two sets of ten lessons. "That tells me you're serious," Rodriguez said. In a membership photograph kept on the center's computer, Jarrah wore a sweaty white T-shirt and glasses with circular frames, a towel over one shoulder, a wan smile on his face. He had dyed his hair a lighter color, blondish, and some people at the center thought he was from Germany. He was agreeable. He said he liked the weather in the United States, thought the people were friendly. He talked about his girlfriend and returning to "Deutschland."

Impressed with Jarrah's skills, Rodriguez asked him if he wanted to enter kickboxing competitions. Jarrah declined. He only wanted to learn to fight. An eager student, he took lessons twice a week, at eight in the morning, for an hour and a half. Once, he asked Rodriguez to help him refine a sleeper hold, in which he subdued an opponent by pressing the carotid arteries in his neck, cutting off oxygen flow to the brain. His student had obviously been practicing the hold on others, and when Rodriguez offered to give Jarrah and his friends semi-private lessons at a special rate, Jarrah responded, "The guys are traveling." At the time, it meant nothing to Rodriguez. He could not have known what Jarrah had in mind. Later, he would be shocked to find out.

"If someone would have said, 'We suspect

one of your members to be a terrorist,' I would have picked out five hundred people before I picked him out," Rodriguez said. "He was playing the perfect role. They sent him because he was the least conspicuous, the most nonthreatening. I was teaching him exactly what he needed to know. I was reaffirming in his mind the art of the ninja. You're fighting for your life. Whether you are a drug agent or a police officer, it's about survival, about using anything at your disposal to survive. I guess he was always planning."

Part of what Rodriguez taught Jarrah was to control his emotions and overcome his own fear and doubts in decisive moments. Unwittingly, the instructor was playing into the hands of the Al Qaeda handbook, which stressed "patience, tranquility and unflappability," the ability "to endure psychological traumas." Even when Rodriguez provoked him, throwing him down and punching him hard, Jarrah did not lose his cool. Three nights before the hijackings, Atta got in a dispute with a waitress over a bar tab at Shuckum's restaurant in nearby Hollywood. Throughout his own training, Jarrah maintained an icy composure. On September 11, his flight was apparently intended to travel the farthest before reaching its target. He, more than any of the other hijacker pilots, would need a practiced calm, a more enduring willingness to die.

He told Rodriguez that he wasn't sure if he would remain in the States or return to Germany, where he claimed to have received a degree in aeronautical engineering. Then, with two pre-paid lessons remaining, Jarrah disappeared from the martial arts center in mid-August. By then, he had not learned how to break bricks with his hands, or cultivated some symbolic fierceness. He had instead acquired the deadly skills of fighting in confined spaces, in an alley, a hallway, a cockpit. He knew how to gouge eyes and clutch a throat with his hands, how to slam the funny bone with a stick or a flashlight and cut the stringy tendons at the elbows and behind the knees, how to slip a punch and slash a throat with a knife, a box cutter, a sliver of glass, how to cause spurting agony by jamming a pencil into a neck, or even a straw with his thumb over the opening. This was not some Olympian discipline he had mastered, but rather the ability to cut easily and hurt immediately.

"He just sponged it up," Rodriguez said. "I showed him everything I possibly could. Obviously, I had no idea of his purpose. He was committed. Certain things are admirable, even in villains. Commitment is admirable. Some people commit to the wrong things. That's the problem."

By the middle of August, the hijacking plan

gained a barbarous inevitability. One exit up Interstate 95 from the martial arts center, Jarrah lived for the final couple of weeks in Lauderdale-by-the-Sea, on Bougainvillea Road, a strip of apartments and beach hotels where impermanence was expected and trusted and transacted in cash payments.

In early July, he had rented an apartment there from Charles Lisa, who was retired from a career in property management. Jarrah was courteous, always waved and said hello, even parked his red Mitsubishi Eclipse on the street instead of in the driveway next to his landlord's bedroom window. Lisa had traveled to Hamburg in the 1950s and had a recreational pilot's license, so the men talked easily about their common experiences. Jarrah said he was from Lebanon, training to become a commercial pilot, but he also included a practiced feint in his résumé, telling Lisa that his father was a professional engineer living in Germany. "He said his father was annoyed with him that he couldn't find a vocation, and was happy that he was taking courses to get a pilot's license," Lisa said.

When Lisa suggested that Jarrah take him flying one day, he said Jarrah "sort of laughed." The subject never came up again.

"He wasn't nasty," Lisa said. "He didn't brush me off."

Given Jarrah's apparent genial nature and the atrocious act he would soon commit, Lisa later wondered whether his tenant had been a lost soul, searching between two worlds, Christian and Muslim. The landlord also wondered how soon in advance Jarrah knew of his suicidal mission. In June, Jarrah had dropped off a suit to be altered at Lord & Taylor, perhaps in connection with a relative's wedding.

"He was too happy a man for a guy who knew he was going to die in the next ten days or so," Lisa said, perhaps underestimating the clever deception of his tenant and the pull of martyrdom that tugged at Jarrah.

This apartment, like his previous one, was on the ground floor, tucked in the back of the property, not easily visible from the street, conducive to a quick getaway if necessary. Jarrah made no remarks when Lisa hung his American flag outside for the Fourth of July, and never mentioned the nude statue that served as a base for a lamp in his apartment. They did talk politics once, when Lisa mentioned the two hundred forty-one Marines killed at their barracks in Beirut in 1983. Jarrah said his family had moved to Germany by that time. He did receive visitors at the apartment, but they came on foot at night. This was consistent with a textbook Al Qaeda approach for meetings. Its handbook advised operatives to take public transportation and "alight on foot," or to park a car away from a meeting spot "to maneuver it quickly at any time."

When Jarrah spoke of traveling to Las Vegas for a few days, following a pattern similar to other hijackers, Lisa assumed he had taken a solo flight to gain his instrument rating. Jarrah seemed keenly interested when his landlord showed him a photograph of the cockpit of a Cessna 172 that had been blown up and made into a poster. Lisa said he also offered to sell to Jarrah some flight gear that he was looking to unload, headphones and a global positioning device, but that his tenant declined. On July 25, Jarrah traveled to Germany, in part to see his girlfriend for what would be the last time, and returned on August 4. While he was away, on July 30 he was granted a license — apparently commercial — to fly a single-engine aircraft, *The Los Angeles Times* subsequently reported. Jarrah later received correspondence from the Federal Aviation Administration, his landlord said. On August 17, Jarrah took a flight to test his proficiency at an airport in Fort Lauderdale. Five days later, he purchased an antenna for a global positioning system, a handheld device that allows pilots to navigate to a position using pre-programmed coordinates. (No evidence of such a device was found at the crash site, the FBI said.)

That same day, Jarrah purchased diagrams of the cockpit instruments on a Boeing 757, according to the Justice Department. He also came to possess flight manuals for Boeing 757 and 767 aircraft. The aircraft had common cockpits, which made it easier to train pilots on the two jets, but also made it more convenient for the men who would hijack them.

By then, Jarrah also had a roommate. In late July or early August, a tall, thin man named Ahmed Alhaznawi arrived by foot to live at the apartment on Bougainvillea Drive. He became one of the four hijackers on Flight 93. Alhaznawi was twenty and was from Saudi Arabia, the son of a mosque prayer leader. He reportedly trained in bin Laden's camps in Afghanistan and recruited two distant cousins, Ahmed and Hamza Alghamdi, who became members of the hijacking team that crashed United Flight 175 into the World Trade Center. Alhaznawi spoke halting English, walked two blocks to the beach early each morning, perhaps to pray, and seemed deferential toward Jarrah, driving him to early-morning appointments. The visitor also had a certain melancholy about him. "He was a sad boy," said Lisa, the landlord. "A smirk for a smile. He bowed his head when he said hello." Alhaznawi would later be pictured with a mustache after the hijacking, but he was clean-shaven in August. The two tenants seemed so inseparable that their landlord initially wondered whether they were lovers. Lisa warned Alhaznawi against smoking and chided him to keep the place clean when it became messy. But the landlord also brought an extra bed into the apartment for Alhaznawi. Lisa said he also applied hydrogen peroxide to an infected gash on Alhaznawi's left leg, directing him to Holy Cross Hospital in nearby Fort Lauderdale to be examined by a doctor.

The New York Times later reported that an attending physician, Dr. Christos Tsonas, had examined Alhaznawi in June at the hospital and concluded that the dark lesion was consistent with cutaneous anthrax. This led to speculation that the hijackers might have played a part in the anthrax letter attacks that followed September 11. His own assistance of Alhaznawi's injury exacerbated Lisa's sense of betrayal after the hijackings. He said that he ended up at the same hospital, suffering from stress and high blood pressure. Hours after the terrorist attacks, he pieced together the seemingly harmless activities of his tenants into a suspicious puzzle. The FBI, Lisa said, later found Arabic newspapers and a notebook tucked beneath a mattress in the rental apartment.

"How could we all be sleeping as a society?" Lisa said. "I beat myself up for not knowing. You think a terrorist in your apartment would fit a profile. I blame law enforcement for keeping the public in the dark."

In an urgent pinballing, Jarrah shuttled between South Florida and the Washington, DC, metropolitan area in late August and early September. He checked into the Pin-Del Motel in Laurel, Maryland, on August 27, and paid for three days. He checked out the next evening at dinnertime, and did not argue when the owner, Suresh Patel, said he would refund the room rate of forty-four dollars for only one night. On September 4, Nawaq Alhamzi, one of the hijackers on the jet that would crash into the Pentagon, also checked into the hotel for a brief stay. Other members of that terrorist team stayed less than a mile away, at the low-cost Valencia Hotel.

The last time that Lisa saw Jarrah in Lauderdale-by-the-Sea was at the very end of August. From financial statements that arrived later, the landlord noticed that Jarrah had withdrawn a hundred dollars a day in the final week he lived at his apartment, and that he ended up with seven dollars in his account. Jarrah also spent two thousand one hundred dollars on one-way airfare, Lisa said. The tenant and landlord spoke again in early September, and on the third of the month, Jarrah came by to pick up an overnight mail package sent from either American or United airlines. Lisa left the package outside his door, wedged beneath the shutter of a window. When he last spoke to Jarrah, the landlord reminded him that he might have money refunded from a security deposit. Where could he forward the money? Lisa asked.

"I'll send you a postcard," Jarrah replied.

On September 5, about four in the afternoon, Jarrah and Alhaznawi arrived at Passage Tours in Lauderdale-by-the-Sea. The travel agency was located near the apartment the men had recently vacated. International flags flew out front, and a carved wooden giraffe stood inside the door. A travel agent of Iranian descent greeted the two men. She said that Jarrah meant "doctor" or "surgeon" in Farsi and asked if it meant the same in Arabic. "Yes," Jarrah responded. The woman remembered him as being handsome and polite, and that his companion became irritated and cut off the conversation.

Seven days earlier, Alhaznawi had purchased a ticket for United Flight 93 from Newark to San Francisco on September 11. At Passage Tours, the two men each paid one hundred twenty-four dollars and seventy-five cents in cash for Continental Flight 1500, which would leave Fort Lauderdale on September 7 at twelve-thirty p.m. and arrive in Newark at three twenty-eight. The agency's records showed the men rebooked on Continental Flight 1600 that was to depart at five fifty-five p.m. and arrive at eight fifty-five.

Earlier on September 5, Saeed Alghamdi and Ahmed Alnami walked into another travel agency in Lauderdale-by-the-Sea. Mile High Travel was located across Commercial Boulevard from Passage Tours, down about half a block. The two men comprised the other half of the hijacking team on United Flight 93. They carried a sharp body odor, and the travel agent who assisted them kept embellishing the service fee for the tickets, hoping they would go away.

Alnami, twenty-three, had reportedly studied Islamic law in Saudi Arabia and had not returned home from a pilgrimage to Mecca six months earlier. Authorities knew little about Alghamdi, twenty-five, who may have stolen the identity of an innocent person, perhaps a Saudi pilot. One of the men spoke English and wrote down both of their names for the travel agent. They wanted to fly on September 7 from Fort Lauderdale to Newark on Continental Airlines, but were persuaded to fly Spirit Airlines, which was cheaper. The two men each paid one hundred thirty-nine dollars and seventy-five cents in cash and left without waiting for their receipts, or two quarters in change.

Two days after his scheduled flight from Fort Lauderdale to Newark, Jarrah appeared one final time in the Washington, DC, area where plans for the hijackings were being completed. He drove a red Mitsubishi, but this time it was a rented 2001 Galant instead of the 1991 Eclipse that he had driven in Florida. Shortly after midnight on September 9, Jarrah sped north on Interstate 95 when he was stopped by a Maryland state trooper for going ninety miles per hour — twenty-five miles per hour above the posted limit. This was exactly the kind of transgression he had been trained to avoid. "One should possess the proper permit and not violate traffic rules in order to avoid trouble with the police," the Al Qaeda handbook admonished. If he were detected now, the entire plot could be uncovered.

If he was nervous, however, it did not show. The trooper, Joseph M. Catalano, described Jarrah as "calm and cooperative." Jarrah produced a valid Virginia driver's license, apparently obtained through a loophole in the state's residency requirements. The trooper peeked inside his car and saw no weapons or suspicious papers. Apparently, this was not the first time Jarrah had been stopped by authorities. *The Chicago Tribune* and the Associated Press reported that he had been detained briefly in Dubai, the United Arab Emirates, on January 30, 2001, after a two-month trip to Pakistan and Afghanistan, the stronghold of Osama bin Laden.

The United States had requested that Jarrah be stopped because he was known to support terrorist organizations, the *Tribune* reported. He had an American visa, so he was sent on his way, reportedly to Germany to visit his girlfriend and to Lebanon to visit his ailing father, who had undergone heart surgery. According to a copy of his visa, Jarrah re-entered the United States on February 25.

His family disputed reports that he had been detained in Dubai, saying Jarrah had arrived in Lebanon five days before January 30. And the Florida Flight Training Center said he was enrolled there until January 15, the same time he was allegedly in Pakistan or Afghanistan. This, his relatives believed, gave credence to the possibility that someone may have stolen his identity. "How could he be in two places at one time?" asked Jamal Jarrah, Ziad's uncle.

The uncle also denied published reports that Jarrah's girlfriend had called the family in late 1999 or early 2000 to report that Ziad had gone to Afghanistan. The Justice Department said all nineteen of the September 11 hijackers had trained in camps in Afghanistan. But Jamal Jarrah said that Ziad had never been out of communication with his parents for longer than ten days. This occurred, he said, when Ziad moved in 1997 from Greifswald, Germany, to Hamburg.

The traffic stop on September 9 was as unavailing as the customs stop in Dubai. Baltimore Mayor Martin O'Malley later complained to the United States Senate Judiciary Committee that this ineffective screening signaled an alarming lack of cooperation between federal, state and local officials. However, Mike Clemens, the assistant special agent in charge of the FBI's Maryland-Delaware division, disputed this, saying that in mid-September Jarrah did not appear on the federal government's "radar screen" of suspected terrorists. He was given a ticket and a fine of two hundred seventy dollars.

"You're free to go," Trooper Catalano told Jarrah. After the hijacking, the ticket would be found in the glove compartment of the car at Newark International Airport.

Hours after receiving the speeding ticket, Jarrah called his family in Lebanon and confirmed the receipt of seven hundred dollars sent to him on top of his two-thousand-dollar monthly allowance. He had asked for the money for "fun." His family expected him home in ten days for the wedding of a cousin. His girlfriend would be there, and their own wedding was planned for the following summer. The family had bought Jarrah a new Mercedes-Benz and joked that one of his sisters would take the car if he did not come home soon enough.

"His father told him about the car, and Ziad was joking, 'Don't play with me, that is a cheap present,'" Jamal Jarrah said. "He confirmed that he would be attending his cousin's wedding. He had bought a wedding suit."

Shortly after midnight on September 11, three men drove up to the Newark Airport Marriott in a red Mitsubishi Galant, said a parking attendant named Tommy, who was on duty.

"Pull up," the attendant instructed the men.

They would only be a minute, the driver said.

The three men entered the hotel, two of them with small roller bags, the parking attendant said. The third man walked back out and drove away in the Mitsubishi. The men stayed on the fourth floor of the hotel, employees said, and left behind maps and flight-related documents.

Jarrah would not be going home, after all.

Before boarding the plane, Jarrah placed one final call to his girlfriend, Aysel Senguen, in Bochum, Germany. Later, she would report him missing. Authorities would find what they called aviation documents in her apartment, and a distraught Senguen would enter a witness protection program. A letter mailed from Jarrah to Senguen with an incorrect address would be returned to the United States and discovered by American investigators.

"I have done what I had to do," Jarrah wrote in the farewell letter. "You should be very proud. You will see the result and everyone will be happy."

With Jarrah apparently at the controls of Flight 93, a jetliner carrying thousands of pounds of fuel headed directly for Washington. Many officials later said they thought the target was the United States Capitol, whose neoclassical dome stood nearly three hundred feet above the base of the building. The White House was not as visible, and an inexperienced pilot might have faced a troubling slalom around the Washington Monument. However, eight months later, the Associated Press reported that the intended target was indeed the White House. The information was apparently obtained during a government interrogation of Abu Zubaida, an Al Qaeda terrorist leader then in U.S. custody. Other officials theorized that the plane was headed for the Pentagon or CIA headquarters. Whatever the target, the hijacker flying Flight 93 had made a bomb threat. Commercial pilots on Jarrah's frequency, along with the air traffic controllers directing them from Cleveland, could not believe the chilling words they were hearing.

Cleveland center: "You're unreadable. Say again, slowly."

Executive Jet 956: "Did you hear the transmission where the airplane just said he had a bomb onboard?"

Cleveland center: "Say again? Was that United 93?"

Executive Jet 956: "Yeah, that transmission you said was unreadable, it sounded like someone said they have a bomb onboard."

Cleveland center: "That's what we thought. We just, uh, we didn't get it clear. Is that United 93 calling?"

After the plane turned eastward, Jarrah spoke again.

"Hi, this is the captain. We'd like you all to remain seated. There is a bomb aboard. And we are going back to the airport. And they have our demands, so please remain quiet."

The Cleveland air traffic center began ordering other jets to turn away from Flight 93.

Cleveland center: "It's United 93 calling? United 93, I understand you have a bomb onboard. Go ahead."

The controller asked the pilot of Executive Jet 956 if he understood the transmission from the United flight.

"Affirmative," the pilot said. "He said there was a bomb onboard."

Cleveland center: "Uh, that was all you got out of it, also."

Executive Jet 956: "Affirmative."

The United jet was now headed southeast, toward Washington.

"United 93, do you hear Cleveland center?"

No answer.

The plane's transponder had been shut off, so the air traffic center in Cleveland and United's operations center in Chicago could not determine Flight 93's altitude. The Cleveland center asked the Executive Jet pilot if he could change course and attempt to visually spot Flight 93. The pilot saw the 757, lost it, then saw it again. It was headed right for him, causing the Executive Jet to make an evasive turn.

"United 93, do you still hear the center?"

"United 93, do you still hear Cleveland?"

Twenty more times the controller would call Flight 93.

Twenty more times he would get no response.

"United 93, United niner three, do you hear Cleveland?"

"United 93, United 93, Cleveland . . ."

9

Deena Burnett had awakened to get her daughters ready for school. Her twins, Halley and Madison, were five and had been in kindergarten for a week. Her youngest daughter, Anna Clare, was three and on her way to the first day of pre-school. They hopped on the bed to rouse their mother, and as usual, Deena went downstairs and turned on the television to check the weather. She lived in a gated community in San Ramon, California, in the East Bay, about forty-five minutes from San Francisco International Airport. Her husband, Tom, was due home from his business trip to New York. Deena switched the television on, and every channel carried urgent news about the World Trade Center being hit by an airplane.

What about Tom? Deena wondered. *He was staying in Manhattan, at a Marriott hotel. Was that near the World Trade Center?* She kept trying to remember what time he was leaving, what flight he was on, what time he was scheduled to arrive home. As she watched, a second plane rammed the World Trade Center. Deena thought of calling Tom's mother in Bloomington, Minnesota, to ask whether Beverly Burnett knew what flight he was on. The phone rang. It was Tom's mother, wanting to ask her the same thing. As they spoke, the call-waiting on Deena's phone clicked. It was Tom, calling from the plane on the cell phone he had nearly lost in a sporting goods store two days earlier.

"Tom," she said. "Are you okay?"

"No," he replied. "I'm on United Flight 93 from Newark to San Francisco. We're in the air. The plane has been hijacked. They already knifed a guy. One of them has a gun. They're saying there is a bomb onboard. Please call the authorities."

He hung up.

She scribbled down what Tom told her and noted the time: six twenty-seven (nine twenty-seven in the East). Later, she would wonder whether Tom called before the hijackers had taken control of the cockpit. Her husband had spoken quietly, quickly, as if he were being watched. The entire conversation had lasted ten seconds. Tom, who had been assigned seat 4B, used an ear bud with his cell phone, the mouthpiece attached to a cord that hung over his shoulder.

A guy had been knifed, he had said. Tom's father was an English teacher, and he was so precise about his own language. Deena assumed Tom meant a passenger. Surely he would have been more specific if the pilot or co-pilot had been stabbed. She had asked before he hung up, and he confirmed, yes, it was a passenger. Most likely, it was Mark Rothenberg, who sat in 5B. All of the other first-class passengers later made phone calls.

A jolt of adrenaline shot through Deena, sheer terror coursing her body. She felt herself quivering. *What do I do? Who do I call for a hijacking?* She paced the kitchen, trying to clear her mind and calm herself down.

Okay, she thought. *First thing, dial 911. Maybe they'll know who to call.*

Deena reached a 911 dispatcher in Contra Costa County, California. Her call was recorded, like all emergency calls, and the tape was later provided to her. She spoke quickly, with fear in her voice, but she'd once been a flight attendant and she knew what to say in an emergency.

"My husband just called me from United Flight 93," Deena said after introducing herself. "The plane has been hijacked. They just knifed a passenger and there are guns on the airplane."

The dispatcher, confused, asked, What plane was he on?

United Flight 93. Tom had departed from one of the New York–area airports and was bound for San Francisco. He was on the plane, and he had to hang up.

186

"He said one of the passengers had been knifed and there are guns onboard and to please let someone know," Deena said.

She didn't know whom to call. Hold on, the dispatcher said, transferring her to the police. She told her story again. The police seemed not to believe her, but they didn't treat her call as a hoax. Finally, she was transferred to an FBI agent. She repeated what Tom had told her. The agent misunderstood. Was her husband's flight one of the planes that had hit the World Trade Center?

"No," she said. "This is another flight."

The night of September 10, after a round of meetings, Tom had dinner with the president of the eastern subsidiary of his company, Thoratec, which manufactured medical devices. Tom was the company's chief operating officer. He also phoned his parents from his Manhattan hotel room and spoke about the throb and blink of neon in Times Square. He urged his mother to take her first trip to New York City.

"You need to go someplace other than where you can play golf," he teased her.

He was thirty-eight, but she still called him Tommy in the youthful way that parents did when their children's lives began with exceptional achievement and seemed to arc in unbroken ascent. He had graduated with honors from Thomas Jefferson High School in

Bloomington, and, in 1980, as quarterback of the football team, he had guided the Jaguars to a conference championship. He won an appointment to the Air Force Academy, obtained his MBA from Pepperdine, became a successful businessman, possessed a ravenous intellectual curiosity. He had a genius-level IQ, his wife said. At six foot two, two hundred five pounds, Tom carried his size with such grace and agility that people rarely realized how big he was until they stood next to him.

A political conservative, Tom valued qualities like sacrifice, valor, courage, patriotism, honor, dignity and citizenship, and longed for a time when these words carried weight and were not hollow platitudes. He seldom used the word "hero," and, even though he played quarterback briefly at St. John's University in Minnesota, he grew irritated when it was conferred on something as casual and frivolous as athletic performance. A student of military history, he made three visits to the D-Day beaches of Normandy. Yet, he avoided speaking to the veterans walking through the cemetery above Omaha Beach, considering it selfish to intrude on such a solemn moment. According to Deena, he lived by two guiding aphorisms: "If you don't stand for something, you'll fall for anything," and "Live every day as if it is your last, for surely one day you will be right."

Adorning Tom's office were busts of Abraham Lincoln, Theodore Roosevelt and Winston Churchill, strong leaders who had acted decisively and according to their conscience in times of crisis, even in the face of public opposition, men who could rally others to their cause by the sheer force of their character. Political leaders of the day often disappointed him with their tentativeness and lack of conviction. President Bill Clinton's moral failings were an embarrassment to him, and a waste of immense potential and intellect. At the same time, he was proud to have the same birthday, May 29, as John F. Kennedy. Had he been born two decades earlier, Tom said, he might have voted this once for a Democrat in a presidential election.

"Moral values, he believed, were not debatable," Deena said. "Tom believed there was right and wrong, and no in-between."

Deena was giving the FBI agent her husband's flight number and destination, when her call-waiting interrupted again. It was Tom. Again, Deena noted the time: six thirty-four on the West Coast, nine thirty-four on the East Coast.

"They're in the cockpit," Tom told her, using an Airfone this time.

The man who had been knifed was dead. Tom had tried to help, but he felt no pulse.

Deena quickly told him what she knew. Two planes had hit the towers of the World Trade Center. Terrorists seemed to be hitting designated targets. Tom immediately pieced things together. The hijackers could be planning to use his plane for a similar purpose.

"Oh my God," he said. "It's a suicide mission."

Deena heard Tom relaying the information she gave him.

"Who are you talking to?" Deena asked.

"My seatmate," Tom replied.

Were commercial airlines being hijacked? he asked. Which airlines? How many planes were involved? Who was involved?

Deena answered with what little information she had. Television newscasters were speculating that the hijacked planes were cargo planes, private planes or commercial jets. When she was a Delta flight attendant, she became familiar with the distinctive markings on various airlines, but she could not identify the planes she'd seen on television.

His plane seemed to be turning east, Tom reported, then said, "Wait, wait, we're turning back the other way. We're going south."

What could he see? Deena asked. He said it was a rural area, just fields.

"I've got to go," he said.

Deena called the FBI again. Her phone

was ringing constantly now, calls coming in, going out. A local police officer arrived to stay with her. She tried to feed the kids breakfast and get them upstairs to brush their teeth and make their beds. Ten things were happening all at once, and she attempted to go about her business, keeping order in the upheaval of the moment. She called a friend to pick her kids up for school. Things would work out. They always did.

We have a perfect life. A good job, great kids, health. Nothing bad ever happens to us.

She was tall, honey-blond, her native Arkansas still in her voice, composed, able as mothers are to manage the scatter of young children. Then her composure left her. Television reported that the Pentagon had been hit. *It must be Tom's plane.* She sat in a leather recliner and started wailing, a keening despair so strange and full of loss that it startled her. *Why is this coming out of my body and why can't I stop it?* Her daughters sat on the sofa, and they thought she was playing a game with them. They started laughing.

The phone rang. It was Tom, a third time, calling again on his cell phone. It was six forty-five, nine forty-five in the East. For a fleeting second, Deena thought Tom had miraculously survived the crash into the Pentagon.

"Tom, you're okay?"

"No, I'm not," he said.

191

A third plane had hit the Pentagon, she told him.

He repeated her words to others sitting around him. What else could she tell him?

The planes seemed to be commercial airliners originating on the East Coast, Deena said.

Tom gave the impression that he was walking around, perhaps trying to see where the hijackers were positioned.

"Do you know who's involved?" he asked.

"No," Deena said.

Again, he seemed to be relaying information, his voice growing muted then louder again. He asked about the likelihood of a bomb onboard. Before Deena could answer, Tom said, "I don't think they have one. I think they're just telling us that."

Had she called the authorities?

Yes, Deena told him. "They didn't seem to know anything about your plane."

The hijackers, Tom said, were talking about crashing the plane into the ground. "We have to do something."

He and others were making a plan. "A group of us." Don't worry, he told Deena. "I'll call you back."

Tom and D. Keith Grossman, the chief executive officer of Thoratec, often relied on a Churchill quote for encouragement in building their company, "Never, never, never,

never give up." The life-preserving medical devices that his company made gave Tom an opportunity to achieve what he strived for — to make a big mark, to engage in something noble, to serve some purpose larger than himself. He was driven, competitive. His only real fear, Deena said, was of failure, of being a footnote, of not making a difference.

"What we accomplish in life, our pursuits, our passions, echo in posterity through our children, our neighbors, and in our souls," Tom had told Thoratec employees in a speech seven months earlier. "Treating people that would otherwise die has a resounding effect on those around us. The struggle to preserve life enriches all of us, and our humanity is fortified by the process. To deem life important, and to act, affects all of those that bear witness to it."

While he privately marveled at his financial success, Tom adhered to a lifestyle of Midwestern simplicity and frugality. He and Deena did not exchange birthday or anniversary gifts. He considered jewelry a waste of money. When he gave his wife a diamond ring upon their engagement, he told her, "You need to understand, this is the last jewelry you're going to get." His car was seven years old; his wife's was ten. Money, he believed, should be spent on travel and education. His two great passions were evident on the wall of his living room: a rack of moose antlers and a hardbound collection of the Great Books. In the Burnett house, books seemed to pile up like cordwood. They spilled into the garage, into Tom's car. Recently, while planning a Las Vegas retreat for his management team, he had ordered four books on blackjack. He didn't yet understand how to win at the game, but he was certain that if he read the books, he'd beat the house.

He was fascinated by Civil War history, particularly by Nathan Bedford Forrest, the Confederate general who began his service as an uneducated private from Tennessee and ended the war as a revered cavalry officer, despite having been wounded four times and reportedly having had twenty-nine horses shot out from under him.

"One of his most telling exploits occurred when his unit was surrounded and outgunned two to one," Tom told his Thoratec employees in his speech months earlier. "The opposing commander expected Forrest to surrender, as did many in his own command. Instead, he quickly organized his force and charged. Imagine the strength of courage required to issue that order and, most remarkably, the strength of faith to follow it. The courage to be decisive, coupled with a faith and trust in each other, carried the day. Forrest and his men not only escaped the entrapment, but looped back and killed or captured the entire opposing force."

Forrest's strategy was deceptively uncomplicated: Get there first with the most men.

"This simple thought, when executed thoughtfully and with passion, is the essence of what is taught in every single military college and business school today," Tom continued. "Identify what needs to be done before your competitors, concentrate your resources on what is most important, then execute with speed. Focus on what is important, prioritize and move. Move quickly. Make your competitors react and respond to you. Pick the battlefield and engage. Speed is a strategic imperative. In all things, speed. Make intelligent decisions with speed, make mistakes with speed and quickly get to the right outcome. The outcome being the most important thing. We will win when we are decisive, when we take action, when we demonstrate commitment versus ambivalence, and when we have faith in ourselves and, most importantly, in each other."

He had acted decisively in his own life, leaving the Air Force Academy after an initiation boot camp, and later receiving his undergraduate degree from the University of Minnesota. He realized he had accepted the appointment to please his father. He did not want a life of submissive adherence to orders, having become upset over the humiliating treatment of a friend who was suspected of deficient leadership. On one of his first dates with his wife, at an Italian restaurant, in July of 1989, Tom became so distracted by a lamp that hung low between them, he reached up, grabbed the bulb and tossed it over his shoulder. "I'm trying to create an atmosphere here," he said, "and this light's not helping."

Possessed of an outdoorsy vigor, the kind of man who liked wine, cigars and venison, Tom appreciated Teddy Roosevelt's rough-rider forcefulness and Ernest Hemingway's terse manliness. "He liked the notion that you could sit down and discuss world events and philosophy and still enjoy hunting and fishing, which are not always considered intellectual pursuits," said Grossman, Thoratec's CEO. Tom liked to orate, and on Friday afternoons, he and his boss would retreat to a deck at the company office to talk and smoke cigars. He also liked to fire off e-mails with his barbed, humorous observations of the day's events.

On animal rights groups attempting to gain publicity during the flurry of summer shark attacks: "Miserable rat bastards. The reason shark, bear and mountain lion attacks are up is because they have been overprotected. I'm for dragging a net around the coast of Florida and having an all-you-can-eat shark barbeque."

On abortion rights: "Everyone wants rights.

No one wants responsibility."

On alleged attacks by a mysterious "monkey-man" on the residents of East Delhi, India: "I need no more convincing. Effective immediately, all travel to East Delhi is suspended."

From age three or four, while his father taught summer reading programs at Camp Lake Hubert in the Minnesota pine country, Tom had become an avid outdoorsman. Even then he knew that bass gathered in the shadows on hot days, and, fishing through the slats in a dock, he caught a four-and-a-half-pound lunker before he entered kindergarten. He learned to sail and shoot a bow and arrow and fire a twenty-two-caliber rifle, to ride horses and bird-dog for his father when they hunted pheasant in Iowa. Later, in the company of his father and intellectual priests, he fished for walleye and northern pike in Western Ontario, attracted to the campfire camaraderie and rugged solitude. As a boy, he sometimes was so quiet that his parents worried that he might have difficulty speaking properly. This story amused his adult friends, who never found him at a loss for words. Eventually, Tom became an entertaining mimic, cracking up his two sisters and his parents with his walk-into-the-walls impersonation of the comic Bill Murray.

At age ten, he convinced his parents to let him travel, alone, two hundred miles by bus

197

to visit his grandmother in Sioux City, Iowa. That same year, Tom and his father traveled to Lac Seul in Ontario. The excursion was enlivened by visitors from Chicago whose fishing tackle included a jug of mixed Manhattans and whose business practices may or may not have had hooks in organized crime. In any case, the visitors got lost in the swirl of darkness and alcohol. Tom and a priest set out on the lake with a flashlight, searched all night and escorted the wayward boaters safely back to camp.

Tom had fished for marlin and dolphin in Mexico, and had scheduled a salmon expedition to Alaska for next summer. He became so enthusiastic about his trips that he made his wife read Stephen Ambrose's *D-Day*, and urged his father to watch *The Longest Day*, before taking them to Normandy. Wondering whether he would have possessed the same bravery as soldiers who charged onto Omaha Beach into the storm of German gunfire, Tom told his father, "I don't know if I could do that." Every Thanksgiving, he sat rapt while his father recited *Gunga Din*, his favorite poem, and at Christmas he insisted that the whole family watch *It's a Wonderful Life*. He thought of building a log cabin on his farm in Wisconsin, and he sometimes mused about how Teddy Roosevelt had been able to leave his family and go on elaborate hunting trips.

"What a life that guy had," he'd say to Deena. "If I did that today, I would be stoned." To which she would reply: "Fine, now change that diaper."

Tom had not spoken elaborately in his first three phone calls from the plane. He was pumping Deena for information. He said nothing about the pilot or copilot, did not describe the hijackers. She didn't ask many questions. He wasn't whispering sweet nothings of farewell. He was making a plan so he could get home safely to his wife and children.

She couldn't accept that he was going to die.

We are the golden couple. Everything good was showered on us. Nothing bad ever happened.

"He never failed at anything he did," Deena said. "If he said he was going to do something, he did it."

Flying had become an integral part of his life. Because Deena was a flight attendant when they met, essentially they dated at thirty-five thousand feet. She would fly cross-country to have breakfast with Tom, or jet from her base in Atlanta to Los Angeles so they could make the return trip together. He seemed to know where everything was located on a plane, even how the galley was stocked. "He would tell *me* where things were," she said. He flew more than one hundred thousand miles a year, and, having anticipated the unlikely but real possibility of a crash, Tom and Deena had worked out a plan in case something did happen to him. When they traveled without their children, they flew separately so their daughters would not be left parentless if one of the planes went down.

Earlier in his career, Tom sometimes talked of getting his doctorate, retiring from business at forty and teaching history. But three years earlier, after the birth of his third daughter, Anna Clare, his focus changed. For weeks, then months, he stopped coming home for lunch. One evening, Tom asked Deena if she had noticed. She thought he had just grown too busy at work.

"I've been going to daily Mass," he told her.

He had a vague feeling that he was being called to do something. He did not know what, but he believed that his thoughts might coalesce if he spent more time in church. Whatever God had planned for him, Tom thought, it would have a big effect on a lot of people, a good effect. He thought it might even involve Washington and the White House, perhaps a career in politics. Deena and Tom began discussing a possible run for office when he turned forty. He could run for the United States Congress or the Senate and maybe, at some point, the White House.

"If you had asked him what he wanted to do, he would have said, 'Be president,'" Deena Burnett said.

They did not share all of the details of this imprecise calling that Tom felt, and his boss, D. Keith Grossman, later would be surprised when Deena told him of Tom's daily visits to church. Tom had mentioned, however, that he might like to run for office. His mother-in-law had even done some preliminary research into campaign financing. His mother told him, "You should run, Tom. You could win, because you're honest."

A vague sense of mortality also began to inflect Tom's life. Shortly after his third daughter, Anna Clare, was born on February 24, 1998, Deena's mother talked about a possible fourth child, so Tom could have a son.

"No, Mom, God's not going to give us a son," Deena responded, as if the words were coming from someone else. "Tom's not going to be around to raise his son, and I can't do it by myself."

Sandra Burchfield, Deena's mother, thought that her daughter meant she was getting a divorce. She began to panic. Deena said, "I think Tom is going to be killed. I can't see us growing old together."

Stunned and troubled, Burchfield quickly ended the conversation, saying, "This is strange. I don't want to talk about things like that."

Never having mentioned this to her husband, Deena said she was caught off-guard a year ago when Tom broached the subject as they stood in the kitchen. This had been a troubling time for the Burnetts. Halley, one of the twins, had become ill with what Tom and Deena feared was cystic fibrosis. (It was not.)

"I've always felt like you thought I was going to die young," Tom had said, according to Deena.

"Why do you think that?" she said.

"I don't know, I just kind of always thought that," he replied.

Maybe she would be the one to die young, she said, adding, "But I've always had the feeling that we're not going to grow old together."

The next day, Deena said, Tom attempted to double their life insurance policies but was denied because he had been diagnosed with sleep apnea. They never discussed the matter again, she said. Later, Deena would remember her husband's beautiful hands, what his mother had called "healing hands," warm and soft. Deena's hands had many lines, but Tom's were smooth and not so criss-crossed. The so-called lifeline curved halfway up his palm and stopped. She had never seen anyone's hands look like that.

Tom called a fourth time. Again, Deena

noted the time: six fifty-four, nine fifty-four in the East. Tom had sounded hurried on the first call, but now he was speaking in a normal voice, calm.

He asked about their three daughters. They wanted to talk to him, Deena said. Tom told her he would talk to them later.

He and others had come up with a plan to regain control of the airplane over a rural area.

"No," Deena admonished him. "Sit down, be still, be quiet, and don't draw attention to yourself."

"If they're going to crash this plane into the ground, we're going to have to do something," Tom said.

There was no time to wait for the authorities. What could they do anyway? "It's up to us," he said. "I think we can do it."

"What do you want me to do?" Deena asked.

"Pray, Deena, just pray."

"I love you," she said.

"Don't worry," Tom said. Then, after a long pause: "We're going to do something."

Deena sent her kids to school and held the phone, thinking Tom would call again and say everything was okay. She had every confidence that he would march into the cockpit and fly that airplane. In the fright-hope of the moment, she did not allow herself to think otherwise.

10

Ziad Jarrah's heinous plan was about to unravel. The forty-minute delay prior to the departure of United Flight 93 had provided passengers with two things those on other doomed flights did not have: Information and time to act. Passengers and crew members, calling on cell phones and Airfones, had learned that the crashes were deliberate. Their plane had traveled nearly as far west as Cleveland before the terrorists took over and made their turn toward Washington. Why had the hijackers waited so long? Were they adhering to some pre-arranged timing? Did they begin to lose their nerve? Perhaps it was something as mundane as waiting until breakfast carts were cleared from the aisle.

In any case, they had picked the wrong plane to hijack. The terrorists apparently had studied these flights carefully, making dry runs since the spring. They knew that few people would be onboard, but they could not have known what kind of people — self-directed, independent thinkers, people who could assess a situation and work in teams, people who would not allow forced enormity.

Teams of five terrorists had boarded the other hijacked flights. There were only four on United Flight 93. Ramzi Binalshibh of Yemen failed four times to receive a visa to the United States in 2000, when Jarrah attempted to enroll him in a Florida flight school. He later became a fugitive. Zacarias Moussaoui, a Frenchman of Moroccan descent, was also suspected of being the intended twentieth hijacker. He was arrested in Minneapolis on August 17, less than a month before the hijackings, when his behavior raised suspicion at a flight school. Moussaoui was later indicted for allegedly conspiring with Osama bin Laden and his Al Qaeda network to kill thousands of people, using airplanes as weapons of mass destruction. He pleaded not guilty.

And while the terrorists were already a man short on Flight 93, something else remained puzzling. On all phone calls made from the plane, passengers reported seeing only three hijackers. Not a single caller reported four hijackers. This raised several possibilities. One was that the fourth hijacker was in the cockpit the entire flight, riding in a jumpseat reserved for observers. Investigators, pilots, flight attendants and United officials tended to discount this theory. If there were seats available in first class — which there were — it was standard practice for pilots hitching a courtesy ride to be given one of those empty seats.

Paperwork would have to be filled out in advance if an observer requested to sit in the cockpit. No request was made for Flight 93, United officials later reported. It was possible that a captain might let someone who showed proper credentials — or what appeared to be proper credentials — into the cockpit briefly, to observe as the plane took off and landed. But Flight 93 was hijacked approximately forty-five minutes after it left Newark. Other pilots agreed that Captain Dahl likely would have requested that any observer return to his regular seat by that time. Some family members of the passengers and crew, however, later remained suspicious that one of the hijackers was in the cockpit from takeoff.

Perhaps one of the terrorists got cold feet when told that this flight would be a suicide mission. Perhaps he did not identify himself, remaining anonymously among the passengers to assist his partners in the event of a revolt. Or, because the 757 was so long and narrow, perhaps the passengers received an obstructed view of the takeover. Eyewitness testimony in moments of stress was often unreliable. As investigators noted, it was not uncommon for bank customers to witness a robbery and to swear that the robber wore neither a hat nor a mustache, both of which later appear clearly on a replay of the bank's videotape system.

The terrorists were slight men, smaller than the former athletes aboard Flight 93, and, as a group, they may not have been as well trained in self-defense as some of the passengers. The hijackers apparently were not as well armed as Tom Burnett believed, either. Bob Craig, the FBI agent who coordinated evidence collection at the crash site, said that no evidence of a firearm was found in the wreckage.

"Expect the response, or a reaction, from the enemy," the letter of preparation had reminded the hijackers during their last-night ritual. The response was about to come.

Richard Guadagno was a small, wiry, muscular man, five foot eight, gentle and introverted, but as manager of the Humboldt Bay National Wildlife Refuge in Eureka, California, he was also a federal law-enforcement officer. He received the same training in hand-to-hand fighting as drug enforcement agents, alcohol, tobacco and firearm agents and the border patrol. As did other federal agents, he had also been trained in how to respond to a hijacking. He was licensed to carry a firearm on the Humboldt refuge and he was known as a gung-ho adherent to the letter of the law. He could also bench-press three hundred fifty pounds, double his body weight.

"He was a quiet, reflective guy, but when he wore that law-enforcement hat, the world was black-and-white for him," Dave Paullin, his supervisor, said. "Either you were right or you were wrong. There wasn't a lot of gray."

As a boy in Ewing, New Jersey, Richard showed no interest in Little League, and when his father took him golfing, he often stole away to a pond to look for frogs. He preferred catching butterflies to catching footballs, and he spent time with several older men in the neighborhood, exchanging ideas on gardening. He grew tomatoes, beans and lettuce, harvested fig trees and planted seedlings that grew into huge evergreens. This green thumb, and an intense appreciation for wildlife and the environment, flowered into a dual major of biology and land management at Rutgers and a seventeen-year career with the U.S. Wildlife and Fisheries Service.

"He had an innate connection with nature from the get-go," his sister, Lori Guadagno, said. "He appreciated the beauty and sensitivity in the world."

In meetings, Richard was generally reserved, but when he undertook a project to restore a creek or protect a wetlands, his voice would become animated and his arms would fly around as if he were conducting an orchestra. "Rich, I got it, slow it down," Paullin, his boss, would say to him, to which he would reply, a slight twang in his voice, "What do you expect, I'm an Italian from Jersey."

At the Humboldt Bay Wildlife Refuge, Richard lived in an A-frame house with a view of the Pacific and the bay, and he indulged his varied passions: surfing, fishing, gardening, cooking, scuba diving. When he moved into the home a year earlier, he cleared the vast undergrowth and planted one hundred fifty trees and shrubs. He built a greenhouse and a sun porch and grew vegetables, orchids, bonsai plants, so many plants that it took him three hours to water them. He rode motorcycles, dabbled in photography and stained-glass art, built furniture, fashioned mobiles from rocks that he cut and polished. He rolled his telescope onto his deck, which provided an unfettered view of the sky. He collected eight custom-made guitars and built one of his own. He even taught himself taxidermy, cluttering his place with deer heads, ducks, a fat beaver, a river otter and a coyote. His sister Lori joked that his house looked like it belonged to the Addams Family.

In his love for nature, Richard grew irritated with those who befouled it. He was a perfectionist, and as a law-enforcement officer, he went by the book. He would sit for hours, waiting to ticket hunters who trespassed onto the refuge to shoot ducks. Once, he was out jogging at night with a flashlight and jumped in front of a truck to cite two men who had been shooting up road signs. Another time, he admonished his own mother not to pick wildflowers on a hiking trail. When his father picked him up at the Philadelphia airport five years earlier and complained that he had gotten a speeding ticket, Richard said, "You deserved it."

"He was a compassionate man, but he had a lot of cop in him," his father, Jerry Guadagno, said. "He didn't like people who broke the law."

Richard had traveled to New Jersey to celebrate his grandmother's one-hundredth birthday. The night before he left, he entered the kitchen from the garage with a small pickax that he put into the bag he would carry on the plane. The one thing Richard did not have was a cell phone.

"If people were conspiring to charge the cockpit," Paullin said, "he would not have been the type of person to sit back and say, 'Let me know how it turns out.'"

Louis J. Nacke II did not back down from anyone. He liked to be in charge. He was five foot nine and weighed two hundred pounds, with a weight-lifter's physique, and he had a garrulous charm about him. He reminded his friend Domenic D'Errico of the voluble characters on the *Sopranos,* a non-felonious wiseguy.

He seemed indestructible. When Lou was a boy, dressed in Superman pajamas and a cape, he ran through a glass door, leaving a deep gash under his left arm that required numerous stitches. Later, he had a red-and-yellow Superman logo tattooed on the arm. He loved to drive fast and blast the radio and blow by people on the highway, and when his wife, Amy, would caution him to slow down, he would say, "No one will ever take me down without a fight."

If people said something to him, he'd say something back. He had a temper. He was not a guy to let things slide. Once, when a driver nearly ran over his younger brother Dale in a supermarket parking lot, Lou punched the guy through the window of the car. Over Labor Day weekend, he had confronted another driver who cut him off on the road, getting out of his car at a red light and seething, "You got something to say to me? I'll knock you back into your Generation X." He was not a man who would wither from confrontation.

His immediate family called him Joey. When his sister, Paula Jacobs, was a senior in high school, Joey disliked the way one of her dates looked, so he and his brother Kenny hung the guy off the backyard deck by his ankles. "I never had another date with him," Paula said. "He said, 'Your family's crazy.' "

Sometimes Lou liked to provoke people just to get a rise out of them. He would get his brothers or sister in a head lock and say, "I love you." He'd make a smart-aleck remark and say "Just kidding," or grab his wife, Amy, and hold her in a bear hug until she'd had enough. He'd release her with a devilish smile and all would be forgiven.

At a previous job at a K-Mart distribution center, where he was D'Errico's assistant, Lou did not hesitate to wade into the middle of a tense attempt to organize a union. "He was on the floor, taking on issues, challenging people," D'Errico said. "Lou was an in-your-face kind of guy. He would not back down. He would cause a conflict just to make sure you understood his viewpoint."

Lou Nacke, who now managed a Kay-Bee Toys distribution center in Clinton, New Jersey, had just celebrated his forty-second birthday two days earlier, on September 9. On the tenth, he was out to dinner in New Hope, Pennsylvania, with Amy and his father-in-law, Dr. Robert Weisberg, when he got a call. It was eight p.m.

"You need to hop the first plane to San Francisco," his boss told him.

Kay-Bee had just signed a huge contract

212

with a customer, and something had happened to a shipment of toys. Lou would have to smooth things over. He seldom traveled for his job. Two, maybe three times a year. On this trip, he would fly out in the morning on United 93 and return the same night. It would be a long day.

"Get someone else to go," his wife said at dinner.

"I should, but I can't," Lou replied.

He left home at four-thirty a.m., traveled an hour to the distribution center in Clinton, then had someone drive him to the airport in Newark to catch his flight. He checked in and received seat 12F. If anyone could solve the problem of this toy shipment, it was Lou. He would work things out. He loved to talk and was not bashful about speaking his mind, whether it related to current events, the reason he used four-inch nails instead of five-inch nails to attach drywall, or the latest culinary delight he had spotted on the Food Channel.

"Even if he knew little or nothing about a topic, he could make it up — he could BS with the best of them," said Lou's brother-in-law, Jeff Trichon. "He just didn't want to stop talking, and often never did."

Lou watched Emeril Lagasse, the television chef, with the same devotion that people once afforded Walter Cronkite. And he loved girl talk. His friend nicknamed him "Louise" because Lou always called Dom D'Errico's wife, Lisa, to trade recipes and chatter endlessly. Lou didn't really cook much, but he had a discriminating palate. He read every cooking magazine he could get his hands on. He would come home with a ten-dollar tub of butter or a twelve-dollar candy bar, and his wife would say, "Ten dollars for butter?" and he would respond, "This is the best you can buy." He was a perfectionist that way, lining up all the clothes in his closet from light colors to dark. "A clean freak," Amy Nacke called him. Lou once had a red Corvette and he cleaned the inside vents with a Q-tip. He ironed his clothes each morning and carefully wiped down the sink after he brushed his teeth. Everything had to be immaculate.

When he wanted to know more about a certain topic, he immersed himself. His father-in-law collected wine, and Lou began collecting, too. The previous September, he and Amy went to Napa Valley on their honeymoon. Lou studied wine catalogues, read wine magazines, sought out the owners of wine shops, purchased cases of wine until he became an expert. He'd laugh and tell his father-in-law, "When you're not around, I go in your wine cellar, get naked and roll around."

At other times, Lou could be sentimental, big-hearted. On his bureau, he kept a small wooden box carved in the shape of a turtle, which his sister had given him thirty years ago. On the sun visor of his car, he placed a childhood picture of his brother Dale. After he divorced his childhood sweetheart, Patricia Alexander, they remained friends. He bought her a car and visited her mother in the hospital. "A rock with a soft spot in it," D'Errico said of him. Amy didn't particularly like Lou's red Corvette, or the money it cost for upkeep while they were having a house built. So Lou sold the 'Vette and bought her a pair of diamond earrings for a wedding present.

This week was to be a celebratory one. Lou had just turned forty-two. His first anniversary was coming up on September 16. Lou and Amy would go to dinner, open a bottle of rare wine. In a few days, they would be moving into their new four-bedroom house with cathedral ceilings. Lou had two teenage sons from his previous marriage — Joseph was eighteen, Louis Paul was fourteen — and he and Amy were talking about starting a family of their own.

He phoned her from the airport before boarding and told her he loved her. "I'll call when I get there."

If anyone could formulate a plan, organize a team of people, it was Lauren Grandcolas, seated in row eleven. A keen sense of planning and preparation ran in the family. Her father, Larry Catuzzi, had coached football with Woody Hayes at Ohio State. She had spent a career in marketing and advertising, most recently for *Good Housekeeping* magazine. Each morning, when she woke up, she had coffee and made a list. Lauren kept lists for everything. Lists for the day, lists for the year, lists for her lifetime. The previous Christmas, she had finally weaned herself from handwritten lists and switched to a Palm Pilot. GET BUSY LIVING OR GET BUSY DYING, said a note on the refrigerator of her home in San Rafael, California.

She was the kind of person who began packing three days in advance of a trip, who bought travel guides and highlighted the relevant passages, who cleaned the house before the maid arrived. "She wanted to make sure she accomplished something every minute of the day," said a friend, Nancy Lee. And, as might be expected of a football coach's daughter, Lauren knew how to improvise. Once, when a friend sprained an ankle during a road race, Lauren drove the friend home, operating a stick shift for the first time, puttering over the Bay Bridge from Oakland to San Francisco in second gear the whole way. Earlier in the year, when she fell ill during a trip to Thailand and had to stay behind while her husband, Jack, went scuba diving, Lauren could not simply stay in bed all day. She made a list of tropical fruits and vegetables, shopped for them and chopped them up to give Jack a facial when he returned. "I had all this goop in my face and hair, things on my eyes," Jack said. "I looked like a cross between a salad and a milk shake."

Lauren kept fit by riding bikes and rollerblading, and, always in pursuit of a new adventure, she booked a skydiving trip for herself and her husband on her thirtieth birthday. Jack was hesitant. Free-falling through space was not exactly his idea of fun at a birthday party, but Lauren had done all the research and had signed them up for a two-hour preparatory course. "I wasn't going to do it, but then I realized here was this size-two woman with a heart the size of Texas," he said. "I had to do it."

In her spare time, Lauren volunteered at AIDS walks, food distribution centers and adopt-a-kid programs, the United Way and Habitat for Humanity. "She always had time for other people and she gave it unconditionally," said her husband, Jack. "She was probably the most unconditional person I ever met." Lauren liked to make light of herself, too, pulling out old dresses and putting on what she called a Mary Tyler Moore fashion show. "A sparkle in a gray-suit world," she had been called several years earlier after cleverly winning an important boxer-shorts account as marketing director of Pricewater-houseCoopers. Lauren was also a certified emergency medical technician. She had come to the assistance of a woman whose foot got trapped in an escalator in San Francisco, of a man who choked on gum at a Dallas health club, of a drunk man who had driven a car into a ditch near her home. In each of these situations, she had secured the area, comforted the person and instructed someone to call 911.

"I never saw her panic," said Deanna Shapiro, a friend who was riding bikes with Lauren five years earlier when they saw a man pull out of a driveway and back into a steep ditch. "She got off her bike, told me to slow down traffic, crawled into the car, asked the guy if he was okay. She was asking him a lot of questions, who the president was, the day of the week, his name. She told someone to call 911. The police came and she told them that the guy seemed inebriated. She was totally cool. She just took over right away."

On September 11, Jack Grandcolas awakened, looked outside and felt a kind of oddness. The clouds seemed to have strange shapes. He turned the television to ESPN, watched sports for a few minutes and switched to the news. He sat there horrified. Planes had flown into the World Trade

Center. His brother was a pilot for American Airlines, so he called to make sure he was okay. His brother-in-law worked near the World Trade Center. He was okay, too. When he saw that planes had been grounded, he felt certain that Lauren would be safe. Her flight was not due to take off until nine-twenty.

Lauren's sister Vaughn called.

"Have you heard from Lauren?" she asked. "We need to find out where she is."

Lauren had taken an earlier flight, Vaughn said.

"You're kidding me," Jack said.

He went downstairs and saw two messages on the answering machine. The first said she would be home early.

In the second message, Lauren seemed calm and hopeful. It sounded to Jack as if she were driving home from the grocery store or ordering a pizza. Still, there was urgency in her voice.

"Honey, are you there? Jack, pick up sweetie," Lauren said, calling from Flight 93. "Okay, well, I just wanted to tell you I love you. We're having a little problem on the plane. I'm totally fine. I love you more than anything, just know that. I'm comfortable and I'm okay for now. I'll, I . . . just a little problem. I love you. Please tell my family I love them, too. Bye, honey."

Jack was trying to hold out hope, but he

was overwhelmed and he could barely speak. He dropped to his knees.

"No, my God, no."

Captain Jason Dahl
(FAMILY PHOTO)

First Officer
LeRoy Homer Jr.
(FAMILY PHOTO)

Flight Attendant
Lorraine Bay
(FAMILY PHOTO)

Flight Attendant
Sandra Bradshaw
(FAMILY PHOTO)

Flight Attendant
Wanda Green
(FAMILY PHOTO)

Flight Attendant
CeeCee Lyles
(FAMILY PHOTO)

Flight Attendant
Deborah Welsh
(FAMILY PHOTO)

Todd Beamer
and son David
(FAMILY PHOTO)

Alan Beaven
(FAMILY PHOTO)

Christian Adams
(FAMILY PHOTO)

Mark Bingham
with mom
Alice Hoglan
(FAMILY
PHOTO)

Deora Bodley
(FAMILY PHOTO)

Marion Britton
(FAMILY PHOTO)

Tom Burnett Jr. and
daughters Halley,
Madison and
Anne Clare
(FAMILY PHOTO)

William Cashman
and Patrick Driscoll
(FAMILY PHOTO)

Georgine
Corrigan
(FAMILY
PHOTO)

Patricia
Cushing
(FAMILY
PHOTO)

Jane Folger
(FAMILY PHOTO)

Edward Felt and wife Sandra
(FAMILY PHOTO)

Colleen Fraser
(FAMILY
PHOTO)

Andrew
Garcia
(FAMILY
PHOTO)

Jeremy Glick
(FAMILY PHOTO)

Kristin White
Gould with
daughter
Allison Vadhan
(FAMILY
PHOTO)

Lauren Grandcolas
(FAMILY PHOTO)

Donald Greene
(FAMILY PHOTO)

Linda Gronlund and
Joseph DeLuca
(FAMILY PHOTO)

Richard Guadagno
(FAMILY PHOTO)

Toshiya Kuge
(FAMILY PHOTO)

Hilda Marcin
(FAMILY PHOTO)

Nicole Miller with
boyfriend Ryan Brown
(FAMILY PHOTO)

Waleska Martinez
(FAMILY PHOTO)

Louis Nacke II
(FAMILY PHOTO)

Donald and Jean Peterson
(FAMILY PHOTO)

Mark "Mickey"
Rothenberg with
wife Meredith
(FAMILY PHOTO)

Christine Snyder
(FAMILY PHOTO)

John Talignani
(FAMILY PHOTO)

Honor Elizabeth
Wainio with her
father, Ben
(FAMILY
PHOTO)

11

At six forty-four on the West Coast — nine forty-four in the East — the phone rang at Vaughn Hoglan's ranch-style home in Saratoga, California. It was the beginning of yet another busy day in the home. In the past two years, Vaughn and his wife, Kathy, had become parents to five babies by surrogate mothers. Alice Hoglan, Vaughn's sister, had delivered four of the babies herself. Just six months earlier, at age fifty-one, Alice had given birth to triplets. "Just lending out the womb," she joked. Alice was a flight attendant for United and was staying at her brother's house to help care for the kids. When the phone rang, a family friend and baby-sitter, Carol Phipps, answered in the kitchen. It was Mark Bingham, Alice's son.

"Get Kathy or Alice quickly," he said.

Carol walked down the hallway to Kathy Hoglan's room.

"There is an urgent call," Carol said. "Come quickly."

Kathy hurried out of bed and ran into the kitchen.

"Kathy, it's Mark. I'm on United Flight 93 and it's been hijacked."

Kathy Hoglan grabbed a piece of paper and wrote "United 93." Mark sounded calm, matter-of-fact.

"I wanted to call to tell you, in case I never see you again, that I love you," Mark said.

Kathy's mind raced. *They'll negotiate, land the plane safely, everything will be okay. How did he make the call? Is he in danger from making the call?* Mark's voice sounded as if a situation had been resolved in his mind. He sounded like a person who knew what was going to happen, or might happen, and maybe things were not going to turn out the way he would like. As if he felt he might die but that he still had hopes of making it through.

"Oh my gosh, let me get your mom for you," Kathy told Mark.

Alice Hoglan had heard her sister-in-law race down the hallway and say, "Well, we love you, too, Mark."

She got to the kitchen and Kathy told her, "Talk to Mark, he's been hijacked."

"Hi, Mark," Alice said.

There was a stiff formality in his response. "Mom, this is Mark Bingham."

Alice had not been expecting her son home

232

until the weekend. He had a business meeting in San Francisco, and he was to serve in the wedding of a friend. Mark was accustomed to a frenetic pace of living. He had spent the summer in Italy, running with the bulls in Pamplona, Spain, attending the Southern Decadence Festival in New Orleans, operating a public relations firm with offices in New York and San Francisco. "You're living high on the hog," his friend, Matt Hall, had told him the night before he left on Flight 93. "Have you ever thought about why you're doing this?"

Adventurism ran in the family. Mark's great-grandfather had helped to build Hoover Dam. A number of his friends, in their early thirties, were at a point where travel had become a more urgent priority than work. Mark had another answer for Hall. He had grown up poor, and he wouldn't live like that again. As his mother described it, Mark was a welcome consolation from a failed marriage. Alice Hoglan said she left Phoenix with Mark when he was three weeks old, and headed for South Florida. There had been a reconciliation with her husband, but it did not last. For a considerable period, Mark and his mother made their own way. At one point, Alice was estranged even from her own family. When Mark was two, he and his mother rented half of a front porch from a Cuban family in Miami for a few months.

Alice attended classes at Florida International University by day, finishing her degree in education and history, and at night she worked as a Playboy bunny. This was the winter of 1973. They didn't even own a can opener, and ate cans of beans and franks with pop-up tops. The next year, while Alice taught school, they lived on a houseboat on the Miami River, so close to the Orange Bowl that they could hear cheering on Sundays during the Miami Dolphins' games.

Later, Mark and Alice relocated to northern California, settling in Monterey. Alice was a blithe spirit. She had been a fan of John Steinbeck, and Monterey was the site of his novel *Cannery Row.* They blew into town on the Fourth of July, 1980, essentially destitute and transient. Mark was ten at the time, and for several weeks, he and his mother lived at a campground, sleeping in the back of an Isuzu pickup truck. They camped at night, and during the day Alice went job hunting. A few times Mark fished for dinner along the Monterey wharf. He and his mother went to a local grocery store to buy aluminum foil and vegetables, and they steamed the day's catch over a campfire.

Alice tried to sell real estate, but a recession was on and interest rates soared. She did secretarial work, too, and they held together, rented an apartment. "I know those were hard times for Mark," Alice said. At one desperate point, she said she even borrowed from a cigar box the last six or seven dollars that Mark had collected from odd jobs, writing her son an IOU. Later, Mark's high school friends would joke that he always appeared in photographs wearing someone else's clothes, and that any item of clothing left near him became public property. "Those were bad times, but we got through them," Alice said. Once Mark's public relations business had become profitable, she would be amazed that he paid more in taxes than she made yearly as a flight attendant.

This was why he lived so high on the hog, Mark had explained to Matt Hall. He had been through times when he had nothing. He and his mother had landed on their feet, built reliable careers, he as a public relations executive, she as a flight attendant. When opportunities came his way now, he would take them. Mark had told friends that he was happily single and planned to spend the next year or two seeing the world. He thought of living in Paris for six months, maybe a year. Mark lived for the moment with a comedian's affinity for ad-libbing through life. In the spring of 1980, when Mark was again hopscotching from school to school, this time as a fourth-grader in Redlands, California, he made a decision that kids seldom get to make. He named himself. He had been born Gerald Kendall Bingham, and his mother did not want to call him Jerry, his father's name, so she massaged his middle name and came up with Kerry. Except that other kids kept teasing him that Kerry was a girl's name. As mother and son walked to school for the first time in Redlands, having moved there the day before, Alice told him, "Kerry, you're going to a brand-new school, no one knows you here. If you want to change your name, now is the time."

As Alice remembered it, he looked at her and said, "Okay, I'll be Mark."

On the phone now, Mark told his mother that he loved her. He kept a sign in his San Francisco office that said ALICE HOGLAN IS A GODDESS. It was not unusual for Mark to call Alice to express his love, but it was unusual for him to do it at six forty-four in the morning. His voice sounded controlled and rattled at the same time.

"I'm on a flight from Newark to San Francisco," Mark said. "There are three guys aboard who say they have a bomb."

"Who are these guys, Mark?"

There was a long pause. Alice listened and listened. Mark did not answer for what seemed like five seconds. She heard voices, nothing suggesting violence or threats, no yelling, no accented voices. It sounded as if someone were speaking to him confidentially. It reminded Alice of an office setting, the kinds of ambient noises a person heard if someone laid the phone down for a minute, or turned away.

Then Mark came back on the line. "Do you believe me? It's true."

He was seeking assurance.

"I do believe you, Mark," Alice said. "Who are these guys?"

There was another long pause. Alice visualized ominous things. Mark said he was calling from an Airfone. He might be in full view of the hijackers. He was probably in first class, she thought, and the hijackers were probably up there. She worried that he was drawing attention to himself, making himself a target.

A long pause followed after she asked him who these guys were. It was as if he did not hear his mother, or someone else was speaking to him. Then the line went dead. She worried that he had been thrown off the phone or that the hijackers had knifed him.

By then, her brother Vaughn had turned on the television in the living room. They saw a horrific replay, one tower of the World Trade Center in flames and the other tower being approached by what appeared to be a slow-moving airplane. It seemed surreal to Alice, like a horror movie.

At that moment, Alice understood. She felt that Mark knew what he was up against, that maybe someone had organized a plan, that he knew the situation was dire and he was calling to say good-bye in case he did not see her again.

Then news came of a third plane hitting the Pentagon. It was apparent now that Mark's plane was a piece of a larger horrible mosaic. Alice and Vaughn and Kathy thrashed about for something to do, some way to help, and Vaughn said, "Get Mark on the phone and tell him it's a suicide mission. Tell him they need to do whatever they can to try to get control back."

Alice dialed Mark's cell phone number. Later, she would retrieve the message from the phone company, one of more than forty urgent messages sent to her son.

"Hey, Mark, this is Dad," Jerry Bingham said from Florida, emotion in his voice. "I'm just calling to see how you're doing. Uh, I'm looking at that big wreck, man," a reference to the World Trade Center. "I hope you're not too close to that. So give me a call when you can," he said, his voice breaking.

Other friends called Mark's cell phone, and so did his assistant at his public relations firm, wondering whether he was flying, reminding him that she had set up a business call for him.

A friend named Ken called. "I'm in absolute shock now," he said in his message. "I can't get over what is happening. Oh my God, this is just devastating."

Then Alice called the cell phone. "Mark, this is your mom," she said. She gave the incorrect time, ten fifty-four. It was actually nine fifty-four in the East. "The news is that it's been hijacked by terrorists. They are planning to probably use the plane as a target to hit some site on the ground. If you possibly can, try to overpower these guys, 'cause they'll probably use the plane as a target."

She was nervous and she kept saying "target" instead of "missile."

"I would say, go ahead and do everything you can to overpower them, because they're hell-bent," Alice said. "Try to call me back if you can. You know the number here."

She gave two numbers.

"Okay, I love you sweetie, good-bye."

To act in the face of danger or fear would not have been out of character for Mark. He had been a sensitive, awkward kid, insecure about his physical ability until high school, when he began playing rugby. By then, he and his mother were living in the Santa Cruz Mountains south of San Francisco, in a rustic cabin whose roof once collapsed in a rainstorm. By virtue of geography, Mark attended public high school in the wealthy enclave of Los Gatos. Alice Hoglan would stand on the sideline in agony, watching her son fulfill the game's motto: Give blood, play

239

rugby. Mark's coach could not remember another player who bled so much or got injured so often. His nose became a career's crooked résumé. But with rugby, Mark's social and physical ungainliness disappeared. In motion, he was a different person, bold, ceaseless, as if awkwardness could be overcome like inertia. His friends were amazed to see him running, headlong, his huge body amped on unpadded adrenaline, craving clean, hard, disruptive contact. There were no protective helmets or shoulder pads in rugby, no plastic-and-leather shock absorbers, nothing but the grunting slap of muscle and bone, the great satisfactory jab of a shoulder into an opponent's chest, that one crystalline instant of domination, that absolute, presiding moment over failing legs and helpless exhale.

"He was like a guided missile, head down, going," said Dave Kupiecki, who attended the University of California at Berkeley with Mark and in whose wedding Mark served as best man. "He wasn't that fast, but he was everywhere. No matter how hard a guy ran into him, he kept going. I was overwhelmed. I'd never seen anyone play sports who was always moving."

Cal won two national rugby championships while Mark was on the team in the early 1990s. It was a social sport as well as a brutal physical one, rough bloody games followed by the striped-shirt bonding of song and drink in a local bar. He and other rugby players liked to quote from Shakespeare's *Henry V*: "We few, we happy few, we band of brothers. For he today that sheds his blood with me shall be my brother." His inhibitions seemed to shed like unwanted weight. Mark became president of his fraternity at Cal, Chi Psi, and something of a prankster-legend in the Greek life, attempting to tackle the mascots of Wisconsin and arch-rival Stanford at football games, snatching ducks from a local aquatic park for a Polynesian luau, sitting in a wheelchair while wearing a Cal football helmet and crashing into stacked milk crates as a human bowling ball, driving a junker car fifteen miles an hour from Oakland to Berkeley so that it could be trashed in the fraternity garage as a way of blowing off steam from final exams. He became fascinated with video cameras after taking a film class in community college. Mark did crazy, wild things as he and his friends made their own videos, such as jumping backwards off of a shipping container so that he would appear a superhuman spy when the film was shown in reverse. It was Mark, too, who scared the hell out of his friends a decade earlier by leaping off a fifty-foot cliff in Maui and splashing into the Pacific. In November of 2000, he served as best man when his father, Jerry Bingham, remarried, which gave him control of the wedding video. "Everybody was three sheets to the wind and Mark was asking trivia questions about Notre Dame football," Jerry Bingham said.

Emboldened by his athletic success, self-assured, his confidence having filled out along with his physique, the social outsider having become an insider in campus athletic and fraternity life, Mark made an announcement in August of 1991 that his family and friends found stunning: he was gay. He first told his mother after they spent a day together, driving home into the sunset from the East Bay. They were more brother and sister than mother and son, and they leaned on each other, talked about everything. On this day, Alice was grousing to him about a man she was dating, when Mark said, "There is something I promised myself I'd tell you before the sun went down."

She could tell by the tone in his voice that something serious was weighing on him.

"I'm gay," Mark said.

Alice was grateful that her son had told her, but astounded at the same time, and she did not remember much else of what was said.

"It's news I don't think any parent really wants to hear," Alice said. "I could tell it meant a lot to him that I would be accepting. I struggled with it. I made calls, researched it, educated myself. Essentially, I hid my chagrin from him. I was riddled with stereotypes. It was weeks, months maybe, before I was able to come to peace with it. I knew it was not a choice that he had made. I knew the last thing Mark needed was resistance or rejection from his loved ones."

He had been afraid to come out, his friends said, not because he was ashamed but because he worried that intractable beliefs might make others think less of him. Mark Wilhelm, a friend who said he met Mark Bingham in 1990, wrote that Mark had sensed since he was twelve that he was gay, and that he feared his friends and family would find out. "I'd have to kill myself," he remembered Mark saying, afraid his family would no longer love him. Mark eventually made this difficult admission while a member of two groups long known for homophobic behavior: Frat boys and jocks. His acknowledgment shook up the belief systems of many who knew him, shattered stereotypes. Mark could be defined only in the sense that he was undefinable. He was a rugby player, a frat boy, a yuppie, a Libertarian who would later help organize a fund-raiser for John McCain's Republican presidential campaign, and he was gay.

"He didn't like anyone trying to put him in a box; that drove him nuts," said Todd Sarner, a longtime friend. "He brushed aside old prejudices about what a jock or a gay person is."

And yet, so resistant was he to being stereotyped, said a friend, Bryce Eberhart, that on Mark's laundry list of personality traits, being gay "was number eight or nine, behind being a decent pickup basketball player."

Certainly, Mark was not fearless, Sarner said, but he took action anyway. He was fiercely competitive, on and off the rugby field. And he protected those closest to him. Mark and Sarner were in Vancouver, British Columbia, visiting a waitress friend, when a group of rowdy teenagers attempted to drink and leave without paying their bill. The teenagers swarmed a waiter and Mark jumped in the middle. Later, in an e-mail, he wrote, "A bar brawl ensued. I skinned up my shin, and my knuckles are still sore from repeated blows."

In the summer of 1991 or 1992, Mark and his family were on a raft trip along the American River in the Sierra Nevada range, when his uncle Lee Hoglan jumped into the water to save a girl who had fallen out of another raft. The girl swam to safety, but Lee went over a small waterfall and became disoriented and helpless in the cold water, as if a rope had been tied around his body. "Are you okay?" Mark yelled at him. "I can't move," Lee said. Mark went in and fished him out. "Without him, I think I probably would have drowned," Lee said. "It was pretty dicey for a while."

In 1995, Mark was walking to a San Francisco bar with his partner at the time, Paul Holm, when the two men were attacked from behind by a pair of muggers, one of whom had a gun. The men demanded Mark and Paul hand over their money and their watches.

"The guy with the gun was bigger than Mark," Holm said. "Mark started fighting with him and the guy started hitting him in the head with the gun. Mark was wearing a white T-shirt, and there was blood all over him. But he wouldn't stop fighting. The gun got kicked away and it skittered under a car. The guy got up and left. It just showed that Mark was willing to jump into action against two big guys to protect himself. I wasn't happy. I thought we should have just given them our wallets, but that's not the way Mark was."

Apart from this dangerous moment, Holm thought of Mark as a "huge Labrador retriever bounding around through life," a gregarious, vibrant, driven man of boundless spirit, a Francophile and a gourmet who drew people to him the way a magnet drew iron filings, a fun-loving goofball who dressed one recent Halloween as a "big-assed" Brandi Chastain and another as a transvestite lumberjack. When Amanda Mark, who would later be his roommate in New York, visited once from overseas, Bingham announced over the public address system at San Francisco International Airport, "Would Amanda Mark please go to Gate 43, we have a keg of beer waiting for you."

"He would make you feel you were his best friend after meeting him once," Amanda said. "If you gave him your number, he'd call you and you'd be a friend forever."

Once hesitant and vulnerable, Mark had compensated for his timidity with a personality so outgoing that he forged a career in public relations. He was famous for wading into crowds of strangers, smiling, sticking out his hand and saying, "Hi, I'm Mark Bingham, who are you?" He had recently walked up to Tom Cruise on the street in New York and introduced himself. Matt Hall, whom Mark was dating, was too shy to approach strangers, fearing rejection, but Mark had told him, "You don't understand how much you can affect people just by saying hello." Sometimes, after a deal was completed, he would make a pair of parentheses with his fingers and say, "All I had to do was get them to talk."

"He was a big, strong, gentle guy," Holm said. "Beneath his bravado, he didn't want to hurt anyone's feelings. He never wanted to hurt anyone. He was always thinking about how things would impact other people. Maybe to a fault. And he had this wonderful trait of looking out for people who were not so strong, either physically or in a work setting. He always looked out for the guy who got picked last in dodge ball."

To his longtime friend, Todd Sarner, Mark had seemed distracted for the last year or so, always in a hurry, as if he had to be somewhere. "Maybe on some level he knew his time was limited," said Sarner, a therapist who held a master's degree in psychology. The two had spoken in a general way about Sarner's fascination with the possibility that some big international change might occur in their lifetimes, perhaps some traumatic moment that would begin a shift away from collective self-centeredness and entitlement. They had even spoken about a possible film project to explore the idea. His close friends knew that Mark longed to make his life great, to make a difference. In July, he and his roommate, Amanda Mark, had talked about writing a novel. Bingham had even gone to the library to check out a book on writing. One of the exercises the book suggested was to write his own eulogy.

"What can we do to be remembered long after we're here?" Amanda recalled the two of them saying. "What can we do to change the world and make it a better place?"

Another close friend, Dave Kupiecki, thought it curious that Mark had traveled to Italy alone during the summer. Yet, he was his old self with friends in Pamplona in July, dressing in a white shirt and pants and a red scarf and running through narrow streets with charging bulls. The first day had gone without incident, he said in an e-mail to his mother, but the group had returned for a second running. This time Mark had found himself briefly caught on the head of a bull, between the horns, and, when he fell, the bull had stepped on him, leaving a red crescent *C* as a souvenir hoof mark on his left thigh. "He wasn't going to be happy unless he drew blood," said Eberhart, a friend and rugby teammate. It had all seemed a bit surreal, Mark told his mother. The incident happened in the bull ring. After people realized he wasn't badly hurt, several ran up and shouted, "Dude! That was awesome! Your hat didn't even come off!" Then a diminutive Spanish man came up and asked him for a cigarette.

"We adjourned promptly to the Café Iruna [made famous by Hemingway in *The Sun Also Rises*] and ordered four beers and a pitcher of Sangria," Mark e-mailed his aunt, Candyce Hoglan. "It was eight-forty a.m."

There would be more contented blood to draw this season, with the San Francisco Fog rugby club. The club had begun as a gay-friendly place for athletes who wanted to participate in organized sport. About a year earlier, the club heard a rumor that a former Cal player was interested in the Fog. That player turned out to be Mark Bingham. He wandered over from a flag-football game one day in a San Francisco park and, as was his style, he began to play fiercely, knocking people to the ground.

"We had a lot of new guys who had never played a contact sport," said Eberhart, one of the Fog's founders. "We had been taking it easy on them. Mark didn't. He came in like a freight train and a lot of guys didn't like him at first. After practice, he went up to the guys, learned all their names, mentioned something specific that they did well or could improve upon, and endeared himself to everyone."

He played with the team at a tournament in Washington, DC, in May of 2001, and a couple of familiar things happened. Mark dislocated his shoulder, and he also led a postgame sing-along with the Fog's opponent from Buenos Aires, warbling "Don't Cry for Me, Argentina." For the upcoming season, the Fog had been accepted into the mainstream Northern California Rugby Union. Though he was shuttling between San Francisco and New York now, Mark would play when he could. Upon the team's acceptance into the rugby union, he sent a passionate e-mail to his teammates:

"When I started playing rugby at the age of sixteen, I always thought that my interest in other guys would be an anathema — com-

pletely repulsive to the guys on my team —
and to the people I was knocking the shit
out of on the other team. I loved the game,
but knew I would need to keep my sexuality
a secret forever. I feared total rejection. As
we worked and sweated and ran and talked
together this year, I finally felt accepted as a
gay man and a rugby player. My two irrecon-
cilable worlds came together."

He continued: "Now we've been accepted
into the union and the road is going to get
harder. We need to work harder. We need to
get better. We have the chance to be role
models for other gay folks who wanted to
play sports, but never felt good enough or
strong enough. More importantly, we have
the chance to show the other teams in the
league that we are as good as they are. Gay
men weren't always wallflowers waiting on
the sideline. We have the opportunity to let
these other athletes know that gay men were
around all along — on their Little League
teams, in their classes, being their friends."

After calling her son's cell phone, Alice
Hoglan hung up. Then she called Mark again
and left a second message. Her voice was
hurried, pressing, but not panicked.

"Mark, apparently it's terrorists and they're
hell-bent on crashing the aircraft," Alice said.
"So, if you can, try to take over the aircraft.
There doesn't seem to be much plan to land

the aircraft normally, so I guess your best bet would be to try to take it over if you can, or tell the other passengers. There is one flight that they say is headed toward San Francisco. It might be yours. So, if you can, group some people and perhaps do the best you can to get control of it. I love you, sweetie. Good luck. Good-bye."

At her apartment in nearby San Jose, California, Candyce Hoglan had a troubling dream. She was Alice Hoglan's sister. Both were United flight attendants. She dreamed of a plane going down, of people begging for their lives, of passengers screaming, "No, no." She awoke disturbed. The dream had been so real. A few minutes later, the phone rang. It was her brother Lee Hoglan. Their nephew Mark was on a plane that had been hijacked.

12

With her husband Jeremy leaving on a business trip, Lyz Glick and her infant daughter, Emerson, had gone to stay with her parents in the Catskill Mountains village of Windham, New York. After a late night with the baby, Lyz awakened just before nine o'clock. A few minutes earlier, the first plane had hit the World Trade Center. She did not think immediately that Jeremy was in danger. They were saying on television that it might have been a commuter plane. A second plane hit, and she knew it must have been a terrorist attack. Two planes don't fly into the World Trade Center by accident. Still, she did not worry about Jeremy. These were probably planes from JFK Airport. He was flying out of Newark. At least the crashes happened early, she thought. Many people likely hadn't arrived yet for work. She went through her address book. *Okay, I don't know anybody who would be in the Trade Center.* She felt slightly guilty. *I'm going to escape this without feeling any emotional impact. I feel really bad for ev-*

eryone else who has lost somebody.

Lyz went downstairs to make breakfast and noticed the nervous looks on her parents' faces. She wanted to watch television, but each time she walked into a room, her parents turned the TV off. Her father, Richard Makely, had a bad feeling about this. The second plane that hit the World Trade Center looked as if it might have swung around from Newark, only a few miles away. "This isn't good," he told his wife, Jo Anne. Lyz was in the kitchen when the phone rang down a long hallway in the family room. It was nine thirty-seven. Jeremy was on the line.

"Jeremy, thank God you're okay," Jo Anne Makely said. "We've been so worried."

He was not okay.

"There are very bad men on the plane," he said. "Let me speak to Lyz."

Lyz heard a scream, or something in a voice that told her to hurry into the living room. "Oh, my God, not Jeremy," she said. Her parents appeared ashen. She knew something was wrong. Her mother handed her the phone. "It's Jeremy," Jo Anne Makely said. "He's okay for right now."

Jeremy repeated what he had said to his mother-in-law. There were very bad men on the plane.

It had been hijacked, Jeremy told Lyz. He had been sitting in Row 11, near the front of coach. The hijackers had a Middle Eastern appearance. They looked Iranian. They put on red headbands and the three of them stood up and yelled and ran into the cockpit. They sent passengers to the back of the plane, and they were threatening to blow it up. They claimed to have a bomb. It looked like a box with something red around it. Jeremy was calling now from the rear of the plane. He sounded calm, but there was adrenaline in his voice. He did not seem panicked but rather confused, sad. "I can't believe this is happening to me," he said.

He kept saying it over and over. "I can't believe this is happening to me." He was too young. He had married his high school sweetheart, and they had a brand-new baby. His life was perfect.

Jeremy and Lyz had met as ninth graders at Saddle River Day School in New Jersey. Even now, he could remember the perfume and the dress that Lyz wore the day he noticed her in biology class. He always said that he knew he would marry her the first time he saw her. He was like that, bold, uninhibited, bull-rushing his way through life as if it were a judo opponent that could be put into submission with a chokehold. He had an outsized body and an outsized personality. He was a man who did not want to be constrained, always fidgety in his clothes, always leaving for a weekend of camping and hiking when he lived in claustrophobic Manhattan, changing jobs every two years or so when he became restless or bored.

"He liked challenges," his older sister, Jennifer Glick, said. "When he got to the point where he exceeded the people above him, or he couldn't stand them telling him to do moronic things, he left. That he had no tolerance for at all. You knew where you stood with Jeremy. You were either a friend or he didn't have anything to do with you. That's where you fell."

Jeremy was the third of six children — all of whose names began with the letter J — and his greatest feature as a boy was a glorious Afro that piled atop his head. He did not cut his hair until he was five, thinking that, like Samson, he might be sapped of his strength. He had a great affection for superheroes, calling his mother Wonder Woman and once accidentally wearing his Superman pajama top to elementary school. Several weeks ago, he had gone wakeboarding on costume day at his house on Greenwood Lake in northern New Jersey, and he had dressed as the Green Lantern. He favored movies like *Braveheart*, which featured a central hero, and, as a child, he and his older brother Jonah created extravagant rescue-and-adventure games based on the television series *Emergency*.

Lloyd and Joan Glick ran a strict household, wanting their children to focus on their educations. There were periods when television was forbidden except on weekends, and a luggage lock was placed on the plug of the TV set when the parents left the house. Whatever their kids did, Lloyd and Joan Glick told them, they should try to be the best. A steel bar was placed in the doorway of the playroom, and the kids were expected to do a chin-up each time they walked through. They lifted weights and used hand grippers while sitting around the living room, knowing that the Olympic wrestling champion Dan Gable had used grips to strengthen his own hands. Someone was always using a stopwatch to time the others at various neighborhood games. On weekends, the entire family ran laps at a local high school. The older kids were so competitive, they would flip over the game board, scattering pieces and paper money, rather than lose at Monopoly. None was more competitive than Jeremy, who made everything a contest. He ate the fastest, did more chin-ups, held his nerve the longest down a steep hill before applying the brakes on his bicycle, played his music the loudest, wanted to have the most friends and the most fun.

"He definitely liked to win," said Jonah Glick, Jeremy's brother. "We used to joke that when we'd go out to dinner, Jeremy always ordered the biggest shake or the biggest portion, whether he'd eat it or not. Even when he was an adult, he bought the biggest pickup truck and had the really giant television."

Like many teenagers, he and his friends went through a defiant period, sneaking out of the house at night, pushing the family car out of the driveway and joyriding through Oradel, New Jersey, stopping at red lights and running naked outside in a so-called Chinese fire drill, pulling all-nighters, jumping off of bridges into dark water, sleeping under bridges, covered in newspapers like hobos. His senior year, Jeremy shaved his head into a Mohawk haircut and pierced his ear, using an ice cube and a bottle of ouzo for anesthetics. Shortly after getting his driver's license, he disobeyed his parents, drove to New York City for a high school English class trip and flipped his car on the West Side Highway. The impact was severe enough that an imprint of his head was left in the roof of the car, but he walked away, having saved the life of his classmate, Gillian Connell, who suffered displaced vertebrae in her neck. In the retelling, it became another Jeremy adventure, in which things always worked out, and he and his friends always pulled through. "A car sideswiped us, and we hit the divider and flipped several times," Connell said. "I didn't have my seat belt on. Jeremy did. The car flipped on the passenger side first and the window blew out. He literally grabbed me by the seat of my pants and threw me in the back seat as we were flipping. I'm sure I would have gone out the window onto the highway."

At one point, Lyz Glick began to lose it on the phone. "Oh, my God, they've got a bomb and Jeremy's on the plane," she said, the dam of her emotions starting to break. But Jeremy said something comforting, and her father heard her say, "I'll be strong, I'll be strong."

Jeremy told Lyz he loved her and he said, "I don't think I'm going to make it out of here." Lyz had seen him cry only when his daughter was born, and now he seemed to be crying again.

Lyz tried to comfort her husband, to give him hope that he would come through this ordeal safely. "You're being silly," she said. "That's not going to happen."

They kept saying "I love you," over and over, "I love you," until it seemed as if they had said it two hundred times. The words seemed to calm them.

"I need you to be happy in the rest of your life," Jeremy told Lyz. "I'll support any decisions that you make." He told her to love their baby and to tell Emerson how much he loved her.

Lyz's father retrieved the cell phone from the car and her mother dialed 911. What was the flight number? the 911 dispatcher wanted to know.

Where was the plane headed?

How many passengers?

What was the nationality of the hijackers?

What did they look like?

What did the ground look like beneath the plane?

Were they circling?

The plane had made a turn, Jeremy said. They were somewhere around Pittsburgh, still high in the air. About thirty-five passengers were onboard. He could see a rural landscape.

At some point, the New York state police seemed to patch in. Lyz heard a click late in the conversation. Questions were being asked and relayed, and answers were being handed from person to person, like buckets of water being used to fight a fire.

Jeremy seemed bewildered. The hijackers said they had a bomb, but passengers were hearing on their phones that planes were crashing into the World Trade Center. Was it true about the Trade Center? Were the hijackers blowing planes up?

He didn't say it, but he seemed to think that if the terrorists intended to blow the plane up, it might be futile to rush the hijackers. If the terrorists were going to crash it into a building, maybe the passengers had a chance to do something.

"Are they going to blow this plane up?" Jeremy asked.

She didn't know, Lyz said, but, yes it was true that two planes had crashed into the World Trade Center. By now, it was almost ten o'clock. At nine fifty-eight, the south tower collapsed in a telescoping of smoke and metal and glass and crumbled rescue.

Were they going to crash his plane into the World Trade Center? Jeremy wanted to know.

"No," Lyz said, almost laughing. "They are not going there."

Why? Jeremy asked.

One of the towers had just fallen.

"They knocked it down," Lyz told him. The north tower was wounded, too. Be strong, she said. The hijackers could be taking the plane somewhere else.

As much for day care as for training and discipline, Lloyd and Joan Glick enrolled their kids in judo lessons when Jeremy was eight. First, it was twice a week, then three times, then almost every day. The Glicks did everything rapaciously. If one kid liked a certain cereal, they bought twenty boxes and ate the same cereal until everyone got sick of it and demanded a new brand. If someone liked a particular shirt, they bought the same shirt in every color. At judo school, the kids would stay all day on weekends, helping to clean up, sometimes getting a ride home from the instructor. Boxes and boxes of trophies accumulated through the years, and judo tournaments became family vacations as Jeremy and his younger brother Jared won national championships at the junior level.

Judo does not allow kicking, and thus requires great balance, leverage, speed and upper body strength to score points. Victory is scored by "ippon," which is achieved by a clean throw, by holding an opponent down, mainly on his back, for thirty seconds, or by putting him into submission with a stranglehold, chokehold or a lock applied against the elbow. Nagayasu Ogasawara, the family's instructor, or sensei, always urged the Glicks to win by "ippon" instead of relying on scoring by the judges. "You never want to have your decision and your fate decided by someone else," he told them.

In 1993, while at the University of Rochester, Jeremy won the national collegiate championship in the one hundred seventy-two-pound category. By that time, Ogasawara had lost touch with Jeremy, and was coaching the West Point team at the championships in San Francisco. He was surprised to see Jeremy walk in alone, no coach, no teammates, so he offered to sit in his corner. Jeremy had done little judo training in college until his senior year and then had practiced on his own at a dojo in Rochester. Yet, when the tournament was over, he had won a national title and had been named the most valuable judoka. Soon after, he was awarded a black belt.

"It was amazing," Ogasawara said. "He really hadn't been doing a lot. But he had a good attitude, a fighting spirit. He kept going and going. Jeremy didn't hold back. He wasn't afraid of anything."

This kind of athletic fearlessness is what drew coaches at Saddle River Day School to name Jeremy captain of the soccer and wrestling teams. Joe Augienello, the school's athletic director who coached Jeremy in soccer, remembered Jeremy as a defensive enforcer, a right fullback "with shoulders out to the moon," tenacious, the kind of defender that made opposing forwards play with their eyes up for fear of a collision.

"Some guys like to say, 'I'm fearless,' but they draw the line somewhere," Augienello said. "I don't think Jeremy drew too many lines."

When his four sons had roughhoused with each other, Lloyd Glick would tell them to "take it to the mat" in the family playroom. The Glick boys loved sports like wrestling, judo, soccer, rugby and lacrosse, which involved minimal padding and maximum contact. "You could fight and not get into trouble," Jared Glick said.

Whatever sport he attempted, Jeremy seemed to be successful. He was a natural athlete. If he did not succeed immediately with talent and technical proficiency, he did eventually with desire and relentless assertion. On one family vacation to Venezuela, while he was still in high school, he entered a bowling tournament on a lark and won a trophy. Later, he became an expert skier and a certified diver. He rented videotapes to improve his technique in alpine skiing and wakeboarding, taught himself to juggle, became skilled performing tricks with a yo-yo. "He was able to get over the frustrations of learning something new," Lyz Glick said. And he could not stomach losing. Two years earlier, after he did poorly in a skeet-shooting competition against his father-in-law, Jeremy practiced secretly until he was adept enough to win the next contest.

His appetite for milk was as insatiable as his appetite for winning. Lyz bought a gallon a day. Jeremy couldn't get enough, and she grew accustomed to hearing him awaken in the middle of the night, open the refrigerator and drink straight from the container. Once, he apologized for drinking all the milk at his in-laws' house, to which his father-in-law, Richard Makely, responded, "That's okay, it was sour."

Of all the sports, it was judo that came to define him and the way he approached life. As a junior in high school, he lost a match at the national championships to a Cuban-

American opponent in Miami. On the plane ride home, Lloyd Glick explained to his son that while Jeremy wanted to win, the other boy could not conceive of losing in front of his family and friends. His son's outlook changed, Lloyd Glick remembered. Jeremy learned to think things through, to consider the consequences of his actions, how they would affect himself and others. Later, as he progressed in the business world and began to hire his own employees, Jeremy invariably asked this question during interviews: "Do you love to win or do you hate to lose?"

There was only one correct answer.

"You had to be an idiot not to want to win; everybody wants to win," Lloyd Glick said. "If you want to truly be successful, you have to hate to lose. You can't stand losing."

In high school wrestling, it had been instilled in Jeremy and his teammates that finishing second was to be disdained, despised. Finishing second meant that you had reached the final of a tournament and lost. "When you're at the ultimate end, that's when you have to win," said Kim Bangash, a close friend and teammate. "That's when you have to call upon whatever you have to excel. That carried weight with him. Number two is terrible. It's far worse to be number two than number three. If you finished third, that means you won your last match."

Apart from that aggressive physical side of

him, Jeremy had an easy, charismatic, persuasive way with people, which made him popular. He was a man of grand gestures and mischievous eyes, said Paul Burgett, vice president of the University of Rochester. Jeremy and Lyz were king and queen of the high school prom. Jeremy was president of his college fraternity. He could be a jokester, the kind of unbridled kid who wore a diaper to high school for Halloween, who put on a powdered wig and a kilt when his soccer team visited England and Scotland. He was so personably convincing that he once walked into a rental agency to return a car and walked out with a job. His family could not remember him going to a single job interview where he was not offered employment. At the University of Rochester, while working to get his fraternity back into the good graces of the school after some members were suspected of selling marijuana, Jeremy hugged Burgett, then the dean of students. The two shared a chuckle over the rare sight of two large men embracing each other. At a recent Macy's Thanksgiving Day Parade in New York, Jeremy carried his nephew on his shoulders and walked right up to Mayor Rudolph Giuliani to shake hands.

"He was one of those persons who lived well in the moment," said Jim Best, a longtime friend and the best man at Jeremy's wedding. "He was always excited about the things he was doing. He made you feel like wherever he was, that was the best place to be, around this person and all this energy."

When they were younger, Jeremy and Best had been drawn to each other by their reserved personalities. They often mumbled under their breaths and were teased by other kids. "We were the only ones who could understand each other," Best said. Later, as he grew more confident, Jeremy became the voice of his family, the one who spoke for the others, proposing toasts at dinners and making speeches at graduations. He was the one who received a citizenship award in elementary school for his good deeds. It was Jeremy who practiced on oranges so that he could properly administer insulin shots to his diabetic brother, Jared, when they went away to judo camp. Jeremy was the one who served as protector in junior high for a shy frail wallflower student. The boy later wrote to the Glicks that Jeremy had stopped others from picking on him and had been the only one of two dozen kids who did not reject an invitation to his bar mitzvah. Not only did Jeremy show up, but the natural showman in him emerged, and he entertained the crowd with his break dancing.

At other times, he appeared formal and almost sheepish in his reticence. He formally asked his in-laws for permission to marry Lyz and shopped for weeks for an engagement ring, learning everything he could about diamonds. The first time Jeremy and Lyz visited her parents after the wedding, he would not go upstairs to bed until Lyz finally told her mother and father, "Will you please tell Jeremy he can come up and sleep with me, we're married."

He could also be so determined, so single-minded and strong-willed, that "he stepped on other people's toes," Jonah Glick said. Kim Bangash, a friend since kindergarten, said he would find himself at Jeremy's house in northern New Jersey, sweating away the weekend, piling cords of wood or mowing the lawn or pulling docks out of the lake before the winter freeze, and wondering, "How the hell did I get up here?"

"We would ask him and he would laugh," Bangash said. "That was Jeremy. Such a good salesman. But he was self-aware enough to ask himself, 'Am I selfish?' To be troubled by it. We had talked about Dr. Jekyll and Mr. Hyde, about the duality of a person, and how people remember you, how they remember the good and the bad."

At his first substantial job out of college, working for a company that sold music kiosks, Jeremy caught a colleague pilfering a list of potential customers, pinned him against a wall and told him in no uncertain terms, "Don't ever do that again." A few years later, before he was married, he and a group of friends were out on the Upper East Side of Manhattan one night when a man accused them of kicking over his garbage cans. Identifying himself as an off-duty police officer, the man pulled a gun on one of Jeremy's friends, and Jeremy threatened, "If you don't put that gun down, I'm going to rip off your face." It was a case of mistaken identity, and the moment was defused before anyone got violent.

"I said, 'Jeremy, the guy's got a gun, he wins,'" Best recalled. "He was like, 'It doesn't matter.' His first instinct was to go after the guy. He didn't look for fights, but if you did something wrong to Jeremy or got in his way, God help you. He couldn't stand it. In sports, he couldn't stand losing. You were in his way, he wanted to succeed. He took it personally. That's the way he looked at things. It translated to work, to the way he lived his life."

On his shoulder, Jeremy wore a yin-yang tattoo, and he sought a kind of balance in his own life. He had a contemplative side to match his physical ardor. At Rochester University, Jeremy studied English and philosophy, wrote poetry, worked with kids at the local YMCA, took a year off from school to help his parents out financially, loading trucks at a department store. He read Hunter S. Thompson and Stephen King, listened to the music of the Grateful Dead, and at some point, he became drawn to the essayist and poet Ralph Waldo Emerson, after whom he would name his daughter. Among other things, he appreciated Emerson's definition of heroism: "A hero is no braver than an ordinary man, but he is braver five minutes longer."

After taking that year off from school, Jeremy seemed to grow more serious. He wanted to make his mark. In a discussion about Eastern philosophies with his longtime friend, Bangash, he disagreed with the belief that the dead know only one thing, that it is better to be alive. "He took a contrarian view," Bangash remembered. "He thought some things were worse than death. There are things you can do to yourself, regretful things, and you end up less than zero. Or, in *Sophie's Choice*, where the mother had to choose between her son and daughter at Auschwitz. He said, 'Wouldn't you rather die than make a choice like that?'

"This is not something you think you'd be engaged in with the captain of the wrestling team," Bangash said. "But ideas were facile for him. He was hungry for information, to learn about the world around him, to experiment. Not just in the Hunter S. Thompson alcohol-and-drug sense. He really thought his mind was just as much a muscle as his triceps and biceps."

What should he do? Jeremy asked Lyz from

the plane. It didn't feel like a normal hijacking. Should he do anything?

They were problem-solving. Lyz asked Jeremy about the United pilots. Were they alive? He didn't know. Had the real pilots said anything to the passengers over the public address system? No.

Did the hijackers have any automatic weapons? Lyz asked. Even a former judo champion like Jeremy would be no match for guns.

No guns, Jeremy said. "They have knives."

How could people have gotten on the plane with knives and a bomb? he wanted to know. And then he made a joke that was typical Jeremy. "We just had breakfast and we have our butter knives."

He said that they were taking a vote. There were three other guys as big as him. They were thinking about attacking the hijackers. Was that a good idea? What should they do?

Lyz shook as she talked to her husband, but when she heard that the hijackers didn't have guns, she thought Jeremy would be okay. He could get stabbed, or get his hand sliced, but he might not even feel it in the adrenaline rush. Getting stabbed wouldn't kill him. *The only hope is if they take these people over and get control of the plane.*

"I think you need to do it," Lyz told Jeremy.

"Okay," he said. "Stay on the phone, I'll be right back."

There was a sound of conviction in his voice. Not anger, but a sense of purpose. He wanted to get home to his wife and daughter.

They were going to jump on the hijackers and attack them, Jeremy said. He didn't come out and say it. Lyz got the impression that the terrorist claiming to have a bomb would not provide much resistance.

Put a picture of me and the baby in your head, Lyz said to Jeremy. Think good thoughts.

He went away, and it sounded as if he were talking to people.

She couldn't bear to listen and handed the phone to her father.

Jeremy had begun to consider his own mortality two weeks earlier, when Lyz's grandmother died. Driving home, Jeremy and Lyz talked for the first time about their wishes for their own funerals. Jeremy said he didn't want anything elaborate, and he didn't want to be buried in the ground. The week before September 11, he and his friend, Jim Best, had watched the movie *Alive*, about a rugby team that had suffered a plane crash in the Andes and how the survivors had turned to cannibalism. Jeremy had been impressed by how the crash and the survival scenes appeared so real, so lifelike. In high school, he had written a poem that Lyz would find eerily prescient after September 11. The poem,

271

Best said, was titled "Redemption in the Sky," and it contemplated good and evil on a doomed flight. The plane was going down and there was pain, and ultimately a soul was freed.

But death seemed so remote now to Jeremy. He had celebrated his thirty-first birthday on September 3. He was a top salesman for Vividence, a Web management company. He had been married five years to a wife he had fallen in love with in junior high. He had a new baby, a house on Greenwood Lake with a swimming pool and a ski boat, a professional life that accommodated his desire to spend a great deal of time with his family. "He was feeding Emmy with a tube, and he said he wished he had breasts," Best said of Jeremy. "He was jealous of women. To see this big he-man developing into a sensitive father was wonderful to watch." If Jeremy made his sales quota on Wednesday, he could take Thursday and Friday off to spend on the lake, or to play with his daughter. Lyz, who had a master's degree in anthropology, taught university courses over the Internet. Jeremy had made a pledge — he would never work in an office again.

His judo days were over. He had undergone surgery four years earlier to have a disk removed from his neck, Lyz said, and he wore a helmet when he skied or wakeboarded to prevent further concussions that had come from judo. He thought he might have reached the level of the Olympics if he had kept at it, but those desires were behind him. His family mattered most now. He and Lyz talked often through each day. She sent e-mail photographs of Emerson, and Jeremy showed them to his clients before he started his meetings. They talked about plans for travel, about going to Africa, maybe trekking in Nepal. His brother Jonah would be getting married in the spring, in Japan, and Jeremy thought he might climb Mount Fuji.

"We knew that we would have a good life together," Lyz said. "We had known each other for eighteen years, but each day was new. We had created a nook, something that people dream of and wait their whole lives to do. We really went after what we wanted."

13

At nine fifty-three, Linda Gronlund called her sister from Flight 93. She had phoned earlier, before boarding, to give the flight number. Linda had sounded so excited on the earlier call. She was beginning a vacation trip with Joe DeLuca, whom she had been dating for several months. They had known each other for years and shared a passion for racing sports cars. In two days, they would celebrate Linda's forty-seventh birthday. Linda was manager of environmental compliance at BMW North America. Joe, who was fifty-two, designed computer software systems for Pfizer Healthcare. They were headed to the vineyards in Napa Valley. Linda knew vintage wine the way she knew vintage cars.

She had forgotten the charger for her cell phone, she said on the first call, so the battery would be running down soon. Write down Joe's number, she told her sister, Elsa Strong, who lived in New Hampshire. The sisters made plans to talk again on Linda's birthday.

When Linda called back, Elsa had left home for a meeting at her son's school. While driving, she listened to radio reports of planes crashing into the World Trade Center. As Elsa pulled into a parking spot at the school, she heard that one of the planes apparently had been hijacked. Her heart started beating rapidly. Her sister was up there somewhere. Elsa sat nervously through her meeting and then learned that both towers had collapsed. The north tower had fallen at ten twenty-nine. Elsa was devastated. She had lived in New York previously and still felt a strong connection to the city. She sobbed on her way home, shattered by news of the fallen towers, worried about her sister. *Please let there be a message saying, "I'm stuck in Chicago."*

The message light was flashing on Elsa's answering machine. Her mother had called, saying something terrible had happened in New York. Had she heard from Linda? The second message was from Linda. There was anger and urgency in her voice. "This is Lin. I'm on United Flight 93. We've been hijacked. There are terrorists aboard and they have a bomb."

Linda could handle herself. She was tough. She had trained as an emergency medical technician, and once, after falling on an icy morning and dislocating her kneecap, she crawled back inside her house, called for an ambulance and re-set the knee before paramedics arrived. In the 1980s, after she had been mugged, she took karate lessons and rose to the level of a brown belt. But how do you protect yourself against men using an airplane as a missile? Linda and Joe had been seated in first class, in seats 2A and 2B. Ziad Jarrah, the hijacker pilot, had been assigned a seat directly in front of them.

In an emergency situation, Linda went into a different mode, an action mode, deliberate, determining what was needed, taking charge. She was impatient with those who were unqualified or made mistakes. "She always wanted things done right, and done right the first time," her father, Gunnar Gronlund, said. "Never mind whose toes you had to step on."

Linda always brought a certain intensity to whatever she did. Her friends thought that "enthusiastic" was an inadequate word to describe her. Her passion was evident in her firm handshake, her varied interests, her assuredness around cars. No man she knew had a better set of mechanics' tools. At age seven or eight, Linda helped with sanding and scrubbing and go-fering as her father restored a 1938 BMW in Sag Harbor, New York. She also helped him restore a 1947 Lincoln Continental, and by the time she was in high school, Linda and her father built a car they nicknamed the Aardvark, which consisted of a Volkswagen engine and chassis and a fiberglass body. "She could set the points and plugs, and the boys would just look at her," her father laughed. "She was a threat to them. Her female friends just stood back a little bit."

After graduating magna cum laude from Southampton College of Long Island University in 1976, Linda attended law school at American University in Washington, DC. Eventually, she became more interested in protecting the environment than in representing clients. Concerned about the effects of pollution and ozone depletion, she went to work for Volvo, marshaling its effort to switch to an air-conditioning coolant that was an environmentally safe alternative to Freon. At BMW, she worked to develop hydrogen-powered cars. She lived on long, narrow Greenwood Lake that sat like a carpenter's level across the border between New York and New Jersey. Linda had to live near water. She learned to sail as a girl, and, later, to scuba dive. The year before, she went to Colorado to take a course in timber-framing for a house she was planning to build. It would be a place where she could grow old — wheelchair-accessible, energy efficient, devoid of building materials that would emit formaldehyde.

"She was not a granola cruncher," her

sister Elsa said. "She was interested in how to make the world a better place in practical terms."

Within the last several years, Linda had spoken with her sister and her friends about how her life, while successful professionally, had been reduced to work. "We talked about how that just wasn't healthy," Elsa said. They spoke of activities that Linda had loved when she was younger, playing the guitar, riding horses. She had picked up the guitar again and had been giving therapeutic riding lessons to children with autism and other disabilities. "It was a real thrill for her," Elsa said. "It put her back in touch with that earlier part of her life."

As long as her sister could remember, Linda had a need for speed, whether it was in a sailboat or a car. "She tended to be full-speed ahead at whatever she did," said Bill Scully, a friend and co-worker at BMW. She got a few speeding tickets, but "not as many as she should have," her sister joked. Linda had been a member of the Sports Car Club of America for at least two decades. Her composure under pressure had made her a skilled flagger and coordinator at races in the Northeast region. She was also known for her unique salute to friends who won races. Dressed in a zippered jumpsuit, she had on rare occasions flashed more than her smile as the winners took a victory lap.

For fifteen years, she had known Joe DeLuca, and since the spring, they had begun dating. Both were married previously and divorced. Linda had shoulder-length blond hair, Joe was tall and graying. He had been so devoted to racing that he married his first wife at a track, dressed in a driver's suit. The entire wedding party took a victory lap in cream-colored cars. "He did not know how to drive slow," said a friend, Walt Huber. Joe drove sports cars, edited racing newsletters and drew a popular one-panel cartoon about a feline driver named Raymond the Cat. Things happened to Raymond. His car fell off a lift. He polished his car only to watch incontinent birds fly overhead. In one of the cartoons, Raymond got stuck in the snow and used a bag of kitty litter to gain traction. "Well this is great," he said to himself, "but what'll I use when I get home?"

Joe brought books to read to the children of his friends, stopped by with ice cream when people got sick and always did something to keep them laughing. Upon returning from a convention in Denver in 1988, he inhaled helium from a balloon and left this high-pitched message to callers on his answering machine: "Hi, this is Joe DeLuca and I'm not home just now. I'm in Denver, the mile-high city, where the air is much thinner than in New Jersey." Every other day, he took an extended lunch and drove a half

279

hour to visit his mother, Felicia, who had suffered a stroke.

In his condominium in Ledgewood, New Jersey, Joe kept a number of photographs of airplanes. Speed was his passion, whether in the air or on the ground. He had an easy-going personality until he got behind a wheel on a track or a road-rally course.

"They say about racing that when you're going that fast, you have to concentrate, you don't think about anything else," said Joe's sister, Carol Hughes. "I guess that's why he liked it. It made him focus."

Some drivers had problems with state troopers on the road. Joe had a problem with deer. "Joe and deer did not get along," Huber, a friend and membership director of the Northern New Jersey Region of the SCCA, wrote in the club's newsletter. "Actually it was his cars and driving style which did not get along with deer." By Huber's count, Joe had sent seven deer to the Great Salt Lick in the sky. Distraught and mischievous upon hitting his first deer, Joe stood it against a tree with a cigarette protruding from its lips, so it might appear to be taking a rest while hitchhiking.

He once owned a Toyota MR-2 that had been chopped with an ax, as if it were an oak tree, during a fight between the previous owner and her boyfriend. The Lizzie Borden car, Joe called it. His most prized car was a

Morgan, handmade in Britain. He and Linda had spent the weekend before September 11 in Massachusetts, at a Morgan competition, and his car had been awarded first place in its class. Linda said she had sometimes become frustrated finding a man who was strong enough for her. Joe was self-assured, quieter, unthreatened by Linda's more forceful personality. "What do I want from life?" she had confided in her friends, seeking fulfillment on a professional and personal level. With Joe, she seemed to be content. "For the first time in years, she was really happy," said Scully.

At go-cart events, Joe was known to go into his solemn, desperate impersonation of the announcer who witnessed the crash of the Hindenburg zeppelin in 1937, saying, "Oh, the humanity, oh this is terrible," whenever one of the little cars did a harmless flip. Linda could display gallows humor, too, and she could also be impulsive. More than one person had been dismissed with the words "Bite me," when the radiator blew on her temper. And she did not easily take no for an answer. When told that the Z3 BMW roadster did not come in the color of chestnut-brown metallic in the United States, Linda said, "Watch me." She bought the car, along with paint to have it redone herself.

But now, just before ten o'clock on September 11, others were in charge. Terrorists were in control. Joe and Linda remained poised. They took turns calling their families. There were things to take care of. Joe called his father, Joseph DeLuca Sr., and said, "Dad, there are terrorists on the plane. I love you very much."

He sounded sad.

Linda left a message for her sister, Elsa. The passengers on Flight 93 were aware that the World Trade Center had been attacked. "I think they're going to try to do something like that with us," Linda said.

Her will was in her safe, and her safe was in her closet, she said. The call lasted half a minute, and Linda's words turned from anger to uncertainty, resignation. Later, her sister learned that Linda, who had begun the flight in first class, had called from an Airfone in the rear of the plane. It was unclear how many other first-class passengers had been moved to coach.

"I want to let you know how much I love you; please tell Mom and Dad," Linda said. "I don't know if I'll be able to tell you again in person how much I love you. I hope I will. I'm really going to miss you."

Then she said good-bye.

14

The phone rang at Fred's Auto Repair in Queens, New York. Marion Britton was on the line, frantic. Fred Fiumano, who owned the garage, was a longtime friend. Marion was crying. Her plane had been hijacked, she said. Two people had been killed, she told Fiumano.

"They slit their throats," she said.

Marion gave Fiumano a phone number. Write it down, she said. Her cell phone was not working. She gave him the number of another passenger. Fiumano could hear screaming, a lot of noise. Things were happening too fast. He could not tell what was going on.

The plane was making a turn, Marion said.

"We're going down," she said.

What was she going to do on a six-hour flight? Marion Britton had wondered in the days before she left. At fifty-three, she was assistant regional director of the United States Census Bureau in New York City. She didn't appear to enjoy flying. She would often change her mind before a trip, saying she felt poorly, or that she had work to finish. A capacious woman, she suffered from diabetes. Usually, she purchased two seats so that she would be comfortable on a plane. Don't worry about what to do, Ligia Jacquez, a co-worker, told her. "Buy a book," Jacquez said. And don't forget, they would show a movie. "Oh, then I'll be fine," Marion said.

Waleska Martinez was not looking forward to the trip, either. That was odd. Usually, she was the most upbeat person in the office. Waleska was in charge of automation in the Census Bureau's regional office, a computer expert, one of only two women to hold that job in the nation's twelve regions. She and Marion Britton were headed to a computer conference in San Francisco. "I'm not excited about this trip," Waleska told Jacquez. She had never flown cross-country on a non-stop flight. Like her colleague, she wondered how she would keep herself occupied for six hours.

Previously, Waleska had loved trips away from the office. She and Jacquez would arrive two days early for a conference, or stay two days late. They would find a nice restaurant, and always a dance club. Waleska loved to dance the merengue and the salsa. She collected refrigerator magnets everywhere she went, and frames for the photographs she took. At a conference in Phoenix, she and Jacquez had made a side trip to the Grand Canyon. Waleska brought along three cameras and her binoculars. "She was very organized and meticulous," Jacquez said. "She was very much into learning, seeing different places, eating different foods, tasting different drinks, learning different cultures."

She soaked up jazz and the blues on Bourbon Street in New Orleans, and she favored concerts by female pop singers who had maintained their careers through turbulent struggles. Tina Turner, Cher and, especially, Madonna. In recent weeks, Waleska attended Madonna concerts in both Philadelphia and New York, and reported back to her co-workers, "You have to see this woman. She's forty and she looks so good. I've got to go on a diet."

At thirty-seven, she was not unfit herself. Waleska played tennis and softball, and once won a game against the Census Bureau's Philadelphia region with a late home run. Her father, Juan Martinez, had been a softball pitcher in the Puerto Rican Air National Guard. He taught Waleska how to pitch, as well, and how to watch the ball, not the pitcher's motion, when she was at bat. Waleska attended the 2000 Subway World Series between the New York Yankees and the New York Mets. Her affection seemed to shift between the two teams, though she did like first baseman Tino Martinez of the Yankees because they shared the same last name, and centerfielder Bernie Williams, who, like her, had been born in Puerto Rico.

"She liked the Mets, unless they were losing," laughed Jacquez, her co-worker.

Waleska studied business and computer science at the University of Puerto Rico and taught computer science before moving to New York and joining the Census Bureau in 1989. She was first in her class, her father said, and first in her family to get a college degree. He called her "the backbone of the family." She called her parents at least three times a week, and always traveled home for birthdays. Her career was on the upswing. For the 2000 Census, Waleska hired and trained the computer staff for thirty-nine local census offices, somehow managing to keep her employees even though the bureau was not paying top dollar, and the dot.com industry was in overdrive.

"She was a manager's dream to work with," said Tony Farthing, the bureau's regional director. "Very innovative. Made the people around her better. Always smiling. Employees like that don't come around every day. Her potential was unbelievable."

The daughter of a policeman, Marion Britton had grown up along the border of

Brooklyn and Queens in New York City. After tiring of several jobs as bookkeeper for construction companies, she went door to door, asking questions for the 1980 census. She stayed on with the bureau, working her way through the ranks until she became assistant director of the New York region. Two decades later, she still loved to tell stories about the characters she met in her early days with the bureau. She had interviewed inmates at Rikers Island, New York's largest correctional facility, and had been struck by how open and blunt they could be about their crimes. "One time she talked to a man who was a convicted murderer, and he could talk about murdering like someone else talked about selling groceries," said Marion's brother, the Reverend Paul Britton of Huntington Station, New York. "He had these dead eyes in his head. Murdering was what he did for a living."

Five or six times, Marion arrived at a house or an apartment and was greeted by an occupant who answered the door completely naked. Her response was to maintain eye contact and to calmly fill out her questionnaire. "She figured that if that's the way they answered the door, that's the way they felt comfortable around the house, answering questions," her brother said.

Frequently, Marion met people who were in dire financial straits, and sometimes she went straight from her interviews to the supermarket, returning with a bag of groceries. "She had a big heart," Reverend Britton said. "She hated to see people suffering any kind of trouble."

Sometimes Marion grew frustrated by the bureaucracy and red tape of the federal government. On the other hand, she worked hard, and her skills were appreciated and cultivated. In twenty years, she had risen from the bottom to the top of the regional hierarchy. Marion could be forceful and demanding, and her voice had a sharpness that could wound. On occasion, it seemed as if she purposely distanced herself from others. And yet she also created a family atmosphere in the bureau, remembering birthdays, reaching into her pocket to buy cakes and punch, setting aside time for office luncheons. "She was very tough with everyone," said Farthing, her supervisor. "The funny thing about her was that she realized it. It was like, 'Okay, I know you put up with me, here's my appreciation.' She would buy lunch for everyone, or if someone was having trouble, she was the first one there to help you out."

Waleska Martinez's mother, Irma, and her brother, Reynaldo, were visiting from Caguas, Puerto Rico, which further deflated her desire to travel. She worked late on September 10, then awakened in the middle of the night, believing she had heard her mother calling to her. Then she returned to her bed, and, according to her partner, Angela Lopez, Waleska said, "You know, something's wrong. I should never have answered my mother's call. That's bad luck."

"Don't worry, nothing's going to happen," Lopez assured her.

Waleska started trembling. She couldn't stop.

Change the flight, Lopez suggested. She couldn't, Waleska said.

Located on the thirty-seventh floor of Federal Plaza, the Census Bureau looked onto the World Trade Center from six blocks away. Many of the workers in the office watched in horror as the second plane crashed into the south tower. Tony Farthing, the bureau director, was in New Mexico on business. He called the office, telling everyone to evacuate, to run, to head north, away from the burning towers, to shut the door and lock it and get out. Eventually, everyone was accounted for except Marion and Waleska. He tried their cell phones but couldn't reach them.

"We're going down," Marion said on her borrowed phone, talking to Fred Fiumano at his garage in Queens.

"You're just going for a ride," he told her,

trying to give her some reassurance. This was a regular hijacking, he said. "They'll take you to another country. Don't worry about it. You're just going for a ride."

He knew about the World Trade Center. He didn't believe what he was saying, but he said it anyway, trying to console his friend.

"You're not going to crash, don't worry," he said.

"No, we're going to crash," Marion said.

She was crying. He heard screaming. Two people were already dead, she had said. He knew something bad was going to happen.

The call got disconnected.

15

In Catonsville, Maryland, Esther Heymann spoke from her home to her husband, Ben Wainio, vice president of First Union Bank in nearby Columbia. Anxious calls had been coming in, full of worry and uncertainty. The call-waiting signal clicked and Heymann put her husband on hold. Her stepdaughter, Honor Elizabeth Wainio, was on the other line. It was shortly past nine-fifty.

"Hello, Mom," Elizabeth said. "We're being hijacked. I'm calling to say good-bye."

Esther had watched the horrific morning unfold on television. She knew that her stepdaughter was flying that day. They had spoken before the plane left Newark. If she heard Elizabeth's voice again this morning, she knew what it would probably mean.

"Do you know what's going on?" Elizabeth asked.

"No," Esther said.

Her first thought was to comfort and protect her stepdaughter, not to alarm her. If Elizabeth wanted to talk about what was happening aboard the plane, that was her choice. If not, Esther would do her best to make these final moments as peaceful and reassuring and loving as possible.

This "really nice person" next to her, perhaps Lauren Grandcolas, had handed her the phone and told her to call her family, Elizabeth said. Both had been assigned seats in Row 11 before leaving Newark. Elizabeth spoke calmly, but her breathing was shallow, as if she were hyperventilating.

"Elizabeth, I've got my arms around you and I'm holding you and I love you," Esther said.

"I can feel your arms around me," Elizabeth said. "And I love you, too."

Esther looked out the window in her bedroom. She told her stepdaughter that she could hold the hand of the nice person seated beside her. Elizabeth spoke about each person in her family and said how much she loved them. She worried about how her older brother, Tom, and her younger sister, Sarah, would handle this terrible news.

"Let's just be here in the present," Esther said. "We don't know how it's going to turn out. Let's look out at the beautiful blue sky and take a few deep breaths."

Elizabeth's breathing seemed to grow deeper and more relaxed.

At five foot seven, with dark brown hair and hazel eyes, Elizabeth Wainio appeared girlish, younger than her twenty-seven years. "Girl with milk for blood," her brother, Tom, called her because she could never seem to get a tan, no matter how long she stayed in the sun. Yet, her career as a district manager of Discovery Channel stores was guided by a clarity and purpose beyond her age. She had the purity of youthful idealism but an "old soul," her boss said. Even her favorite movies were from another, more romantic era: *The Sound of Music, Breakfast at Tiffany's, It's a Wonderful Life* and *The Wizard of Oz.*

"Don't forget to wake up Dad when the monkeys come," she would unfailingly tell her sister, Sarah, perpetuating a family expression that survived like an heirloom from Lizz's childhood.

Elizabeth seemed to drink in life as if to quench some deep, parched thirst. She had transformed her district, New York and New Jersey, into the most productive sales region in the Discovery chain. When she came to visit her parents, they played music and danced, and, because of her ebullience, it always seemed like Christmas. In her apartment in Watchung, New Jersey, Elizabeth kept a note on her refrigerator, a quote from Henry Miller that said, "The aim of life is to live, and to live means to be aware, joyously, drunkenly, serenely, divinely aware."

At Catonsville High School, it was clear that Elizabeth was going places. Her résumé had been stuffed like a steamer trunk: Four school plays, six all-county orchestras, vice present of the Honor Society, co-chair of the Spirit Committee, president of the Varsity Club, member of the county all-star field hockey team, captain of the cheerleading squad, editor of the school newspaper. Despite peer pressure to the contrary, she joined Students Against Drunk Driving, and she felt self-assured enough to go to the prom without a date. Later, she marched at pro-choice rallies with her parents in Washington.

"She was always comfortable in her own skin," her stepmother said. "She did not need outside people to validate her."

It was in high school, too, several days before her seventeenth birthday, that Elizabeth suffered the death of her grandmother, whom she called Omi, a Jewish refugee from Nazi Germany. Writing about her grandmother's death a year later, as a freshman in college, Elizabeth meditated on the self-centeredness of youth:

"I had never experienced a death before and when I realized that I would never see my grandmother again, I felt completely empty inside. We all expected this to happen at some time, but now that her death was imminent, I couldn't help but think that there was something else I should be doing or feeling. Here I was, almost seventeen years old, so selfishly caught up in my own life that I had never taken the time to think about what this death was going to mean to me. I felt like I was letting someone down, that I should be taking the time to reflect on my grandmother's life and all the time we shared."

Driving to her grandmother's funeral in North Carolina, she recalled Omi's resilience through the war years and through thirty-five years as a widow. How she flirted with the neighbor and asked Elizabeth in her sweet German voice, "Do you have a boyfriend? What's his name? You can tell me." How she wore a disarming smile and overpowering perfume. Her grandmother would want a celebration, not mourning, on the day she was laid to rest. So Elizabeth commemorated her grandmother, and then her own seventeenth birthday. "I know it was filled with sadness," she wrote, "yet at the same time it was probably the first birthday I had ever had that was truly a celebration of life."

After a year at Ohio State, Elizabeth returned home and received a degree in communications from Towson University. She worked while she was in school, and a month before she graduated, she was named district manager of Gymboree, a children's clothing store chain. "A lot of the store managers were women in their thirties, and here was a twenty-one-year-old kid giving them directions," her father Ben Wainio said. "Some people made it very difficult for her. She struggled with that."

Still, Elizabeth's star kept rising in the retail business. In January of 2000, at age twenty-six, she was named district manager for the Discovery Channel's stores in New York and New Jersey, including the flagship store in Grand Central Station. Her management style was the peppy enthusiasm and airy idealism of a cheerleader. "Miss Swiss," she was nicknamed because of her congenial neutrality in company politics. She used quotes from movies and film clips to motivate her employees during meetings, believing that the cinema was a great common denominator. A colleague, Rick Vercellotti, thought that Lizz resembled her favorite actress, Audrey Hepburn: "Her simplicity in her beauty, her expressive facial features, her sense of style and her giving nature." Elizabeth left bouncy music on her phone messages to pump up her employees, and pulled all-nighters, as if studying for exams, to prepare her stores for executive visits. The creative end of the business interested her, and down the road, maybe she would become an entrepreneur.

"She had an agenda," her father said. "A lot of twenty-six- and twenty-seven-year-olds are not as focused as Lizz was. She had a lot of faith in Esther in where she should put her money. She would say, 'What do I do now to become a millionaire?' She didn't want to work hard her whole life. She wanted to get to the point where she was self-sufficient, so she wouldn't have to worry about things later in life."

If there was one thing Elizabeth could not countenance about New York, it was the sports teams. A die-hard Baltimore fan, she mischievously changed the screen savers in her stores from Yankees logos to the Orioles emblem. Hers was a ravenous sports family. Her grandfather played basketball at the University of Pittsburgh in the 1920s, and her aunt had been one of the original cheerleaders for the Baltimore Colts. The first song Elizabeth learned to sing was the Notre Dame fight song. Ben Wainio collected baseball cards, and each year he gave his daughter the card of Mike Mussina, the Orioles pitcher. Then Mussina did the unthinkable. He became a Yankee. "How dare he!" Elizabeth told her father.

In early September, her Orioles again out of the pennant race, Mussina and the Yankees headed toward the World Series, Elizabeth took a trip to Europe, first to Italy for the wedding of a friend, then to Paris for a week. She arrived home on September 9, to prepare for a business trip on the 11th. She had been so smitten by the City of Lights that she told her parents, "After Paris, what could there possibly be?"

★ ★ ★

For eleven minutes, minutes that were terrifying but serene, too, Elizabeth spoke with her stepmother from Flight 93. As if repeating a mantra, Esther Heymann remained at her bedroom window and looked outside and said, "I've got my arms around you, honey. I love you."

"I feel them, and I love you, too," Elizabeth said.

They were quiet for a moment, then Elizabeth thought of her family and said, "It just makes me so sad knowing how much harder this is going to be on you than it is for me."

After a period of silence, she said, "I should be talking. I'm sitting here being quiet, I'm not even talking."

"We don't have to talk, we're together," Esther said.

Then it went quiet again for what seemed like a long time, and Elizabeth said that she knew her grandmothers, both deceased, were waiting for her. There was calm resolution in her voice.

They were quiet again. Esther could not hear another person. She could not hear any conversation or crying or yelling or whimpering. Nothing. The moment was horrible, of course, how could it not be, but it was also tranquil and comforting. Esther's mind raced. Should she be listening for other voices? Asking questions that might help authorities? No, this was clearly the right thing to do. It didn't seem conflicted or complicated. She was embracing her stepdaughter, who had chosen not to act distraught or tormented or shaken. Lizz seemed already to be leaving her body, to be letting go and going toward something good. She seemed to have released herself. Her grandmothers were waiting for her.

And then Elizabeth said, "They're getting ready to break into the cockpit. I have to go. I love you. Good-bye."

She hung up. It was just past ten.

16

"Have you heard what's going on?"

"I've seen it on TV," Phil Bradshaw said from his home in Greensboro, North Carolina. He had been talking to a friend when he received another call. His wife, Sandy, was a flight attendant on Flight 93. She was phoning from the plane.

"Phil, my flight's been hijacked," Sandy said.

"What?" Phil said in disbelief.

"My flight's been hijacked by three guys with knives."

The day before, Phil Bradshaw arrived home from a trip piloting jets for US Airways as Sandy prepared to leave for her transcontinental trip with United. They spoke for about twenty minutes at the Greensboro airport as one touched down and the other prepared to take off. Phil had been away for four days and begged and pleaded with Sandy to cancel her trip.

"I want to spend time with you and the

kids," Phil told Sandy. "You don't need to work. Just come home. Call in sick."

Sandy was due to catch a flight to Charlotte, then connect to her base in Newark. She would fly to San Francisco on September 11, lay over, then return home the following day. This would be her last trip of the month. She had reduced her flying schedule to about four days a month after giving birth to a daughter, Alexandria, two years earlier. Her youngest child, Nathan, would celebrate his first birthday in ten days. She had already bought his birthday presents, and the family's Christmas presents, too. So devoted was Sandy to her children, she took them with her even when she went outside to check the mail in a neighborhood of two-story brick homes and manicured lawns, pulling her daughter in a wagon and pushing her infant son in a stroller. She was also the stepmother of a teenage daughter named Shenan.

"She wanted to be here for them," Phil said.

Blond, strikingly attractive, Sandy had grown up in rural Climax, North Carolina, where her father raised twenty thousand chickens and sold paving equipment. She helped feed and water the chickens, rode horses, always clamored for another pet, raised a calf on her own when the mother abandoned it. She played football and baseball and basketball with the neighborhood kids and later learned to ride motorcycles. "She was up for anything," said her sister, Tracy Peele. She often spoke of wanting to become a flight attendant, and the job seemed to suit perfectly her love for travel, ebullient personality and high-beam smile. "She brightened up any dark room," her husband said.

One had only to take a look at her garden to know how meticulous and organized Sandy was. "She had a plan for everything," her sister said. She was one of five children, and as adults, when the extended family took trips together to the beach or Nashville or Disney World, Sandy called the travel agent, found the place to stay, compiled an itinerary. "We called her The Planner," Tracy Peele said.

Sandy and Phil met by chance in 1987, when she was on a date with his best friend. "The first day I met her, I fell in love with her," Phil said. "Three months later, they broke up and the rest is history."

The couple had been married eleven years, about the same length of time that Sandy had been a flight attendant, first for US Airways, then with United. She preferred to work first class, but she had picked up this trip on Flight 93 at the last minute and would be working coach.

Phil had been asking her to quit since their

infant son was born, and she almost did at one point, but, at thirty-eight, Sandy wanted to maintain her independence. When the kids were old enough to be in school, it would be nice to take a two-day trip and relax in a hotel room, take a break. She wasn't ready to give up flying. What better way to take affordable vacations, snow skiing in the winter and water skiing in the summer, or visiting Australia, the Virgin Islands, Europe. There was another thing. She wanted to save her sick time. Her twentieth high school reunion was coming up at the end of the month.

"I need to go do this trip," Sandy said.

Phil let it go. Sandy was not generally an outspoken person, but she was strong-willed. She was not someone to provoke. "If you made her mad, you better look out," he said. When she was younger, someone sneaked onto her family's property and attempted to steal a three-wheel vehicle out of the driveway. Sandy confronted the robbers as they loaded the vehicle into their truck. They threw it out and drove away with the lights off, attempting to escape in anonymity, but Sandy went after them. "She chased them down and got the license plate number," said Tracy Peele, Sandy's sister. "We found out who they were."

Sandy left for Charlotte on September 10, after seeing Phil, only to get stuck there for six hours. Rain had settled in over Newark, and there was a fire at the airport, forcing delays and cancellations of numerous flights. Phil called her every hour, six or seven times, asking her to catch the next flight home to Greensboro. "Every other day is booked," she told him, referring to available flights on the monthly schedule. "I don't have any other time to go flying." Finally, about nine p.m. on September 10, Phil reached Sandy by cell phone in Newark, where she and a group of flight attendants rented a hotel room near the airport. They each paid one hundred forty dollars a month to keep the room available year-round, a crash pad for sleeping when they had to catch an early flight. Again, he asked her to come home. He knew she wouldn't.

"I'll see you Wednesday night," Sandy said.

Now, as she spoke from Flight 93, there was surprising composure, but tumult, too, in Sandy's voice.

Phil, a pilot, began asking her questions.

"Who's flying the plane?"

Sandy didn't know.

"Where are you?"

"I'm not sure."

"Where's the sun?"

"In front of us," Sandy said.

So the plane was eastbound. "What do you see?" Phil asked.

"I see a river."

Most of the passengers had been herded to the rear of the plane, she said. A few were in first class. She thought she had seen one of the hijackers, a short, dark-complexioned man, sitting in the back row of first class.

Sandy seemed to be in the back of the plane. She said she was boiling water to throw at the hijackers. There were two coffee makers in the rear galley and two warmers.

"Do you have any other ideas?" she asked.

Phil, in shock, couldn't think of anything. He told Sandy, "Be strong and brave and be safe."

Sandy vowed to quit flying if she made it home. But now she had more urgent concerns.

"We're going to throw water on them and try to take the airplane back over." Then she said, "Phil, everyone's running to first class. I've got to go. Bye."

At nine forty-seven, CeeCee Lyles, the second flight attendant working the rear galley, called her husband, Lorne. He had fallen asleep after working the night shift at the Fort Myers, Florida, police department. CeeCee left a message on the couple's answering machine.

"Hi baby, I want you to listen carefully. I'm on a plane that's been hijacked. I'm calling from the plane. I want to tell you I love you. Please tell my children I love them very much. I'm so sorry, I don't know what to say. Three guys hijacked the plane. I'm trying to be calm. I heard planes were going into the World Trade Center. I hope to see your face again."

She began to cry.

"I love you baby," she said.

CeeCee and Lorne talked two dozen times a day when she was on the road. They would hang up, and, five minutes later, one of them would call back and say, "Did I tell you I love you?" Lorne and CeeCee had been married on May 1, 2000, but they still acted like newlyweds, holding hands constantly while relatives teased them about their public affection. Both had been married previously, and their blended family consisted of four sons — Jerome Smith, sixteen; Justin Lyles, eleven; Jordan Lyles, nine; and Jevon Castrillo, seven. CeeCee would come home and do homework with the boys, and she liked to shoot basketball with them at a nearby school. Free nights were reserved for movies. She and Lorne never went to the movies without each other. They loved comedies and action thrillers. Dinner and a movie was a perfect night out. Divorced for seven years, he had felt hardened and wary and stranded, but he was drawn to CeeCee, who was caring, unselfish, down-to-earth. She awakened something in him, softened him, and became his best friend, his joy. She had been a cheerleader in high school, and she still had a cheerleader's fresh good looks. She possessed the kind of beauty that was so precisely achieved as to appear casual and low-maintenance. She would not even go to the grocery store without fixing her hair and putting on lipstick, checking her nails. He loved her feet, the way they were shaped and pedicured. He thought she had perfect feet.

"Just trying to look pretty for you all the time," CeeCee would tell Lorne. "Can't argue with that," he would say, adding that she seemed beautiful just waking up in the morning.

Her beauty, however, was matched by a toughness forged from a previous career as a police officer in Fort Pierce, Florida. CeeCee had been a patrol officer and a detective for six years, working neighborhoods tattered by poverty, crack and prostitution. She stood five foot five and weighed one hundred forty-five pounds and had taken a course in handling herself in close-quarter physical confrontation. She knew how to stun someone with a chop to the neck, how to retain her weapon during a fight, how to gouge at someone with a fingernail file, how to find weak points in an attacker's knee and groin. She knew how to remain calm under duress, when addled crack dealers or robbers drew a gun on her or kicked and punched at her and called her racial epithets.

"We lived for the rush, the adrenaline," said Wendy Burstein, a fellow officer and steadfast friend. "She would always say to me, 'I've got your back,' and she always did." The two of them came to be known as "Peanut Butter and Jelly" for the way they stuck together. "Fort Pierce is a pretty tough place," Burstein said. "We were always getting in fights, having guns pulled on us."

Four years earlier, CeeCee stopped a car being driven by suspected drug dealers. She tried to keep the four men in the car, but they got out and began running. "It was at night, and I could hear the tension in her voice when she called for a backup," Burstein said. "There were four big guys and they weren't listening to anything she said. They all jumped out and three of them got away, but she tackled the other guy and brought him down."

In another case, an eighteen-month-old toddler was severely burned from the waist down when a gasoline can exploded next to a furnace in a modest home. The boy's skin had peeled away from his legs, and his parents and grandparents were afraid to touch him, Burstein said, but CeeCee ran into the house, grabbed the boy and began rubbing his back, cuddling and calming him until paramedics arrived. "After he got home from the burn center, CeeCee went back for months to check on him," Burstein said. "She was so good."

At thirty-three, CeeCee had a particular sympathy for those trapped in unraveled lives. She had been a teenage mother, and so had her own mother. CeeCee had been adopted by an aunt and raised by her birth mother and her mother's older sister. Her extended family was staunchly rooted in the church. Two of her uncles were pastors, and an aunt, Mareya Schneider, founded Restoration House, a shelter for women who had been abused or consumed by drugs and alcoholism, losing custody of their children and control of their lives. CeeCee had helped restore the shelter when it opened six years earlier, and she served as an example of someone who had righted herself without falling into despair or public assistance.

"We try to teach women to get their lives back and take care of their own children without getting caught up in a financial system where people are not motivated to do well because it is being done for them," Schneider said. "CeeCee was a good role model. She taught her sons, 'If you don't work, you don't eat.' "

While she was a patrol officer, CeeCee met Lorne Lyles, who was then a dispatcher for the Fort Pierce Police Department on Florida's Atlantic coast. She encouraged him to become a policeman, and when he got a job in Fort Myers, on the Gulf Coast, she decided to switch careers. She had tired of politics in the police department, and the work could be dangerous and dispiriting. She had two sons to care for. On December 11, 2000, seven months after she and Lorne were married, CeeCee entered flight attendant school in Chicago. Six weeks later, she was assigned to fly out of the United hub in Newark. Lorne loved the way she looked in her uniform, the blue pants and white shirt, tie and vest, and the long-sleeved dress with the maroon stripes. He thought she looked sexy.

Throughout the summer, while her kids visited their fathers and his kids visited their mother — Lorne traveled the country on his days off, meeting CeeCee in Atlanta, Denver, San Francisco, Los Angeles, Chicago, Phoenix. In the spring, they had taken their sons to visit the Statue of Liberty, the Empire State Building and the World Trade Center. "For the last three months, it was like they were on a honeymoon," said Shirley Adderly, CeeCee's mother. "She was so happy, almost exuberant. We would tease them that when school started, they'd have to come back to real life."

Because she was so new to the job, in which attendants requested flights each month according to a seniority system, CeeCee often filled in for colleagues who called in sick.

Her routes were frequently changing. It was like being a reservist in the military, always on call. She liked the trip to San Francisco because it was non-stop, and she could stay the night in town. After a weekend visit to see Lorne's sons in Indianapolis, CeeCee left Fort Myers on September 10, flew to Chicago and connected to Newark. She paid one hundred fifty dollars a month with four other flight attendants to rent a studio apartment, where she could watch television, read, listen to music and sleep during layovers.

At nine fifty-eight CeeCee called her husband again. This time Lorne awakened and took the call. He looked at the time and the Caller ID display on the phone. It was his wife. He assumed her flight had been delayed or canceled.

"Babe, my plane's been hijacked," CeeCee said.

"Stop joking," Lorne said.

"I'm not joking," CeeCee said. "I wouldn't joke about something like that."

Lorne could hear other people in the background. It sounded as if they were crying. He sat up.

"I called to tell you I love you," CeeCee said. "Tell the kids I love them."

They said a prayer. CeeCee told Lorne again how much she loved him and then said, "Aaah, it feels like the plane's going down."

"What's that?" Lorne asked. *Lord, please bring her through.*

"I think they're going to do it," CeeCee said. "They're forcing their way into the cockpit."

Lorne could hear screaming in the background. CeeCee screamed and he heard a whooshing sound, a sound like wind, a sound he couldn't really explain, just that it was like wind and people were screaming and then the call broke off.

17

The hijackers apparently did little to prevent the passengers and flight attendants from making phone calls. People spoke nervously but freely, without fear of immediate retribution. Perhaps, with so few hijackers trying to control so many passengers, the terrorists considered it too risky to intervene. Perhaps the passengers in the rear of the plane were being only loosely watched, or were left unattended. Still, none of the calls mentioned one critical element. If the passengers were able to overpower the hijackers and regain control of the plane, who would fly it?

Had Jason Dahl, the captain, and LeRoy Homer Jr., the first officer, been killed by the hijackers, as many presumed? Or were they still alive, as some investigators considered? Were they debilitated, or could they have recovered to save the aircraft? There was no way to know conclusively. If the pilot and first officer were dead or incapacitated, the slim hope for landing the plane safely rested with two men in coach. Donald F. Greene, seated in Row 27, had a pilot's license. Andrew Garcia, in seat 20C, had trained as an air traffic controller years earlier in the California National Guard.

"I have just found it so unusual that no one mentioned the pilot among them," Claudette Greene, Don's wife, said. "If these guys were trying to reassure their wives on the phone that everything was going to be okay, wouldn't you say, 'We've even got a guy who can fly the plane.' There was never any mention of that. Don was a proactive guy. He would have been in these guys' faces."

Don Greene was licensed to fly an amphibious plane, a single-engine four-seater. He was also qualified to serve as co-pilot on a King Air, a twin-engine turboprop, his wife said, but these two planes were far less powerful and sophisticated than a huge jet like the 757. Steering a plane — keeping it steady, or climbing or descending under normal conditions — would not have been so difficult, aviation experts said. Every student pilot knew the basics of pulling or pushing on the control yoke and making corresponding adjustments to the throttle. If a pilot pushed forward on the control yoke, the trees got bigger. If he pulled back, the trees got smaller. That was flying, reduced to its rudimentary essence. Left to its own design, a 757 was programmed to fly straight and level. But steadying an airliner that was de-

314

scending rapidly and flying erratically at excessive speeds would have severely challenged a pilot unfamiliar with jumbo jets. In 1979, TWA Flight 841 fell thirty-three thousand feet in forty-four seconds while en route from New York to Minneapolis. The Boeing 727 spiraled, uncontrolled for more than five miles, before the pilot was able to save the plane and all eighty-nine people aboard.

Unlike the other three hijacked planes, Flight 93's navigational system was reprogrammed from its original destination to Washington's Reagan National Airport, providing the 757 with steering coordinates toward the nation's capital. Yet, the jetliner had no altitude safety cushion to facilitate a passenger takeover. Flight 93 had descended under ten thousand feet, either trying to fly below radar, investigators theorized, or navigating clumsily because of inadequately trained hijacker-pilots. Ziad Jarrah apparently had never before flown a jumbo jet.

A plane flying less than two miles above ground under great aerodynamic stress provided precious little opportunity for an amateur pilot to make a rescue. Even if the plane had been stabilized after a passenger takeover, landing tested a pilot's skill most stringently and presented the greatest danger of accident. There was an old joke among pilots that flying was the second greatest thrill known to man and landing was the first. According to the Air Line Pilots Association, eighty percent of airline crashes occurred within a few miles of an airport, when a plane was either taking off or landing. Even with help from a control tower, a pilot untrained in the handling of a 757 would have found himself sitting at the controls in a cockpit of enormous complexity. To get the passengers down alive, he would have to master the intricate physics of glide slopes and sink rates and the hydraulic choreography of slats and flaps and spoilers. A tiny, propeller-driven plane responded much quicker to a pilot's commands. If a small plane came in too low and needed to abort a landing, the pilot could hit the throttle and the aircraft would lift almost immediately, like a kite on a string. A one-hundred-twenty-ton airliner possessed a far greater energy, which was not so easily harnessed and maneuvered onto a runway.

"This was not like Sky King in the 1950s, where Daddy conks out and Timmy's flying the plane and they talk him down and everyone's happy," said John Mazor, a spokesman for the Air Line Pilots Association, which represents sixty-six thousand pilots from forty-six airlines in the United States and Canada. "It would be extremely difficult at best. He would have been a real hero."

Donald F. Greene flew a plane affectionately nicknamed the "Flying Canoe," a Lake amphibious craft with a single engine mounted above the cabin. The plane landed in the water on its hull and had pontoons attached under the wings. On trips from his home in Greenwich, Connecticut, to visit his in-laws in northern Maine, Don and his passengers could simply land the plane, sit out on the wing, drop a line and fish. Essentially, it was a boat with wings. "Every excuse he had to do it, he loved to go bobbing around in that plane," said his wife, Claudette Greene.

Two weeks earlier, Don had taken friends from Virginia on a fly-by of Manhattan, providing a bird's-eye view so they could photograph the World Trade Center and the Statue of Liberty.

"On a great day, it was breathtakingly beautiful," Claudette said. "You could fly lower than the top of the towers. It was such a different perspective than commercial airlines or driving."

Donald Greene was born Donald Freeman, in a family whose roots were extensive and complicated. His birth father, Charles Freeman, was an advertising executive, and his mother, Phyllis Saks, was a member of the family that founded Saks Fifth Avenue and came to symbolize elegant living. The Freeman boys, as Don and his three brothers were invariably known, would accompany their grandmother, Elsa Saks, to the specialty store as she said in her aristocratic voice, "I believe I get a discount here." They marveled at how she could smoke a cigarette down to a column of ash and, in their adult lives, they would come to repeat her tender gesture of squeezing their hands three times to mean "I love you," and expecting four squeezes in return for "I love you, too."

When Don was five, his father died of cancer. His mother married Dr. Leonard Greene, an inventor and aerospace scientist who adopted Don and his brothers, Doug, Chuck and Steve. Don's mother died when he was sixteen, and the eventual blended family included a dozen members. "When we went somewhere all wearing the same shirts, we really looked like something," Leonard Greene said.

His adoptive father was such a curious and resourceful man, Don joked, that he thought of eight different ways just to get out of bed in the morning. Leonard Greene was a seminal figure in aviation safety. As the founder of Safe Flight Instrument Corporation, based in White Plains, New York, he invented the stall warning indicator that has been standard on aircraft since the 1950s. On October 25, 1947, *The Saturday Evening Post* called the stall warning indicator "the greatest lifesaver since the parachute."

Leonard Greene also invented the wind shear warning system, and as head of theoretical aerodynamics at Grumman, he wrote an important early paper explaining that it was possible to break through the so-called sonic wall and to exceed the sound barrier. In 1983, he also became the principal owner of the twelve-meter yacht *Courageous*, which had won the America's Cup in 1974 and 1977. He set about creating a winged keel, a bold new design that increased the boat's stability in the water.

Don Greene, who was fifty-two, came to share these same passions for aviation and sailing. He graduated with an engineering degree from Brown in 1971, and later received his MBA from Pace University in 1983. After working in real estate development and for the Department of Housing and Urban Development, Don settled into the aviation business, becoming executive vice president of Safe Flight, whose products are used on two-thirds of the world's aircraft. He guided the company from analog to digital product design and boosted sales by fifty percent. He was expected to be named president in three months at Safe Flight's annual Christmas party.

"Donny was happier at this point than he ever was before," said Doug Greene, his eldest brother. He had come into his own. He had seemed "a bit forgotten" when he was younger, his brother said, the third of four sons, not as independent as the eldest or as indulged as the youngest. Trauma had accompanied the privilege in his life. Both his parents had died by the time Don was sixteen, his career path had not become immediately apparent, his first marriage had ended in divorce. He remarried in 1990, and he was now the father of a ten-year-old son, Charlie, and a six-year-old daughter, Jody. He seemed more fulfilled, self-confident, substantial. His relationships with everyone in his family blossomed, and so did his business acumen. He became a calming influence, a source of familial information and advice.

"I think he wanted to be as successful in his own right as his brothers, wanted to have a family as his brothers did, wanted to be a buddy the way his brothers were," Doug Greene said, adding, "Maybe we were jealous that he was helping run the business and we weren't. He stopped competing and started appreciating. And so did we."

Even as a boy, Don had been organized and meticulous, curious about distant adventure. The wallpaper in his bedroom formed a map of the world, and when a country changed names, he erased the former name and dutifully wrote in the new one. He seemed particularly challenged by the end of colonialism in Africa; in 1960 alone, seventeen nations gained independence. "His whole map, he'd rewritten with a scrawl," his sister Bonnie Le Var said. "It just killed me to see this handmade map. He just wanted to be right."

Don seemed to be a natural coach, whether it was instructing his children or managing flight-safety engineers. He was firm, compassionate, charming, tranquil under pressure. Once, when the landing gear on the family's King Air did not show proper deployment on the cockpit panel lights, he told his brother Doug, "Before we go through all these emergency procedures, why don't we change the bulb?" He did, and, as he suspected, it was the lightbulb that had malfunctioned, not the landing gear.

At the beginning of each day, he meditated for twenty minutes, and at lunch, he took walks with colleagues to exercise his legs and his ideas. He was an attentive father and husband, leaving work promptly at five-fifteen for the twenty-minute commute home in time for dinner. He attended his children's athletic and academic functions, took them to Williamsburg, Virginia, when they studied colonial America, built forts and courses with ropes and pulleys, pulled them around Candlewood Lake in Connecticut on a rubberized banana boat, screaming and laughing as if he were one of the kids.

Don knew how to relax, whether it was in a hot tub after a day of skiing or with a splash of water in his Jack Daniel's. On the slopes, he sometimes carried a ski pole that doubled as a flask. "On occasion, when the weather required, he filled it with brandy," Doug Greene said. "We were very comfortable skiing."

In high school, Don and his brothers were accomplished wrestlers. He also participated in the sport at Brown. While school records indicated that Don entered only two matches in the one-hundred-seventy-seven-pound category, both in his junior year, Elie Hirschfeld, the university's class president of '71, described him "as the strongest man I ever met."

"His body was like a piece of iron, all muscle bundled up in his medium height and strong girth," Hirschfeld said. "We wrestled once or twice and he was always careful not to hurt me or anyone else when he was demonstrating maneuvers. He was a gentle man, with bursting capabilities at the ready, if needed. When we went anywhere together, I knew I was safe."

Don played tennis, golf and rugby before developing a neurological disorder that cost him partial use of his right hand. Still he persisted with scuba diving, sailing and skiing. On the slopes, he could coax the timid, elevate the intermediates, challenge the experts. He had a special ability, said his friend Dan Merrick, "to make you rise above yourself and be the best part of what you could be."

"He was the kind of guy you wanted to sit next to at a dinner party," his wife Claudette said. Which is exactly how they met in 1987. She was executive director of the Westchester Philharmonic, attending a fund-raising event at the Seagram's hangar at the Westchester County Airport in suburban New York. Small planes were brought in to create an intimate space, including the amphibious plane that Don flew up for the occasion. He brought along a tuxedo for the black-tie event and ended up seated next to Claudette, after her brother canceled as her date. She and Don were married three years later, almost to the day.

When the extended Greene family took its annual Thanksgiving resort holiday, more than fifty people joined in what was known as Turkey Week. On September 11, Don was headed with his three brothers on a quieter trip to hike the area around Lake Tahoe, Nevada. From there, he had a business trip scheduled to New Orleans. But his flight had been hijacked, and he was the one passenger aboard who might have had the skills necessary to get the others down safely.

"There is no doubt in my mind that had the passengers been able to gain control of Flight 93, Don, with a little input from the control tower, could have safely landed that airplane," said Peter H. Fleiss, a longtime friend and colleague at Safe Flight, who added that Don had trained on a Falcon corporate jet simulator. "It would have been a hard landing, sure, but he could have gotten it down."

Such a rescue would have required great skill and even greater fortune.

"If a guy was a professional pilot flying all the time, it would have been possible," said Hank Krakowski, a 737 captain who was in charge of United's flight operations on September 11. "If he was an occasional pilot, it would have been a pretty big challenge. You can get a boat into a dock, but it's a lot harder getting a cruise ship into a dock. The problem is the mass of the machine, the energy, the feel. It doesn't have the response of a smaller plane. It has much more kinetic energy. It takes training to get a feel for that. At least the weather was clear. That would have worked more toward a successful outcome than a lousy one."

Another passenger who could have assisted Don Greene in the cockpit was Andrew Garcia. He had worked for United's aircraft interiors division as a purchasing manager in the 1960s and had also served in the California Air National Guard. He did not obtain a pilot's license, but he did train as an air traffic controller. Leaving a friend's birthday party early, he had flown East from northern California on September 9 for a business meeting. He was the founder of a company called Cinco Group, Inc., which sold and distributed industrial products, many of them related to the airline industry. He ran the business with his wife, Dorothy. Andrew tried to get out of the meeting on the East Coast, but could not. At least it would be a quick trip. He booked his return on Flight 93, excited to get home because his daughter Audrey Olive was expecting a child in three days.

Andrew was trim and fit at five foot seven, one hundred forty-five pounds, with salt-and-pepper hair. He was sixty-two but looked much younger. He had been a sprinter and wrestler at San Jose State University, Class of '61, and he still played tennis and golf, did daily calisthenics and ran several miles near his home in Portola Valley, California. "He was a runner, not a jogger," Dorothy Garcia said. "We have friends who go out and do jogging. Andy would sprint for two miles."

He was a devout Christian. Cinco was an acronym for Christ in Company. Andy had grown up in Sunnyvale, California, located between San Jose and San Francisco, where his father owned a grocery store. He worked in the store and also in the nearby apricot, apple and cherry orchards. Even now, he cut and peeled a piece of fruit for his wife each night after dinner.

Retirement was not on the immediate horizon, not complete retirement, but his son,

Andrew, had joined the family business, and succession seemed to be in order. Andrew Sr. and Dorothy wanted to spend more time at a condominium they had bought on the Valley Ranch golf course in Carmel, California. Since founding Cinco in 1991, Andrew had played an important role in changing the government's specification requirements for airport ground power units. These devices sat on the tarmac and provided power to planes while they were at rest.

His business strategy was this: "I don't try to sell people our products, I want them to buy our products." It was a nuanced but important distinction. Andrew went so far as to provide his customers with phone numbers of his competitors if he believed they had a more suitable product. "Noble" is the word that Louis S. Lombardi, a longtime colleague and friend, used to describe him. "He was the epitome of a gentleman, in his personal as well as business life," Lombardi said.

He was also an inveterate prankster from his college days at San Jose State. Andrew would call his wife and pretend to be a customer, or phone his cousins and impersonate Cesar Chavez, the pioneering labor organizer, wondering why they were not contributing money to the United Farm Workers union. While making a speech at the wedding of his daughter Audrey, he spoke in the *Godfather* voice of Marlon Brando. He short-sheeted beds, Saran-Wrapped toilet seats, left the occasional dead fish under the seat of someone's car.

"When his sister got married, he put white shoe polish in her Jergens skin lotion," Dorothy Garcia said. "A couple of days later, she was looking in the mirror wondering why she was getting whiter and whiter and whiter."

Andrew's love of aviation extended to his eldest daughter, Kelly. When she was five or six, he began taking her to the San Jose airport in the family's Volkswagen squareback, and they sat with their legs dangling through the sunroof, watching planes take off and land. "He would point out all the planes and what they were used for," Kelly Garcia said. "Probably by the age of ten, I could identify aircraft by sound." At twenty, she got her own pilot's license, even if she sat on a pillow in the cockpit because she was but five feet tall.

For Kelly's thirtieth birthday four months earlier, Andrew had taken his children and their families to Hawaii for a week. Family time was important to him. When his three children were younger, he made it a point not to miss their soccer matches and swim meets and equestrian events. He taught them not to take themselves too seriously or to treat serious endeavors too lightly. He gave his kids homework, assigning them a stock to track in the financial pages, and when they took riding lessons, he had them clean stalls to pay half of the cost. "He taught us the value of things, how to treat people with dignity and respect, what kinds of standards to set," Kelly said. "And he always made a point of telling each of his kids how proud he was of us. A lot of people leave that unsaid. He always let us know."

The annual Garcia family picnic had drawn fifty people on Labor Day weekend, cousins and aunts and uncles commenting that this seemed to be the best gathering in the last thirty years. A week later, Andrew had a business trip scheduled to the East Coast. He hadn't flown since the trip to Hawaii in May. He spoke to his family on the night of September 10, saying he would be home the next morning.

One of Andrew's employees, Stephen Frasch, traveled with him on September 11 and departed Newark on an American flight bound for Los Angeles. The plane was redirected to Cincinnati after the suicide hijackings began. Frasch called Dorothy Garcia and asked her to make a hotel reservation for him. "I'm sure Andy's flight is fine," he told Dorothy, explaining that his plane and Andy's had taken off at nearly the same time. Dorothy called United and was told that Flight 93 was still scheduled to land in San Francisco at eleven-nineteen.

Her phone did ring another time. "Dorothy," the voice said, clearly her husband's, but after that one word, the call broke off. She assumed it was just a bad connection until her son, Andrew, called later and asked if his father had taken Flight 93.

"Yes," his mother told him.

"Tell me it isn't so," he said.

"What's the problem?" Dorothy asked her son.

"They lost the plane," he said.

18

With a pleasant monotony, William Wright flew across southwestern Pennsylvania in his single-engine Piper Arrow, mapping farmland with an aerial photographer. They were on assignment for the state agriculture department, flying back and forth on a route that extended from about twenty miles east of Pittsburgh down toward the West Virginia border. It was a part of the state where the regional airports were named after such native sons as Jimmy Stewart and Arnold Palmer. There had been talk on the radio about something happening at the World Trade Center, but Wright had gone about his business. He had turned northward when he received a message from the air traffic center in Cleveland. He was to return to the airport in Indiana, Pennsylvania, as soon as was practical. Then another call came: Return home right now. Then a third call: Land immediately in Latrobe, Pennsylvania.

There was air traffic below the Piper, so it could not land right away. The Cleveland center wanted to know if Wright could see a plane off of his left wing. Ten o'clock was the direction.

No, he couldn't. Neither could Holli Joiner, the photographer.

The Cleveland controller seemed to grow frantic. He gave the location of the plane again.

"There it is," Joiner said.

The gray-and-blue 757 was slightly behind them, perhaps a mile away, descending through the Piper's altitude at seven thousand feet.

The jet seemed to move away, then come back, Wright said, doing several steep rolls, dipping one wing, then the other.

"The wings started to rock," Joiner said, so mesmerized that she forgot to take a picture of the United jet. "The rocking stopped and it started again. A violent rocking back and forth, like it was going through turbulence."

Head north, the Piper was told. Get away quickly.

The 757 continued eastward and disappeared from the Piper's view.

It had been a slow early morning at the 911 center in Westmoreland County, Pennsylvania. A new emergency dispatch center was scheduled to be dedicated in the county seat of Greensburg, located twenty-five miles east of Pittsburgh. At nine fifty-seven, dispatcher

John Shaw took a break and walked toward a television to see the commotion involving the World Trade Center. It seemed to be on fire. As he walked across the room, an emergency line rang and he grabbed the call, which shattered the serenity of the morning.

"We've been hijacked," a man said.

"Where are you?" Shaw asked.

The man did not know precisely. He was on United Flight 93 from Newark to San Francisco, and it had been hijacked. He was calling from the bathroom.

Following procedure, Shaw asked for the passenger's name and cell phone number. The passenger identified himself as Edward Felt. There was no doubt that the call was authentic. To Shaw, the caller sounded as though he were crying. He seemed to speak in a quiet scream, as if he wanted to shout at the top of his lungs but felt he couldn't. To others who would hear the tape later, including a government official and Sandra Felt, Ed's wife, his voice sounded pressing, but he was composed and purposeful. All agreed that the caller was attempting to relay as much information as quickly as he could.

"I think he was trying to confirm with someone that the plane had in fact been hijacked," Shaw said.

Typically, Edward Felt flew Continental, but this was a last-minute flight, and he booked United in seat 2D. He tried to get out of the trip, and, late the previous night, he still did not have a hotel reservation. But he was a leading engineer for BEA Systems, a software firm, and his company needed him at a business meeting in San Francisco. It would only be for a few days. He'd be back home in Matawan, New Jersey, on Friday.

Ed was forty-one, and he joked with his two daughters that he wished he'd had a computer when he was a kid. "We only had zeroes then, no ones," he laughed about the binary technology. He made learning fun, the kind of father and engineer who was brilliant but not supercilious or intimidating. As a boy in Clinton, New York, Ed dismantled radios and clocks and put them back together. At age six, he rewired his family's basement, even though his enthusiasm overwhelmed his engineering skills at that age. "I think they went without electricity for a while," said his daughter, Adrienne.

"If I had a school full of kids like him, I'd only have to work one day a week," said Frank Perretta, Ed's middle school principal. "National Honor Society, just endlessly curious and questioning. If you'd say, 'Let's try something you haven't tried before,' he'd say, 'That sounds like a good idea.' "

In high school, Ed and his friends listened to a trivia game played on the Hamilton College radio station. On Friday or Saturday nights, they gathered in the living room with pizza, chips and reference books at the ready and "his team routinely won, they'd beat the college kids," said Gordon Felt, Ed's brother.

Ed went to undergraduate school at Colgate, where he met his future wife, Sandra, on the third day of freshman orientation. While he attended graduate school at Cornell, Sandra worked, and to stretch their meager budget, they played another radio trivia game that asked questions related to math, history, theater. "We won a few free dinners that way," Sandra said. Ed was the kind of guy who read science encyclopedias from cover to cover and pored over math books for fun, fascinated by fractals and chaos theory. At Colgate, he took a chemistry course just to help his roommate, who wanted to get into medical school. "He loved breaking that curve," Sandra said. "All the pre-meds would get very upset."

At BEA, Ed had been one of the lead architects on the Tuxedo software system, which was industrial-strength plumbing that connected business computers. He had also been awarded two patents involving encryption technology.

"A lot of this industry is populated by people with huge egos," said Terry Dwyer, formerly the chief technology officer at BEA and Ed's manager. "Ed was the best of the best. He knew a lot, but it never came off that way. He didn't lord his intelligence over people. He was very unassuming, down-to-earth, willing to talk to anyone, to make time for anyone."

His bright red hair had gone silver-gray, but Ed kept himself in shape, running several miles at night on a treadmill in the basement, watching the news or the financial channel. He also liked to run outside, but he was fair-skinned, and his daughters joked about how he slathered himself with sunblock and pulled his socks up to his knees to keep his calves from becoming pink and blotchy in the heat. To keep his five-foot-eleven, one-hundred-eighty-pound body fit, he switched to a vegetarian diet and also swam at a local club. At BEA, he was famous for taking walks to help himself or others solve problems. On weekends, he brought his fourteen-year-old daughter Adrienne to math enrichment courses, sometimes sitting in. And he drove his youngest daughter Kathryn, who was eleven, to piano lessons. He had begun tinkering with the keyboard himself. Kathryn was also a top age-group runner and he had planned to accompany her to a Junior Olympics competition in Orlando, Florida. He had also taken his daughters to the Arctic to see polar bears, and to the Galapagos Islands to view sea turtles.

"He always turned learning into a game and made it fun," Kathryn said.

Ed loved gadgets: White-noise devices to help him sleep, magnets, woodworking tools, a remote-control car starter, a fingerprint scanner in his office, a device on the family van that beeped when he backed up. He also taught the girls spatial games and exercises regarding the anatomy of movement. Recently, he had become enthralled with a flight-simulator computer game. "He had mastered most of the aspects of flying, except for landing," Adrienne said. "A few days before he left, we were sitting there playing — his computer was next to mine — and we were crashing into things like the Statue of Liberty. Neither one of us could land."

To make United Flight 93, Ed had a car service pick him up at five-thirty a.m. Four hours later, Sandra Felt sat in the waiting room at her dentist's office when she heard someone say something about an airplane. She asked that the volume be raised on the television and was later told by a receptionist that two planes had hit the World Trade Center. Worried, Sandra tried calling her husband on his cell phone, hoping he had left it on, that there had been a delay in Newark. His cell phone rang and rang, and then the call was forwarded to his voice mail at the office. "Where's Ed?" people began asking around the office. "What flight is he on?" His colleagues thought he could not be on United, because he always flew Continental.

In his call to the 911 dispatcher, Ed Felt did not describe the hijackers or mention any attempt to regain control of the plane. Once, he seemed to grow impatient with the dispatcher, but he kept his cool under the circumstances. "We're going down, we're going down," he said at one point, emotion in his voice. It was not clear whether he was calling from a bathroom in the front or the rear of the plane. Later, his wife came to believe he was in the front, because passengers calling from the rear appeared to speak openly. Ed seemed at one moment to be peering out of the bathroom, as if checking to see what might be going on. As she listened to the tape later, Sandra Felt likened the noises to street-level sounds one heard when riding a Ferris wheel — many voices were audible, but none that could be picked out clearly. She also wondered whether her husband had been injured.

After seventy seconds, the cellular call disconnected.

"We lost him," Shaw told his supervisor.

Just before ten a.m., Dennis Fritz took a call in the control tower at the airport in Johnstown, Pennsylvania. It was the Cleveland "en route" center. A large, suspect aircraft was twenty miles south of Johnstown, descending below six thousand feet and traveling east at a high rate of speed. Was Johnstown in radio contact with such a plane?

"No," said Fritz, who was the Johnstown air traffic manager. Eight or nine aircraft had been diverted to the airport after the hijackings began. As far as he knew, everything was down. He would let Cleveland know if he heard anything.

Fritz grabbed his binoculars and scanned the horizon. The Johnstown-Cambria County Airport had no radar. It relied on visual identification of aircraft. Fritz saw nothing over the ridges that rose to nearly three thousand feet.

A short time later, Cleveland called again. The unknown aircraft was now fifteen miles south of the field, heading directly for Johnstown. The tower should be evacuated. Fritz ordered four workers to leave. Still, he saw no sign of a plane through his binoculars.

Forty-five seconds later, the Cleveland center called a third time. Disregard the evacuation. The aircraft had turned south. Cleveland had lost radar contact.

President George W. Bush had received news of the second attack on the World Trade Center while reading to second graders at the Emma E. Booker Elementary School in Sarasota, Florida. The gravity of what had occurred was evident in the look of stunned nonchalance on his face. He finished his reading, and at nine-thirty, he announced on television that the crashes were "an apparent terrorist attack," saying, "Terrorism against our nation will not stand."

He hurried in the presidential limousine to Sarasota Bradenton International Airport and, by nine fifty-five, the president was aloft aboard Air Force One. Vice President Dick Cheney had moved into a bunker beneath the White House. By now, the Pentagon had also been hit by a hijacked plane. All commercial airliners had been ordered grounded.

According to *The Washington Post*, the vice president recommended to President Bush that the military be authorized to shoot down any other jetliner approaching Washington with seemingly hostile intent.

"You bet," President Bush concurred.

"We had a little discussion, but not much," the president told the newspaper.

The president then spoke with Secretary of Defense Donald H. Rumsfeld about the procedures military interceptors would follow before shooting down an unresponsive airliner. Fighter jets would attempt to make radio contact, then visual contact. They might even fly in front of the plane.

A military aide informed Cheney, apparently incorrectly, that a commercial plane was eighty miles outside of Washington and a fighter jet was available to intercept. "Should we engage?"

"Yes," Cheney responded.

When the plane was said to be sixty miles out, Cheney was asked again if the order of engagement still stood.

"Yes," he said.

The decision was "painful" but "clear cut," Cheney later told the *Post*, adding, "I didn't agonize over it."

"You're asking American pilots to fire on a commercial airliner full of civilians," Cheney said. "On the other hand, you had directly in front of me what had happened to the World Trade Center, and a clear understanding that once the plane was hijacked, it was a weapon."

At nine forty-five, Todd Beamer had reached a GTE-Verizon operator. By pushing a latch, Todd had withdrawn the phone from a seat-back and unspooled its cord. He had pressed "0" and reached an office in Oak Brook, Illinois, fifteen minutes from Chicago's O'Hare Airport. The operator at Workstation Fifteen took the call, but the news apparently traumatized her. She handed off the call to Lisa D. Jefferson, a customer service supervisor with seventeen years' experience and a soft, reassuring voice.

"I understand this plane is being hijacked," Jefferson said to Todd. "Could you please give me detailed information as to what's going on?"

She had dealt with bomb threats and medical emergencies, but never a hijacking. There was no training manual for terrorism, no precise list of questions to ask, so Jefferson relied on her instincts and her experience: Get the basic facts, keep the line open, have someone contact the FBI. GTE-Verizon did not routinely tape its telephone calls. As a supervisor, she would have been the one to monitor the taping, but she did not want to risk losing the call.

The caller identified himself as Todd Beamer, from Cranbury, New Jersey. He spoke in a soft, calm voice. Three people had hijacked the plane. Two with knives went into the cockpit and locked the door. The third person stood in first class with what appeared to be a bomb strapped around his waist with a red belt. He ordered everyone to sit down, then closed the curtain that separated first class from coach. There were ten passengers in first class, twenty-seven in coach, and five flight attendants, Todd said, giving Jefferson the flight manifest. He could not see any children.

Two people were lying on the floor in first class, Todd said. He did not know if they were still alive. Lisa Jefferson overheard a flight attendant sitting next to Todd say that the men on the floor were the captain and co-pilot. The flight attendant did not mention them by name, or say that they were wearing uniforms, but she seemed certain.

Todd repeated what the flight attendant had told him.

At the beginning of the call, Todd spoke in a low voice, almost a whisper. If he felt his life was threatened, Jefferson said, he could lay the phone down. Don't hang up, keep the line open, she told him. Todd said he was fine, free to talk.

"Do you know what they want?" Todd asked. "Money or ransom or what?"

He seemed confused.

"I don't know," Jefferson said.

Todd did not seem to be aware of the other hijackings. Jefferson did not have many details, either, but she gathered from co-workers standing around her that the other hijackings had been suicide missions. She did not mention this to Todd, not wanting to alarm him.

His voice went up a bit. "We're going down, we're going down. No, wait, we're coming back up. We're turning around. I think we're going north."

It was disorienting. He said he didn't know where they were going.

"Oh, Jesus, please help us," Todd said.

Todd asked Jefferson to recite the Lord's Prayer with him. They recited it together, then Todd began reciting the twenty-third Psalm:

"The Lord is my shepherd; I shall not want. He maketh me to lie down in green pastures: He leadeth me beside the still waters. He restoreth my soul: He leadeth me in the paths of righteousness for his name's sake. Yea, though I walk through the valley of the shadow of death, I will fear no evil; for thou art with me."

The plane seemed to take another dive, and nervousness came back into Todd's voice.

"Oh God," he said. "Lisa."

The operator thought this was odd. She had introduced herself as Mrs. Jefferson and had not given Todd her first name.

"Yes?" she said.

"That's my wife's name," Todd said.

"Oh, that's my name, too, Todd," Lisa Jefferson said.

"Oh, my God," he said of the coincidence.

He told her about his family, his two young sons, David and Andrew, and his wife, who was expecting a third baby. "If I don't make it out of this, would you please call my family and let them know how much I love them?" Todd asked Jefferson, giving her his phone number.

Of course, she said.

Todd was an account manager for Oracle software. He was headed to the company's headquarters in Redwood Shores, California. His favorite time of the year was approaching. The air would soon chill, and he could wear sweatshirts, and the cornfields outside the family's spacious colonial home would hunch into the arthritic stalks of Halloween. His favorite athlete, Michael Jordan, was coming out of retirement and would be playing a few hours away in Washington, DC. Todd had grown up in the Chicago suburbs, and had eagerly followed Jordan's six championship seasons with the Bulls. He had worn Jordan's number twenty-three for a portion of his own basketball career, and his mother-in-law had even painted a mural in his home office of Jordan's last, victorious shot with the Bulls, a push-off jumper that clinched a National Basketball Association title over the Utah Jazz. As an added touch, she had placed the Beamer family into the stands behind the basket — Todd, Lisa, and their sons — David, three, and Drew, one.

Todd loved his Chicago teams, though, with the exception of Jordan's Bulls, public affection in the Windy City was usually rebuffed by the cold shoulder of defeat. He hung photographs of Wrigley Field and Soldier Field in his home office. He had a Bears dartboard and Cubs pinball machine. He'd even named his cat Payton, after the National Football League's all-time leading rusher, Walter Payton. On their fifth anniversary, Lisa surprised Todd with a trip to Wrigley Field and a meal at Jordan's restaurant. She thought Todd and Jordan had similar qualities. They always seemed to come through.

After his meeting in California, Todd planned to take the red-eye flight home. It was to be a one-day trip. Todd had considered flying out a day earlier, as soon as he and Lisa returned from Italy, but he wanted to spend more time with his sons. He gave them a bath, read a book to them and put them to bed. At thirty-two, he was seeking equilibrium in his life. Like many professionals, he had struggled to find a satisfying balance between his career and his family. On Friday mornings, he attended breakfast meetings with a group of male friends, where that subject was an overriding concern. "We were all trying to strike that balance," said Doug MacMillan, who often hosted the meetings at his home. "How much is enough at work? Where do you draw the line? Todd was talking about cutting back on his travel."

At one point, Todd traveled nearly half the days of each month. Lately, he'd cut back to four or five days a month, remaining in sales instead of advancing into management so he could keep his own schedule. He had begun to work more often out of his home, heading downstairs into his office early in the morning, re-appearing for a shower, and returning to his office until his son David said, "Pack it up, Dad, time for dinner." The family had a number of pet sayings. When it was time for the kids to put away their toys, or put on their shoes for a trip outside, Todd would exhort them with a call of "Let's roll." He was building his nest egg, hoping to retire from sales at age forty. A devout Christian, he taught Sunday school at his local interfaith church, and he thought he might like to teach high school or become a junior high principal in his next career. He would teach and coach. He had played college baseball and basketball at Wheaton College in Illinois, and he loved the life of jeans and ball caps. Perhaps he would even coach his sons.

He had hit a home run in his last at-bat as a collegiate baseball player. SOLO SHOT IN 5TH he scribbled on the ball that he kept in his office ten years later. At one time, Todd hoped to play in the major leagues. Now, he participated in "old fat man's softball," and pickup basketball at lunch, but one thing had never changed about the resolute way he played. He hated to lose. Absolutely hated it. He was a "gamer," said Doug Scheidt, a college teammate and, later, a roommate. Todd was intense, goal-oriented, unruffled by pressure. After college, while Todd was studying for his MBA at DePaul, he and Scheidt played in a three-on-three basketball tournament, with first prize being front-row seats to see Jordan and the Bulls. "It was double elimination, and we were beat," Scheidt said. "Then Todd kicked into another gear. He hit all the big shots and we won the tournament."

In January of 1994, on the weekend that Todd and Lisa were planning to move to the East Coast, a snowstorm hit, leaving him stranded at Newark International Airport and her stuck with a rental van full of their belongings in Chicago. One plane made it back to the gate in Newark, Todd talked his way on, and when the weather cleared, he caught the last flight out to O'Hare Airport.

"That was him," Lisa said. "He always figured out a way to get done what needed to be done. As soon as Todd was around, you always thought, 'Okay, everything's going to be all right.' "

David Kohlmeyer, a classmate of Todd's from fourth grade through high school, had long noticed an uncommon determination in his friend. Their school, Wheaton Christian Academy, forbade athletic participation if a student missed class. One Friday, Todd came to school with one-hundred-two-degree fever so he could play basketball against his team's top rival.

During conditioning drills for soccer, Kohlmeyer said, Todd always beat him by a step or two when they sprinted after a three-mile run. The last time they had seen each other, several years ago, they had played pickup basketball, each game going to twenty-one points. Todd had won again, three or four games, each game by a point or two.

"That edge, that little extra desire, was so unusual," Kohlmeyer said. "I've never seen it before in anyone else."

The Boeing 757 moved erratically and Todd thought he had lost contact with the operator.

"Lisa, Lisa," he hollered into the phone.

"I'm still here, Todd. I'm still here. I'm not going anywhere. I'll be here as long as you will."

He said a few of the passengers were going to "jump" the hijacker with the bomb and try to regain control of the plane.

"Are you sure that's what you want to do?" Jefferson asked.

"At this point, I don't have much choice," Todd said. "I'm going to have to go out on faith."

What did she think?

"I stand behind you," Jefferson replied.

They talked more about their families. She was in Oak Brook, Illinois, and he had lived in nearby Wheaton. She had two kids and he had two kids. He said he was on a business trip. He had thought about calling his wife but did not want to upset her if he did not have to.

"I just want to talk to somebody and just let someone know that this is happening," Todd said.

"That's fine," Lisa said. "I'll talk as long as you want."

Then, in the background, she could hear an "awful commotion," men's voices raised and hollering and women screaming "Oh my God," and "God help us," and "Help us Jesus."

Todd seemed to turn away from the phone to speak with someone else.

"You ready?" he said. "Okay. Let's roll."

19

Flight 93 kept descending to the southeast. Rodney Peterson and Brandon Leventry, auto mechanics in Boswell, Pennsylvania, crossed Main Street in this tiny mining town about ten o'clock when they noticed a jetliner appearing to lumber through the sky at about two thousand feet.

Hijackers had already crashed planes into the World Trade Center in New York and into the Pentagon outside Washington. No commercial flights were supposed to be airborne. This United flight could have been circling and headed to the airport in nearby Johnstown, but Peterson had worked previously at the airport, refueling helicopters and corporate jets. He was familiar with flight patterns, and he knew that jetliners generally approached Johnstown at a much higher altitude.

"Check that plane out," Peterson said to Leventry.

Then the plane did something odd. It dipped its wings sharply to the left, then to the right, casting a blinding glare from the sun.

"Something ain't right," Peterson said.

The wings leveled off but the plane was now heading southward. No local airport in that direction could handle the landing of a Boeing 757. Peterson broke into a run, trying to follow the plane up Main Street, but the jetliner disappeared over a line of trees and houses.

"If they were fighting with the hijackers, I guarantee it happened right here," Peterson said later. "It dipped left and dipped right. No plane that big flies like that."

The hijackers rocked the wings, investigators theorized, to keep the passengers from rushing the cockpit, apparently trying to knock them around like bowling pins. Much of what happened in the final minutes of the flight fell into the uncertain realm of conjecture, according to officials who heard the cockpit voice recorder and read transcripts. The last moments were subjected to the murkiness of interpretation, hopeful imagination. There was no clear determination provided by the voice recorder, which operated on a thirty-minute loop and taped remarks using microphones located in the pilots' headsets and in the cockpit ceiling. Many of the recorders were of 1970s vintage and did not provide stereo quality, investigators said.

There were no definitive answers to questions that families were asking: How did the hijackers get into the cockpit? Were the pilots killed immediately? Did the passengers advance into the cockpit? Which ones? Did the hijackers drive the plane into the ground deliberately or lose control in the chaos of the moment? There was no final avenging "Death to America" assertion by the terrorists, no flag of takeover planted in the cockpit by liberating passengers, no scenario that would provide unclouded drama to the mind's reconstruction. The tape seemed disjointed, many of the voices muffled and muddy.

At the same time, family members later said they were provided an encouraging scenario when they heard the voice-recorder tape: Federal prosecutors in the upcoming trial of Zacarias Moussaoui, accused of being the intended twentieth hijacker, proposed that the passengers used a food cart as a battering ram to enter the cockpit, even if they were ultimately unable to save a plane that was flying too low and fast and was turning upside down.

The final loop on the voice-recorder tape began at nine thirty-one and ran for thirty-one minutes, according to the notes and recollections of families of the passengers. Near the beginning, an accented voice in English ordered someone to sit down. A voice implored in English, "Don't, don't." A woman, presumably a flight attendant, pleaded not to be hurt or killed, saying, "Please, I don't want to die."

After the plane was hijacked, at least one flight attendant pressed a code on her Airfone and reached the United maintenance office in San Francisco, airline officials said. She reported that one hijacker was holding the crew at knifepoint, according to *The Wall Street Journal.* Evidence that at least one flight attendant was bound by the hands would turn up at the World Trade Center, and the same method of restraint was suspected on Flight 93. Patrick Welsh, the husband of Deborah Welsh, the flight's purser, said he was told by United that one flight attendant was stabbed early in the takeover. Presumably, this was learned from a call to United's maintenance center. It was "strongly implied," he said, that his wife had been a victim, given her position in first class and the likelihood that she would have stood between the hijackers and the cockpit. "Knowing Debby, she would have resisted," Patrick said. "She didn't meekly submit to anything. She was feisty, big-boned, formidable. She could handle herself."

At nine thirty-nine, Ziad Jarrah, the hijacker pilot, said in accented English that he was the captain and that there was a bomb aboard the plane, which was headed back to the airport. "They have our demands," he said, urging the passengers to remain quietly seated in an effort to calm them.

After an initial flurry of activity, there were stretches of silence on the tape. Despite what Jarrah said, this was no regular hijacking. There were no demands to be made, only a grim mission to carry out. The hijackers' inexperience was evident. They gave instructions and prayed. Clicks could be heard, along with paper shuffling and knocks on the cockpit door. Coughing noises were also heard. Officials who listened to the tape also reported a gurgling sound. At one point, a male voice said in English, "Oh man," perhaps in surprise at finding someone dead or injured.

A two-tone alarm sounded when the autopilot was disconnected. An alarm also would have sounded because the plane was traveling at five hundred seventy-five miles an hour in the final minutes, far exceeding the design limits of four hundred twenty-five miles an hour below twenty thousand feet and two hundred eighty-seven miles an hour below ten thousand feet. Over the barber pole, pilots called it, referring to the red-and-white needle on the plane's airspeed indicator. "It could have even broken the sound barrier for a while," said Hank Krakowski, who was head of United's flight operations control in Chicago on September 11. The seeming maneuvering of hydraulics also could be heard, along with the rushing of wind in heavy air so close to the ground.

About midway through the tape, one of the hijackers said to another, "Let the guys in now," apparently referring to other terrorists entering the cockpit. A vague instruction was given to bring the pilot back in. What this meant was not known. Was one of the United pilots needed to shut off the autopilot alarm or to set a new course? Was the body of one of the pilots to be brought into the cockpit? Was this a reference to a hijacker pilot?

The fate of the pilots, Jason Dahl and LeRoy Homer Jr., could not be clearly determined by the cockpit voice recorder, which did not document the moment Flight 93 was overtaken about nine twenty-eight. After the gruesome screams of "Get out of here!" were heard on the air traffic control frequency, many investigators assumed the hijackers had barged into the cockpit, killing the pilots immediately by slitting their throats. The hijackers would have had no reason to keep them alive. They were not asking for ransom or to be diverted to Cuba or some other country.

Other investigators, noting the reference to bringing the pilot back in the cockpit, considered different scenarios: If the pilots had been killed in the cockpit, the hijackers might have had trouble removing dead weight from such a cramped space. And they would have risked sending the plane into an uncontrollable spiral. The cockpit also would have become nauseatingly messy and sticky with blood. And the immediate killing of the pilot and co-pilot might have led to a simultaneous passenger revolt. Some investigators believed the hijackers had threatened one of the flight attendants, obtained a key to the cockpit door, learned the secret knock to enter or waited until one of the pilots went to the bathroom. Some pilots later interviewed by investigators said that they would have left their seats, trained in appeasement, asking the hijackers what they needed and where they wanted to go, offering money, food, drinks, anything to calm them, never expecting that the terrorists would take over the controls.

After the hijackings, United flight attendants would report having seen Middle Eastern men knocking on the cockpit door of several flights before September 11, as if they had mistaken the cockpit for the bathroom.

Forensically, it would be impossible to tell exactly when or how anyone aboard the plane died. The cause of death for all aboard Flight 93 would be listed as fragmentation due to blunt-force trauma. According to a letter from the Department of Defense's Armed Forces Institute of Pathology, written a month after the crash, most of the remains consisted of sheets of skin with no underlying bone or soft tissue. "While the injuries are traumatic in nature," the letter said, "they are non-specific and cannot be definitively classified as pre-crash stab or incised wounds [knife wounds]."

Because the 757 had one narrow aisle, passengers would not have been able to rush the cockpit three abreast from the rear of the plane. They would have been forced to charge single-file. What does appear certain, based on telephone calls from the plane, the rocking of the wings and the desperate final struggle aboard, is that the passengers and crew acted with heroic purpose. The hijackers attempted to scare the passengers into docility by warning that they had a bomb on the plane. In the end, though, it was the passengers who unnerved the hijackers.

At nine fifty-three, the hijackers grew concerned about possible retaliation from the passengers. One of the terrorists urged that the plane's fire ax be held up to scare the passengers. Federal officials later told family members that the hijackers, in a bumbling manner, suggested holding the ax up to the peephole in the cockpit door, believing incorrectly that the riled passengers could see through the other end. At nine fifty-seven, one of the hijackers asked if anything was going on, apparently meaning outside the cockpit. Something was. The passengers had begun to retaliate. They were carrying out their plan to take back the plane. "Fighting," one of the terrorists said.

"We don't have all the answers, but there is no question in my mind that the passengers were heroes in the truest sense of the word," said Wells Morrison, the deputy on-scene commander for the FBI, who declined to discuss specifics of the voice recorder or evidence found at the crash site. "Everyone should be proud of their actions."

Flight 93 continued in trouble as it flew over Highway 30, now eighty miles southeast of Pittsburgh and one hundred seventy miles northwest of Washington. Across the state, in the suburbs of Philadelphia, the highway connected the tony cities along the Main Line of the old Pennsylvania Railroad. Four hours to the west, the road undulated through the Laurel Highlands, part of the Allegheny chain, and the terrain was one of steep hills and sharp turns. In this rural area, the connecting roads bore names like Skunk Hollow, and it was not uncommon to see groundhogs lumbering across the blacktop.

The morning fog was just burning off on the western ridge as Terry Butler worked among the metal carcasses at Stoystown Auto Wreckers, stripping parts from a Dodge Caravan. Stripped and smashed cars were stacked in long, neat rows. Butler heard a loud rumbling sound, looked toward the mountains, then turned toward the east and saw the United jet flying above a house. It seemed only five hundred feet above the ground now.

No big plane flies that low around here, he thought. *It will hit a tree.*

The jetliner seemed to gain altitude as it skimmed over a ridge, but it made a sharp right turn and began to roll over on its side. Several miles away, Rob Kimmel, a truck driver, was working in his garage when he saw the jetliner fly overhead, banking hard to the right. It was only one or two hundred feet off the ground as it crested a hill to the southeast. "I saw the top of the plane, not the bottom," Kimmel said. "It looked like something was wrong."

Rick King, the assistant volunteer fire chief in Shanksville, Pennsylvania, spoke on the phone with his sister, Jody Walsh, who lived four miles north in Lambertsville. Modest houses and barns hugged the narrow, two-lane road between Lambertsville and Shanksville. Dairy farms, fields of corn and oats, and woods of oak and maple and pine carpeted the rolling terrain. Only two hundred forty-five people lived in tiny Shanksville, the homes set in terraced rows along the town's three streets. The residents possessed an easy friendliness. Everyone knew everyone else, and that familiarity made them trustful and put them at casual ease with strangers. King owned Ida's Country Store, which made delicious sandwiches and hot meals for lunch, and sold memorial photographs of the late racing car champion Dale Earnhardt. The assistant fire chief was two doors down, at his home, when his sister said, "Rick, I hear a jet."

The mother of two small children, Walsh had the television turned to *Barney*, not to the hijacking calamities, until King's wife phoned her at nine forty-five. Walsh had been scheduled to make green eggs and ham for her son's pre-school project, but now her brother was on the phone, and she could hear a sound that was out of place for this quiet town. She knew that other planes had crashed, and now this one seemed to be coming right over her house, making a noise so loud she could no longer hear her television.

"That's not funny," King said, thinking his sister was joking.

"I'm serious," Walsh said. "I hear a jet coming down."

She was too frightened to look outside.

Cordless phone in hand, King walked onto his front porch. He could hear it too, the screaming engines.

"Oh, my God," he said. "I think it's going to crash."

★ ★ ★

Lee Purbaugh did not hear the plane until it was nearly on top of him. He was working with a blowtorch at the Rollock scrap metal company, standing on a bluff overlooking a reclaimed strip mine. This was his second day on the job. The Boeing 757 flew over his head, thirty or forty or fifty feet above him, he estimated, so close that the bottom of the plane seemed a tan color as it reflected the fields below.

The plane was hurtling along at nearly six hundred miles an hour. There was only a sliver of time for his mind's snapshot, and he was not accustomed to seeing an airliner racing by at the distance of a punted football. Eyewitness accounts were frequently unreliable. That said, Purbaugh was the only person to see the plane go into the ground. The jetliner rolled onto its back, into an inverted position, according to investigators. The wings seemed to be rocking, Purbaugh said. Then the jetliner made a sharp, fatal tilt and dived, one wing and the nose of the plane seeming to hit in an awkward crumpling. The 757 appeared to be swallowed in flames and there was a loud explosion and a dark cloud mushroomed. It was three minutes after ten. What he saw was so horrific and unbelievable that it seemed distant and dislocated, as if he had not viewed the crash live but had watched it on television, *World's Scariest Accidents.*

"Oh, my God, it crashed," Rick King said to his sister. "I gotta go."

He was a mile and a half away, two miles at most, and he could feel his porch rumble. Karl Glessner, owner of a building supply company, was four miles away and the noise to him sounded like lightning and thunder at the same time, a sound that would be made "if you could hear lightning, a crackling and booming and roaring that you could feel in your chest." Rick Yock, a bartender at the Indian Lake Resort, located two miles from the crash, was sitting at home, watching television with his mother. Planes had hit the World Trade Center and the Pentagon, and now he felt a shivering explosion in rural Pennsylvania. The power went off in his house, the lights, the television. The phones went dead. He thought the whole country was under attack.

Rick King ran two doors down to Ida's Country Store, and hollered toward his wife, Tricia, "A plane just crashed. It had to be a jet." She could see the distressed look in his face. Emergency sirens began to wail. He ran a block to the fire station and called the 911 dispatcher in nearby Somerset, the county seat. "Plane down, Lambertsville area," the control center told him. How many fire departments had been dispatched? King asked. Three, he was told.

They must think it's a Cessna, he thought.

"The way the ground shook, this has to be a jet airliner," King said.

He requested that an additional five fire departments be dispatched. En route to the crash, he radioed the Somerset 911 center again and asked for all available ambulances, paramedics and medical helicopters. *There must have been two or three hundred people on that plane.*

Smoke rose above the tree line as Terry Butler watched from Stoystown Auto Wreckers, about one and a half miles northwest of the crash site. He screamed into his walkie-talkie, "Call 911, a plane's crashed." Sometimes the workers at the salvage yard played jokes on the internal radio system, and several of his colleagues thought he was kidding. "I'm serious," he said, and there was a tone in his voice that let others know he was telling the truth. He stood in disbelief for what seemed like ten minutes, watching the smoke rise above the woods to the southeast. Distraught, he walked into the office and told his boss he was leaving for the day.

Lee Purbaugh scrambled down the bluff from the scrap metal company and ran three hundred yards to the place where the plane had crashed. The field reeked of jet fuel. Trees had been singed, branches were smoldering and underbrush was aflame. One of the plane's tires burned. There was a smoking hole in the ground. But why wasn't there more fire? The jetliner had been loaded with nearly ten thousand pounds of highly flammable fuel on takeoff, and Shanksville was in the middle of a drought. Paper had spread more than fire. The plane had been carrying thousands of pounds of mail, and pieces had scattered about, envelopes with California addresses, magazines, paper on the ground and in the trees, some of the envelopes burned, some still in the same unharmed condition in which they were mailed. A mile and a half downwind, at Indian Lake Marina, the sky seemed to be raining confetti a few minutes after the crash. Purbaugh ran to the site to see if he could find anyone alive, but he knew by the terrible way the plane hit that no one had survived.

Something struck him. The plane. Where was it?

"It was unbelievable," Purbaugh said. "Something that big had scattered that quick. There was nothing there. Everything was shredded."

A controller at the Cleveland en route center feared the worst. Flight 93's radar track had been lost. The controller asked a plane in the vicinity, "Do you see any activity on your right side, smoke or anything like that?"

"Negative," the pilot said. "We're searching." Then he radioed again: "Yeah, we do have a puff of smoke now at about, oh, probably two o'clock. It appears to be just a dark cloud, like a puff of black smoke."

At the United system operations center outside of Chicago, the red radar track of Flight 93 just stopped, the image of a miniature plane halting on a video screen as if a computer had frozen. Hank Krakowski, the director of the airline's flight operations, handed a map to a dispatcher sitting behind him in the crisis center. "Map that," he said. The dispatcher determined the longitude and latitude of the last position of Flight 93 and reported that it was south of Johnstown, Pennsylvania. Krakowski phoned the airport in Johnstown, and had trouble reaching anyone because of an apparent power failure. Finally, he reached the airport manager.

"Do you see anything?" Krakowski asked.

Yes, the manager said, about thirty miles to the south, a smoke plume was visible. It was clear to Krakowski that the plane had gone down.

Aboard Air Force One when he learned that a plane had gone down in Pennsylvania, President George W. Bush asked, according to *The Washington Post*, "Did we shoot it down or did it crash?" Condoleezza Rice, the national security adviser, ordered that the

Pentagon be called. Two hours later, to everyone's relief, the Pentagon had a definitive answer: The plane had not been shot down.

Traveling at five hundred seventy-five miles an hour, the 757 had inverted and hit the spongy earth at a forty-five-degree angle, tunneling toward a limestone reef at the edge of a reclaimed strip mine. Because the plane crashed upside down, the engines and the stowed landing gear thrust upward and forward. The ground became littered with the fractured underbelly of the plane, electronics, shredded wiring. The cockpit and first class shattered like the point of a pencil, and remnants sprayed into a line of hemlock pine trees. The fuselage accordioned on itself more than thirty feet into the porous, backfilled ground. It was as if a marble had been dropped into water.

No more than seven minutes after the crash, Rick King arrived in his fire truck, steering it down a dirt road within fifty feet of the crater. He rescued people for a living, and he expected to find survivors from this plane. The twenty-five volunteers in the Shanksville Fire Department brought along self-contained breathing devices and hydraulic arms, known as the jaws of life, to pry open the fuselage. As he approached the scene, adrenaline thoughts raced through King's head. *What are we going to see? Is there going to be a fire in the fuselage? Will people be trapped?* He jumped out of his truck and noticed small fires in different places, but he could not see the plane.

Where is it?

He was sure a commercial airliner had crashed, but he saw only small broken pieces. A 757 is composed of six hundred twenty-six thousand parts, fastened by six hundred thousand bolts and rivets, connected with sixty miles of wire. That's all that he could see now, fragmented parts and rivets and wires, a catastrophic uncoiling. Other firemen and townspeople at the scene had the same quizzical looks. Metal and plastic and paper were everywhere, in the trees, on the ground, a shirt, a shoe, underwear, a backless seat sitting in its aluminum track, a remnant of a seat cushion smoking on the roof of a nearby cabin. The pine trees were peppered with shrapnel. King saw the pushed-up earth and the crater that measured thirty feet or more in diameter, and he knew it had been the point of impact. He sent a crew to hose down the smoldering debris, but still he did not realize what had plunged into the disturbed ground.

"Never in my wildest dreams did I think half the plane was down there," King said.

Maybe it wasn't a commercial airliner.

The rumors started. There were two hundred people on the plane, four hundred.

There were no passengers, only mail. Bewilderment prevailed. No one knew anything for certain. King sent his men into the woods to search for the fuselage, and they kept coming back and telling him, "Rick, there's nothing."

Terry Shaffer, the Shanksville fire chief, sped to the crash from his job twenty miles away in Johnstown and found himself standing around with the others in disbelief. "You wanted to do something and there was nothing to be done," he said.

The force of impact had lifted heavy fieldstones and tossed them more than a hundred yards downwind. The axle for the 757's nose wheels had broken away and tumbled, snapping a tree that was half a foot in diameter, the local fire chief said. A stone cabin one hundred yards from the crater was knocked off plumb, its windows shattered, its ceiling tiles scattered like playing cards, its garage doors blown upside down and inside out. The nose of the jet, known as the radome, which housed a pivoting radar system, flew thirty yards in the woods and folded on itself like a clamshell, Shaffer said. A dog-eared Bible was found near the crater, its cover damaged but its pages still readable. A necktie lay on the ground, still knotted. A snake, sunning on a rock, was seared with its body coiled, its mouth open to strike.

In the hours after the crash, Pennsylvania state troopers said that they had seen no piece of the plane larger than a phone book. Later, an eight-by-seven-foot section of fuselage containing several windows would be found. It was about the size of the hood of a car. A piece of one engine, weighing a thousand pounds, landed more than a hundred yards from the crater, apparently jettisoned upward in a tremendous arc. The cockpit data recorder, one of the so-called black boxes, would be excavated fifteen feet into the crater and the cockpit voice recorder at twenty-five feet. Ash and paper, a canceled check, a charred brokerage statement, traveled eight miles from the crash on a prevailing wind. Brush fires would spark up in the woods for more than a week.

Where were the people? Where were the bodies?

King was puzzled. He hoped to save passengers, but he did not see anyone, no one wandering dazed through the woods, no one trapped in the fuselage, not a single person alive or dead. Wallace Miller, the Somerset County coroner, arrived and walked around the site with King. Bits of plastic melted and fell from the trees and sizzled in the eerie quiet. They walked around for an hour and found almost no human remains.

"If you didn't know, you would have thought no one was on the plane," Miller said. "You would have thought they dropped them off somewhere."

20

After Todd Beamer said "Let's roll," his line remained open to GTE-Verizon operator Lisa Jefferson, but she heard only silence. She kept repeating his name but heard no response. After fifteen minutes, maybe thirty, one of her supervisors said, "Lisa, release the call."

Ilse Homer was on her way to a gym in the Forest Hills section of Queens, New York, when she encountered someone who told her, "Did you hear about the tragedy? Two planes collided accidentally into the World Trade Center." Both planes belonged to American Airlines, the person said erroneously. Ilse couldn't stay at the gym. She bought herself a cup of coffee and sat at a train stop and began crying. *Why am I crying? I didn't know anyone.* Her son, LeRoy Homer Jr., was a pilot for United, and these were American planes. She walked home and left a message on her son's phone: "I hope you don't have to fly today. There's a terrible tragedy. Two American Airlines jets crashed into the World Trade Center." Then she said what she always did to her son: "Stay safe. Fly with God. You are the sunshine of my life. I love you." Not until four-thirty in the afternoon would she find out that her son had been the first officer on Flight 93.

Richard Makely, the father-in-law of Jeremy Glick, took the phone from his daughter, Lyz, after Jeremy said he would be right back on the line. For what seemed like more than a minute, he heard no background noise, only silence. Then came screams, a mass of shouting, no separate voices, female screams more than male screams. Then another sixty seconds of silence, or ninety seconds, followed by another set of screams. It was the kind of sound people made when they rode a roller coaster. All the screams started at the same time, and they all stopped at the same time. Jeremy's call from the plane ended at three minutes after ten, according to phone records. At the operator's request, Makely remained on the line for ninety minutes. He thought he heard the sound of a phone banging against something. It might have been imagined in the stress of the morning. He couldn't really tell. The banging sound and then nothing.

An ambulance arrived, and a paramedic began taking Lyz's blood pressure while her father remained on the phone. *What's this guy doing here?* She tried to call Jeremy's family and some of their friends, but she had trouble with the phones. A New York state trooper drove up, and she borrowed the trooper's phone and got through to Jeremy's mother. At this point, Lyz still had hope. In her mind, she was in her car driving to Newark or Pittsburgh to pick Jeremy up. A minister came to the house and said the plane had crashed, but there were survivors.

If there are survivors, Jeremy has to be one of them, Lyz told herself. *He wouldn't let himself die.*

Lyz Glick phoned the school in Fairview, New Jersey, where Jeremy's mother, Joan Glick, taught as a speech specialist. "Do you know what's going on?" Lyz asked.

"I've heard," Joan said.

"Jeremy's plane was one of those hijacked," Lyz said. "He's okay for now. You need someone to drive you home. You need to get home."

The roads were crowded with people leaving Manhattan for northern Jersey. What was usually a thirty-five-minute commute to Upper Saddle River now took almost two hours for Joan Glick. A friend followed her home, and they stopped periodically to converse, to update each other on what was being said on the radio. Joan could not comprehend that Jeremy's plane had been overtaken by terrorists. She thought he was already in California. He was supposed to have flown out the day before. One of the stops Joan made was at a church. She walked in and the church was empty and organ music was playing.

"That's when I realized that Jeremy's plane had been one of the ones that crashed," his mother said.

At home in Cranbury, New Jersey, Lisa Beamer made breakfast for her two boys and got them dressed for a trip to the grocery store. She and Todd had been away, and there was no milk in the house. Shortly after nine, a friend called and left a message: Was Todd okay, given what was happening with all the flights? Lisa turned on the television to see that both towers of the World Trade Center had been hit.

She watched for a couple of minutes and decided that two planes ramming into the Twin Towers could not be isolated or accidental. She tried to find Todd. Oracle did all of its travel online, so there was no travel agent to call. She knew that he usually flew on Continental, which had a hub in Newark. Continental wouldn't say whether Todd was on one of its planes, but the flights all appeared to be fine. She felt relieved. A few minutes later, Lisa wondered whether he had been traveling on United instead. She tried to get through to United but couldn't, so she phoned friends and asked if they could try to locate Todd. Lisa wasn't really worried, just frustrated with the jammed phone system.

Todd was fine. He was always fine. Todd is the ultimate survivor.

As the morning unraveled, she became more concerned. She called Todd and left a message on his cell phone. "I know you're okay. I'm worried. Call me as soon as you land."

Her phone did ring, around ten o'clock, as Lisa was trying to finish the laundry and keep an eye on the television. The first call rang twice, but she answered and found no one there. Usually the phone rang four times before the answering machine picked up. Either someone had hung up, or the call got disconnected. She carried the cordless phone into her laundry room, and it rang again. No one was there.

A friend, Elaine Mumau, came over to keep Lisa company. As they watched on television, the crash site from Pennsylvania was shown. There was no plane, not even a chunk of a fuselage, only smoke wafting out of the ground. The announcer said the plane might have caught fire or exploded. It was clear there was nothing left.

Lisa stood behind the couch in her living room. A couple of minutes later, the television reported the Pennsylvania crash was a

United flight from Newark to San Francisco. There was no doubt that this was Todd's flight.

"Elaine, no," she said in despair.

"You don't know," her friend said. "He might have gotten on a different plane. The flight might be trying to get down somewhere."

"No," Lisa said, slumping to her knees.

Deena Burnett could not let go of the phone. Her lawn filled up with policemen and neighbors and FBI agents. A police chaplain came in and mentioned something about organizations for widows. It was the wrong thing to say. Deena wanted him out of the house. A priest from her church arrived. What should she tell her daughters? "Tell them Dad's on a long trip and won't be home for a very long time," the priest suggested. This seemed so inadequate. *Next,* she thought. At least it was nice to have someone praying with her. She had no idea what to do, and she hoped the presence of God would come upon her and bring her some comfort. She wasn't giving up yet. She kept thinking her husband, Tom, would call. *I just know it. People survived crashes all the time.* She kept watching TV, hoping to see the crash site so she would know how much of the plane was intact. Then she saw pictures of the crater, and she knew there were no survivors. She put the phone down. She had held it for nearly three hours, and the batteries had gone dead.

After flying a defensive canopy over Washington, DC, for four hours in their Air National Guard F-16s, Captain Honey and Major Lou returned to Langley Air Force Base in Virginia. Essentially, they had flown a holding pattern at six miles a minute, Lou said. That part had been routine. What wasn't routine was the confusion, "the smoke of war," he called it. "No one knew exactly what was going on," he said. But both Honey and Lou said that no one had given them any orders to shoot down a commercial airliner. They did not even learn about Flight 93, or a plane crashing in Pennsylvania, until they returned to Langley, they said.

Only later did they have to confront the possibility that they might have been called upon to fire missiles on American civilians.

"I try not to think about it," Lou said. "I can't say it doesn't cross my mind. We were fortunate and grateful that the passengers stepped up and did what they had to do to put their destiny in their hands. There's no way you can repay them."

A pilot flying a combat air patrol has to rely on superiors on the ground with a broader awareness of a threatening situation, Honey said. "If you're told to intercept, if you're given the order, we have authentication procedures to check the genuineness of the order, then you do it," he said. "You trust people on the ground have a lot bigger picture than you do. But you don't want to be called on to do anything like that. You don't want to kill anyone, especially citizens of the United States. Those folks really kicked butt. They probably saved a lot of lives. You talk about unselfish acts. Words can't explain how impressed I am with people like that."

John Linner had been expecting his friends, Joe Driscoll and Bill Cashman, at Yosemite Park in late afternoon. Linner had taken Flight 93 four days earlier to hike first with his son, John Paul. This morning, they awakened at six, and his son dressed and began his drive to the airport in Fresno, California. He was headed home to Texas. Ten minutes later, he returned and knocked on his father's cabin door. Something terrible had happened at the World Trade Center. John Paul Linner called United and was told that Flight 93 was in the air and on its way to San Francisco. *Okay, the worst that can happen is that they'll ground everything,* John Linner thought. *Joe and Billy will get to San Francisco eventually. They can rent a car and drive from Frisco in four or five hours. As bad as it is, at least they're all right.*

The Linners walked from their cabin to a park cafeteria. John Linner bought a cup of coffee and struck up a conversation with some people from New Hampshire, while his son paid attention to the television. Then John Paul came over and grabbed his father and took him outside. Flight 93 had been hijacked, and it had crashed. Shaken, John Linner called Joe Driscoll's wife, Maureen, in New Jersey. She thought her husband and Bill Cashman had taken an earlier flight. John hoped she was right, but he knew his friends were on Flight 93.

21

It occurred to Allison Vadhan sometime in mid-morning that her mother, Kristin White Gould, might be flying that day. There was no cause for immediate alarm. An insomniac, her mother was not a morning person. Surely, she would not have awakened early enough to take one of these doomed flights. If she was traveling, she would likely have taken a car service from her brownstone on Manhattan's Upper West Side to LaGuardia Airport in Queens. Her plane would be grounded now, along with every other commercial flight in the nation. Allison lived only several miles from John F. Kennedy Airport, and not far from LaGuardia. She expected her mother to show up at her house at any moment. They would talk, maybe even have lunch.

Allison lived in Atlantic Beach, New York, an elbow of sand that nudged into the ocean at the western reach of Long Island. Three blocks wide, this sandbar extended into a series of barrier islands that trail eastward like fins under the belly of the main island. The Atlantic Beach toll bridge served as the marshy film location where Sonny Corleone was machine-gunned in the first installment of *The Godfather*. At least some locals believed this to be true, but memories moved in and out like the tide over three decades. Perhaps it was another bridge. The director Francis Ford Coppola remembered building his own toll booth on a deserted airport runway. In any case, from the bridge the land was flat enough and the World Trade Center tall enough that its towers stood visible fifteen miles away at the lower tip of Manhattan. Allison Vadhan did not find the metallic twin peaks attractive, as she did the Chrysler Building and the Empire State Building. Still, their upper reaches were a gossamer landmark, appearing light gray in the distance against a clear blue sky.

Her own life was inextricably linked to the buildings and their threatened history. Her son Jason — her mother's first grandchild — had been born on February 26, 1993, the same day that a rental van carrying a twelve-hundred-pound bomb exploded in the World Trade Center's underground garage. Six people had been killed, more than a thousand had been injured. So many workers had poured out of the buildings, dazed in sooty escape, their cheeks and foreheads and chins covered in the blackface of terror.

Two years later, Ramzi Yousef, a man whose real name and nationality were uncertain, was arrested in Pakistan and flown back to New York to face charges in the bombing. Eventually, he would be convicted as the plot's mastermind. In the air above Manhattan, an FBI agent accompanying Yousef had pointed at the towers and said, "They're still standing, aren't they?" To which Yousef replied, "They wouldn't be if I had enough money and enough explosives."

On September 11, Allison Vadhan left her gated community in Atlantic Beach and drove toward work. She was a physician's assistant. The doctors she worked with specialized in orthopedic sports medicine, mending the broken bones and rewiring the torn knees of professional athletes, including tennis players, football players with the New York Jets and hockey players with the New York Islanders. As usual, the radio in her sport-utility vehicle was tuned to a news channel. A bulletin interrupted a traffic report. Something, perhaps a small airplane, had hit the north tower of the World Trade Center.

Her cellular phone rang. It was her husband, Dr. Deepak Vadhan, a pulmonary specialist who had left home earlier and was driving to his office in Brooklyn. "Did you hear what's going on?" he asked.

Ten minutes from her home, Allison

reached the Atlantic Beach toll bridge. She could see smoke pluming from the north tower. Workers were repairing the bridge, leaving one lane empty of traffic, and she pulled over, behind a set of traffic cones. "Hey, lady, you can't park there," one of the workers told her. Or maybe he said, "Be careful, lady," but the sight of the burning tower was too compelling to ignore.

She left her vehicle and stood on the bridge. She saw a flash from the south tower in the distance, a mushrooming of red and orange and black. Her jaw dropped. *Was it another plane? A bomb?* Workers on the bridge fell into an urgent discussion. One of the workers had a relative who worked at the World Trade Center. Go home, his friends told him. Do what you have to do. Then the men went back to their business, not yet understanding that the destruction had been intentional. Allison started crying. The workers looked at her as if she were overreacting, growing hysterical. But she knew this was no accident. *This was no idiot not looking up to see and flying into a building.* She was too unnerved to go to work in this condition. She would return home and fix her face and regain her composure. Her schedule was light that day. She would go to the office later. She took her time getting home, driving back roads, thinking, worried.

Once she turned on the television, she

could not turn it off. A third plane dived into the Pentagon. Her mother-in-law watched with Allison, but she was from India and spoke little English, so Allison went to a neighbor's. New York and Washington were under attack. She needed someone to sit with her and provide reassurance and share her disbelief. As she watched television at her neighbor's house, the south tower of the World Trade Center collapsed. She felt the need to run outside and capture this on film. It was such a moment of history. She felt guilty, and too embarrassed to tell her friend, so she made up an excuse to leave and went home and grabbed her video camera.

"I have to do something," she said. "I'll be back."

Before Allison could drive back to the Atlantic Beach toll bridge, the north tower of the World Trade Center collapsed. Dust and debris spewed in a terrible arc, like smoky tendrils from a jester's hat. Nearly three thousand people would be dead. Some had jumped, others died in the explosions or perished in the awful compression. Allison stood on the bridge with her camera. She could not remember for how long, only that she felt obliged to record some permanent reminder. She felt like a gawker, but she could not turn away. A trail of smoke formed a long smear against the blue sky. The smoke would lighten and then it would blacken again in huge puffs that seemed to be exhaled from a bellows. The temperature of fallen steel beams would remain molten for weeks, forcing workers at Ground Zero to change their boots frequently because the soles melted.

As she filmed their smoky remains, Allison felt drawn to the towers of the World Trade Center in their absence, an affection she had never felt when they stood boxlike in the distance. "They never felt that important to me," she said. "But now they felt the same thing to everybody."

It was not unusual to be in the dark about her mother's plans. Kristin White Gould, who had turned sixty-five two weeks earlier, had only in recent years agreed to e-mail her travel itinerary to her daughter. She considered it such a pedestrian concern. She was an inveterate traveler, born as Olga Kristin Osterholm into a family whose history traced to one of the country's seminal voyages. She was a descendant of William Brewster, a passenger on the *Mayflower* in 1620 and a leader of the Pilgrim colony at Plymouth, Massachusetts. He was the Reverend Elder of the Pilgrim church at Plymouth, and in his early fifties, Brewster had been the eldest *Mayflower* voyager to participate in the first Thanksgiving.

As had Brewster, Kristin had studied Latin and ancient Greek. She owned a bracelet made of Byzantine coins, and her idea of a vacation was to visit historical or cultural landmarks. She had traveled down the Nile, visited the Great Pyramid, toured Greece, Sicily, Italy, Spain, Turkey, telling her friends, "As I grow old, I like to do things that involve digging in the dirt."

Her grandfather had been a prominent Long Island physician named Leander Newman, who had treated the Guggenheims, and in his younger days as an intern, had driven the first motorized ambulance at Bellevue Hospital. In 1953, Kristin had been valedictorian of Paul D. Schreiber High School in Port Washington, New York, and she had followed her grandfather to Cornell to study medicine, before being drawn toward her other great interests — literature, acting and writing.

At Cornell, she met her first husband, Mark White, in a course on ancient Greek, and she moved in the same literary orbit as the novelist Thomas Pynchon and the poet-songwriter Richard Farina, who would later marry Joan Baez's younger sister, Mimi, and would include a character named Kris in his novel, *Been Down So Long It Looks Like Up To Me*. Kristin had been involved in one of the early campus protests. The politics were sexual, not military-industrial. She opposed rigid housing rules, including one that prohibited male students from visiting the rooms of female students unless the door was left open and one foot was kept on the floor at all times. "This outraged the more experimental of undergraduates," said C. Michael Curtis, who is now a senior editor at the *Atlantic Monthly* magazine. On May 23, 1958, as many as two thousand students stormed the home of the university president, tossing eggs and trampling flowers and Puritan sensibilities.

"Standing on his front porch, the egg-spattered president vowed that Cornell would never be run by mob rule," Pynchon wrote in the foreword to Farina's novel. "He then went inside and called the proctor, or chief campus cop, screaming, 'I want heads! I don't care whose! Just get me some heads and be quick about it!'"

Four upperclassmen were suspended and later reinstated.

Eventually, Kristin pursued a career that twinned her passions, becoming a medical journalist. She published a book called *Diet and Cancer* in 1984 and grew to be on familiar terms with important scientists, working for such publications as *Medical World News* and the *Journal of Women's Health*, and writing award citations for the Lasker Foundation, the National Institutes of Health and the American Cancer Society. She met her third husband through an ad in the *New York Review of Books*, and she dabbled in poetry. In a poem titled "An Invitation to Reincarnation," she wrote:

I'd love to return as a Cello,
And if you came back as a Bow,
The music we'd make would make continents
quake
And Dolphins would whistle "Bravo!"
If we are not locked in Episcopal Doctrine
And Cosmic Conditions allow,
You'd tenderly stroke all my Strings till they
broke
Into Songs quite unsingable now.
In some sweet Hereafter, when you're a bit
dafter,
And breathe NO_2, not NO,
Your laugh, my dear Fellow, would waken this
Cello,
And you'd be my Favorite Bow.

Kristin seemed to her friends to know something about everything, the advent of the Gregorian calendar, existentialism, the toilet training of standard poodles. "A sponge for knowledge," her daughter Allison called her. She was the kind of woman who would put the top down on her Saab convertible and drive through Manhattan singing Brecht's *Threepenny Opera* in German or quoting e. e. cummings, "I sing of Olaf glad and big, whose warmest heart recoiled at war." At the wedding shower of a friend, she made a frivolous hat out of ribbons and a paper plate, and the next moment, she quoted a passage from *Beowulf.* "This is a woman who spoke in perfect paragraphs," said the friend, Karen A. Frenkel, a science writer and documentary producer.

And yet Kristin's practicality pre-empted snobbish arrogance. As a single mother in the 1970s, with a young daughter to support, she had for a time written articles for the *National Enquirer*, which afforded her a reliable paycheck and the mischief of anonymity. The *Enquirer* in those days was recruiting women "who looked impeccable and upper middle class," said Diane Ouding, a close friend who also wrote for the tabloid. "They would pay you ridiculous amounts and comp your hotel." Kristin wrote stories on medical or scientific events, said a friend, Frances Borden, articles that were "very creative and never hurt anybody."

Kristin also worked in the music business, doing public relations for Atlantic Records. She met Stevie Wonder, Aretha Franklin and Bob Dylan, secured an autographed picture of the Beatles and handled publicity for an early appearance by the Rolling Stones on the *Ed Sullivan Show*. More seriously, she edited an instructional manual for playing the blues harp and wrote musical criticism that appeared in the form of biographical sketches of Paul Anka, Joan Baez, the Beach Boys and Sam Cooke. She loved classical music and jazz, frequented the Metropolitan Opera, Alice Tully Hall and the New York Philharmonic, and it was a rare week that she did not attend some live performance. There was, however, some music which she could not abide. She did not like to sweat, and she especially did not like to sweat in health clubs that played disco music. Recently, she had joined a club upon the reassurance that she could exercise to opera.

She filled her brownstone on West Ninety-fourth Street with books, read inveterately as she chased elusive sleep and carried hard-bound volumes to her friends in heavy bags, as if the tomes were as essential a staple as groceries. She also lent her car to her friends, occasionally paid their doctor bills, even helped put a friend of her daughter's through college. She was an eager, gracious host, and her friends recalled her brunches that were "merry affairs where there always seemed to be a contingent of Irish pundits and poets present." She once became so enthralled with a book about a writer's disconsolate childhood, a book that she considered benevolent and accomplished but destined for obscurity, that she bought one hundred copies and gave them away. The book turned out to be Frank McCourt's *Angela's Ashes*, which won the 1997 Pulitzer Prize for biography.

She preferred to do her own writing long-hand, before transferring the work to a computer, and she hung out at the Lion's Head, a literary saloon for reporters, novelists, playwrights and politicos in the West Village. Once, a woman came into the bar and asked, "Is this the place where writers with drinking problems go?" Kristin responded no, it was a place for drinkers with writing problems.

In June of 1996, in a letter to a friend about the literary life, in which she quoted Yeats, Robert Louis Stevenson and the *Pogo* cartoon strip, Kristin wrote, "I just believe that inside every great poet and elegant thinker there dwells a Winnie the Pooh who must have A Little Something at about four o'clock. Poetry and philosophy aside, enlightened folk recognize each other through shared universal values — a reliable Swiss Army knife, Hunny, songs beside a driftwood fire, a cuddly stuffed animal for sleeping with and a well-shaped dry martini."

Four months later, she had been present into the early morning of October 13, 1996, when the Lion's Head closed after more than three decades. The beer still had a foamy head on it, but the profits did not. A miniature coffin sat next to a guestbook in the back of the bar as patrons came to pay their last respects. "It was a nexus of people who lived by the word," she told *The New York Times.* "Engineers, mathematicians, physicists, if you brought them here, they just didn't get it."

Her own curiosity with words could be comforting and therapeutic. She used a technique in her interviews, dropping a pencil and stooping to pick it up, as if to show deference to her subject. She was of an age that believed it best not to confront men in leadership roles, but to charm them with wit and bright knowledge. She once talked herself out of a mugging, dated a man who met her by dialing her number mistakenly, and turned an obscene phone call by a desperate, lonely teenager into a kind of friendship. "He was a lonesome kid, twelve or thirteen, no one around when he got home from school," said Ouding, her friend. "They ended up having several years of a phone relationship. Obscenity quickly dissolved into having someone to talk to."

Kristin had celebrated her sixty-fifth birthday on August twenty-ninth, and she had three grandchildren, but she refused to be called Grandma. A self-described chubby brown wren in high school, she had later evolved into a swan of elegance and sophistication, even if nature's own work had to be embellished occasionally with bottle-blond enhancement or a scalpel's restorative contour. If a writer's words could be shaped and edited, why not her looks? While Kristin reminded her daughter of Laura Bush, the first lady, Kristin's friends thought that she looked less matronly with her WASPish face, wide smile and cute upturned nose. "She looked like all the women you see in the elevator at

Saks Fifth Avenue," Ouding said. "Perfectly done, hair perfect, teeth perfect, any blemish immediately dispatched."

She had grown blonder as she aged into Scandinavian sturdiness, but for all of her professional accomplishment, Kristin had found a frustrating impermanence in her relationships with men. She had been married three times, divorced twice, widowed. Once, when Ouding was considering marriage, Kristin had leveled with her: "Look, you're never happy for very long. Then it's like pulling a boat up the Volga River." For a husband, she recommended, "Look for a man with quaint hobbies like trains and toy soldiers. Those are the faithful guys."

Still, she did not discount yet another marriage, and the night before Kristin headed to San Francisco to see a companion, she and Ouding e-mailed each other until two in the morning. *Should I wear this, should I wear that? What's my best color?* Kristin was not yet ready to let her high heels or her hair fall flat. She and Ouding messaged each other like sisters, and having built professional lives in the formerly male-dominated career of journalism, they felt it was nice to fall back on silly girlishness.

"She was a bird that did not want to be caged, a free spirit, creative, artistic," said a friend, Dr. Arthur DuBois, a professor at the Yale Medical School. "She had a duality, one side being a conservative background, the other being a free spirit, creative, artistic. Like Hedda Gabler, she didn't want to be pinned down. In that sense, she was ahead of her time. I don't know if her family understood that, or she felt they didn't understand."

As the morning of September 11 wore on, Allison Vadhan began to get worried. Even if her mother had slept late, surely she was awake by now. Kristin must have turned on the television or heard the terrible news about the World Trade Center from a friend. Why hadn't Allison heard from her? She would definitely want to talk about this, let her daughter know she was safe. Ten months earlier, Kristin had been traveling in Sicily during the disputed American presidential election. She had called Allison and chatted for hours from across the Atlantic. Maybe she was caught in transit to or from the airport. In 1993, while New York was in shock from the truck bombing of the World Trade Center, Kristin had not cowered at home. Instead, she had driven from Manhattan to be present for the birth of her first grandchild.

"She was not one to scare; she would never take no for an answer," Allison said.

But why hadn't she heard from her mother? Allison thought she'd better quit filming on the toll bridge and go home to check her computer. If her mother was traveling, maybe she had forwarded an itinerary. It was funny how her mother often took the most obscure airlines to save money. Anyway, she loved to sleep late. It would not be like her to take a flight as early as the ones that had crashed. Allison returned home, went to her son's room and turned on the computer. She began to grow numb. Her mother had done something unusual. She had scheduled herself on an eight a.m. flight out of Newark for San Francisco. United Flight 93. The television in the room was tuned to CNN, and just as she looked at her computer, someone announced that a plane was down in Western Pennsylvania, a United Airlines flight from Newark, Flight 93. Had her mother, who spent her life in appreciation of preserved monuments, died in the same attack in which missile-planes attempted to destroy America's financial and military monuments? It was too much to absorb.

Allison was trained to keep her cool in medical emergencies. This is how she made her living. She prided herself on remaining calm in times of stress. But now she was confused. Information was coming at her too fast, and she grew bewildered by the swirl of flight numbers and destinations and planes that had fallen from the sky. They were talking about a plane down in Pennsylvania, and the flight number matched her mother's itinerary, but her mother was going to San Francisco, not Pennsylvania.

Was she imagining all this? Everything was racing and she could not trust her own eyes. Allison's adrenaline was pumping and she began to think three steps ahead and she wondered if she was hallucinating. She walked next door to her best friends' home and said, "I need you to come over and take a look at this."

Her own voice was excited and scared, and it seemed to Allison that her neighbors did not believe her.

The neighbor, Jay Sessler, opened the e-mail and realized that Allison had not been imagining this. Her mother had booked herself on United Flight 93. Maybe she took another flight, Sessler said, trying to comfort Allison. Nothing definite was known. But Allison knew. Her mother's itinerary showed Flight 93, and now they were reporting on television that the flight had crashed in Western Pennsylvania. Allison called her aunt in Connecticut, and her aunt was crying.

"Why are you crying?"

"Allison, don't you know?" her aunt said.

Allison hoped that her aunt was crying over the events of the morning, over the tragedy at the World Trade Center. But she knew the truth without having to be told.

"I think I know," Allison said.

She went numb. Then she thought she would have to be strong for her children. She thought of Jackie Kennedy.

Carol Sullivan's flight on Continental from Newark to San Francisco was diverted to Grand Rapids, Michigan. She was director of the German Wine Information Bureau in New York. The pilot of her flight said that terrorists had attacked the World Trade Center and the Pentagon. He did not mention that airplanes had been used as missiles, but said there was a national emergency. All planes had been grounded. Sullivan took the in-flight magazine out of its pouch and looked at a map of the United States, trying to figure out where Christian Adams' plane would be grounded. The deputy director of the German Wine Institute, Christian was traveling on United Flight 93. *No big deal,* Sullivan thought. *He has my cell phone number. We'll hook up in San Francisco.*

The German Wine Institute promoted the export of the country's vintages. The United States imported a million cases of German wine per year, and Christian had traveled for a pair of wine tastings, one that ended on September 10 in New York, and another that was to begin September 13 in San Francisco. He would also have a chance to see his brother, who lived in the Bay Area. Christian, who was thirty-seven, held a marketing degree from the University of California at Davis, but trips to the States had been rare in recent years. He ran a winery in Biebelsheim, Germany, owned by the family of his wife, Silke. The couple had two young daughters. Usually, the American tastings were held at the end of September, corresponding with the fall harvest in Germany, for which Christian had to remain at home. This year, because of the Jewish holidays, the tastings had been moved to earlier in the month.

The son of a German wine official, Christian represented a diverse industry by deftly avoiding the political minefields that came with his job. His decision-making, like his style of wine tasting, was carefully considered, never rash. And in a business where egos were as commonplace and pointed as corkscrews, he had a certain open friendliness and willingness to pitch in.

"As a woman in this business who came up through the ranks, I saw that it was usually the men of position who stood around watching me do the grunt work," said Sullivan, who ran the German Wine Information Bureau, a publicity arm of the German Wine Institute. "Christian was ready and willing to do whatever needed to be done, xeroxing, lifting cases, whatever. He let me boss him around and thought nothing of it."

After the wine tasting in New York,

Sullivan and Christian had checked into the Marriott at Newark Airport on September 10. He could not have known that he stayed in the same hotel as the men who would hijack his plane. He was scheduled on United Flight 93 to San Francisco, while Carol was to leave fifteen minutes earlier on a Continental flight. Their flights were departing from different terminals, so Christian said he might sleep in for a few more minutes. He might meet her for the six a.m. airport shuttle, or he might not. When he did not show up in the lobby, Carol and her assistant, Caroline von Bistram, left without him. "He'll be fine," von Bistram said. "He's a big boy." They would meet in baggage claim in San Francisco.

Now, grounded in Grand Rapids, Sullivan and other passengers clustered around television monitors. A woman who had been sitting across the aisle from her on the Continental flight had a son who worked at the World Trade Center. She had been nervous, but later she talked to him. He had stayed home sick that day. He was fine.

"Did you hear of another flight out of Newark that's missing?" the woman asked Sullivan.

"I felt a wave of horror coming from her to me," Sullivan said. Across a television monitor scrolled a message that United 93 had been lost.

She went to the United counter and demanded an explanation. What did that mean, lost?

Later in the day, Sullivan received a call from United saying that Christian had not been on the plane.

Were they positive?

Yes.

She knew that was wrong. Eventually, she spoke with Christian's brother. Yes, it was true. He was on Flight 93. After trying to ignore the burning and tightness in her chest, Carol Sullivan said she ended up in the hospital for two days with a heart attack.

For seven hours after they were diverted to Toronto, Ryan Brown and the other passengers on his Northwest flight sat on the ground, not allowed into the terminal for security reasons. Frantically, he spoke with the sister and mother of Nicole Miller, his long-time girlfriend, who had taken United Flight 93. They kept phoning and leaving messages and everything was confused. United reported that Nicole was not listed on the flight manifest.

"I hope you're right," Brown said to Nicole's sister, Tiffney Miller. "But I checked her in for that flight. If they didn't let her on the plane after that, I don't know."

His hope kept dimming. He felt as if he were in shock.

Another message from Nicole's family said she was still not confirmed on Flight 93. Brown held out some slim hope. Maybe Nicole had taken another flight. She might be stranded in Toronto, too. Maybe he would see her when he got off the plane. There were long lines as he went through Customs, and he kept looking for Nicole among all the bewildered, frustrated passengers. He did not see her. Then he called Nicole's mother, Cathy Stefani, in California.

"Where's Nicole?" Brown asked.

It had been confirmed, her mother said. Nicole was on Flight 93.

Falling to his knees in the airport, Brown began sobbing.

22

The enduring image of Flight 93 is one of pastoral devastation, a smoking hole in a rural field, a place of blowing paper and shredded metal and fragmented debris that might have marked a landfill instead of a plane crash. Yet, had the 757 remained aloft for only two or three more seconds, many more people might have been killed. The jet may have crashed into the cluster of houses in Shanksville, or into the renovated Shanksville-Stonycreek School where four hundred ninety-four students in pre-kindergarten through twelfth grade had begun another day of classes.

"It could have been a lot worse had it gone a few seconds longer," said Wells Morrison, the FBI's deputy on-scene commander.

Twenty minutes longer, and United Flight 93 would have reached Washington in a finale of suicidal fireworks. "The strikes must be strong and have a wide impact on the population of the nation," read an Al Qaeda terror manual obtained by the Associated Press months after the September 11 attacks.

The manual recommended hitting buildings "with high human intensity" in the United States and Europe, such as skyscrapers, airports, nuclear power plants, monuments and sports stadiums. "Four targets must be simultaneously hit in any of those nations so that the government there knows that we are serious," the manual read.

The day after the crash of Flight 93, as he spoke to reporters in a tent placed in a cornfield near the site, U.S. Representative John P. Murtha of Johnstown said that the target undoubtedly had not been a reclaimed strip mine in rural Pennsylvania. Arlen Specter, the U.S. senator from Pennsylvania, later proposed a Medal of Freedom, the highest civilian honor, for those who had thwarted the hijackers' apocalyptic intentions. Rick Santorum, the junior senator from Pennsylvania, presented workers at the crash site a flag that had flown over the U.S. Capitol and expressed sober gratitude for the disruptive actions of the passengers.

"Somebody made a heroic effort to keep the plane from hitting a populated area," Murtha said. "I would conclude there was a struggle and a heroic individual decided, 'I'm going to die anyway. I might as well bring the plane down right here.'"

Ten miles away in Somerset, the seat of Somerset County, Pennsylvania, Governor

Tom Ridge presided over a sunset memorial three days after the crash. Fifteen hundred people crowded around the county courthouse, which had been draped with an oversized American flag. Small flags solemnly decorated every business in the downtown district. In the hushed twilight, a bell tolled for each of the forty passengers and crew members aboard Flight 93. A candle was lit for each victim, and the flames were used to light smaller candles held by townspeople who attended the service.

The hijackers had failed in their mission, Ridge said. "They did not destroy our spirit, they rekindled it. They did not destroy our patriotism. They did not — and we will not let them — take away our way of life."

By fighting back against the hijackers, the passengers and crew "undoubtedly saved hundreds, if not thousands, of lives in the process."

"They sacrificed themselves for others — the ultimate sacrifice," said the governor, who would later become the federal Director of Homeland Security. "What appears to be a charred smoldering hole in the ground is truly and really a monument to heroism."

Six days after the crash, families of the passengers and crew members gathered on a bluff above the soft, cratered soil where Flight 93 had been entombed. They cried and prayed and left remembrances of their loved ones, flowers, photographs, a Chicago Bulls' hat and M&Ms for Todd Beamer, a GOT MILK? poster for Jeremy Glick, a Japanese flag for Toshiya Kuge. He had been a huge fan of the Pittsburgh Steelers. He brought his Steelers' jersey with him on the flight, and he died not eighty miles from where the team played its games. His mother, Yachiyo Kuge, would return to the site later for a Buddhist ceremony of salt and rice and water and burning incense. Even months later, she would keep waiting for her son to call, to walk back into her home. "He was a bright and illuminating presence in our lives," she said. "Our house has darkened."

Bernadine Healy, then the president of the Red Cross, surveyed the bucolic scene in the Pennsylvania mountains, the stubble fields of corn and the autumnal hint of color in the trees, and said she felt "a certain peace, a certain beauty" in the place where Flight 93 had crashed. This was, she said, "a kind of Gettysburg for the first heroes of the war on terrorism."

Juan Martinez attended the memorial in honor of his daughter, Waleska, who had been seated in Row 10. He had never told his family the secret he kept for a decade. A master sergeant in the Air National Guard, he dreamed repeatedly of an airplane crashing. Over and over, he saw pieces of plane,

404

parts of people. "I always thought it was going to be me," he said. On September 9, he walked past a photograph of his daughter at his home in Caguas, Puerto Rico, and unsettling images came into his head. Waleska would die in a plane crash, not himself. So unnerved was the father that he dropped to his knees in the hallway and began praying: "These images can't be for real. Please, God, don't let this occur." Now, as he stood on a bluff above the crash of Flight 93, looking down at burned trees and FBI agents in hazardous-materials suits, everything felt familiar and sickening. These were the same scorched trees and white suits that came into his head two days before the plane crashed.

Carrying the cremated remains of their brother, Alan, who had died in a car accident on his honeymoon, Mitchell and Glenn Zykofsky began a bleak drive across country from northern California. They had another memorial to attend, this one for their stepfather, John Talignani, who had been aboard Flight 93. The nation's air fleet was grounded, so they drove rental cars into the pitch black of the Donner Pass, beyond the gaudy lights of Reno, Nevada, through unrelenting rain that forced them once to pull off the road in a blinding storm. Finally, they reached Shanksville, Pennsylvania, for the memorial service on September 20.

"While we were driving back, we were informed by the airline that there was a memorial in Shanksville," said Mitchell Zykofsky, a New York City police sergeant. "We had to race across country. It was a bizarre journey, driving in the rain with the remains of my brother in the back of the car. It was sad, but the people in Shanksville were special. They lined the roads and held up signs. You could tell how they were affected by this."

On September 24, families of the passengers and crew were invited to the White House, where President George W. Bush and First Lady Laura Bush met individually with each family. The president spoke plainly, not from a script, shaking hands, hugging relatives, letting them cry in his arms, assuring them that those aboard Flight 93 were heroes, and that they had not given their lives in vain. The families were then greeted by a line of White House staff members who stood on both sides of a hallway in the East Wing, giving thanks that their lives might have been spared by the bravery of passengers and crew members on Flight 93. For some relatives, it was their most heart-rending moment in the aftermath of the crash. One staff member, who seemed to be in her early twenties, could not look Deborah Borza in the eyes. She appeared to be only slightly older than Borza's own daughter, Deora Bodley.

Borza hugged the woman and said, "You're here because your job is not done. It was my daughter's privilege to die for you. Honor her and do your job."

Other families felt too overwhelmed by grief to take any solace from the gratefulness of the White House staff.

"I just wanted my daughter back," said Esther Heymann, the stepmother of Honor Elizabeth Wainio.

The courage of those on Flight 93 continued to resonate with the president. He began to regularly incorporate Todd Beamer's call to action into his own speeches. In the State of the Union address on January 29, 2002, President Bush said, "None of us would ever wish the evil that was done on September 11, yet after America was attacked, it was as if our entire country looked into a mirror and saw our better selves. We were reminded that we are citizens, with obligations to each other, to our country and to history. We began to think less of the goods we can accumulate and more about the good we can do. For too long our culture has said, 'If it feels good, do it.' Now America is embracing a new ethic and a new credo: 'Let's roll.'"

The morning of October 7, more than three hundred people boarded a dinner-cruise ship in Honolulu, Hawaii, and traveled the short distance to Diamondhead for a memorial service for Georgine Corrigan. A pod of dolphins jumped and spun near the boat. A helicopter swooped in and dropped a scoop of soil from the crash site in Pennsylvania. Laura Brough, Georgine's daughter, and the other mourners tossed rose petals into the water. Forty doves, one for each passenger and crew member aboard Flight 93, were released into the sky. A friend of Georgine's read an Indian proverb: "When you were born, you cried and the world rejoiced. May you live your life so that when you die, the world cries and you rejoice."

That same day, the American bombing campaign began in Afghanistan.

On November 12, two months and a day after the crash of Flight 93, American Flight 587 came apart shortly after takeoff from John F. Kennedy Airport. The Airbus A300 plummeted to the ground in Belle Harbor, a serene neighborhood in Rockaway, Queens. Bodies fell out of the sky, and houses burst into flames in an area that had been home to a number of firefighters who perished in the attacks on the World Trade Center. All two hundred sixty people aboard the plane died, along with five people on the ground. Five miles away, Allison Vadhan was at home in Atlantic Beach, New York, terrified that another terrorist attack was underway. Her mother, Kristin White Gould, had been aboard Flight 93. "I thought the whole thing was happening again," Allison said. "I was looking for smoke." Her husband, Dr. Deepak Vadhan, had driven through the area fifteen minutes earlier. He called and said, "Don't go to work right now. Don't go anywhere. Let's see what happens." She called her boss, an orthopedic surgeon affiliated with the New York Jets. "I've got another plane in my backyard," Allison said. "It feels like I'm under attack."

As the day wore on, investigators said that evidence did not point to a terrorist act. The tail fin of the plane fell off. This led investigators to examine whether the crash was caused by rapid movements of the rudder after the wake of another jet buffeted Flight 587. When it looked as if no other planes were crashing that day, Allison left for work, feeling an odd relief. "Any other year, people would break down and be dumbfounded and exhausted by this tragedy," she said. "It's horrible, but instead everyone was saying, 'Thank God it was mechanical problems.' They were just grateful it wasn't terrorism."

Arriving at the airport in the dark of early morning, Lisa Beamer took the same Newark –to–San Francisco flight that her husband Todd had taken six weeks earlier. By then,

United had discontinued operating a Flight 93. Lisa's was named Flight 81. She felt some anxiety, and a friend had asked that the GTE Airfones be covered on the backs of the seats. Still, Lisa said, she refused to live her life cowering in dread.

"The terrorists had quite a few missions on September 11," she said. "One was to wreak havoc on our nation. Another was to hold us captive to fear as to what might come next. If we allow them more control than they already have, that's allowing them an additional victory, which I refuse to do."

Articulate, photogenic, the holder of a degree in economics, resolute in the face of tragedy, she became the most visible spouse of a passenger aboard Flight 93. Lisa received an avalanche of mail saying that her husband's story and her own public strength had consoled others and made them resilient in the wake of September 11. War veterans began sending her their medals, including Purple Hearts. President Bush invited her to attend a speech before Congress. Her family Christmas was shared nationally on CNN with Larry King.

However misdirected, a backlash developed in occasional letters to the editor and in private remarks by some families of Flight 93 passengers. The letters and whispers suggested that Lisa received too much attention, that she was attempting to make her husband the preeminent hero. This was the insidious rippling of September 11. Terrorism did more than take three thousand lives. It created rifts inside of brittle families. And it divided other families, previously unknown to each other, who had been united by their suffering. Resentment sprung from inconsolable grief and scattershot anger. Bitterness welled in the perception that passengers aboard Flight 93 had attained unequal status in their deaths, that heroism had been divided into the ranks of generals and privates. There existed a desperate wanting for reassurance that everyone aboard had acted within character, that all had trumped fear with nobility.

The majority of the Flight 93 families thought the snippy criticism of Lisa Beamer was unfounded. They noted that she started a foundation for the surviving children of the passengers. That she lobbied on Capitol Hill for tax relief. That she thoroughly researched the federal government's offer of compensation and explained to the other families its benefits and shortcomings. That everyone should be allowed to grieve in the manner they find appropriate.

"I try to do what's right, whatever the consequences," Lisa said. "You can't be critical of anyone who is grieving. They don't act the way they would under normal circumstances. You have to give them a grace period, to do what they need to do, and hope they come out healthier and stronger than they were to begin with."

Lisa said she chose to play a public role, in part, because her own father had died of an aneurysm when she was fifteen, and her younger brother later had found it troubling not to know more details of his dad's death. By giving interviews, and appearing on talk shows, she could build for her young children an archive of news clippings and videotape about their father, to show them as they grew older. By keeping her husband's name in the spotlight, she hoped by extension to keep the memories of all those who died on September 11 in the spotlight. She also found it comforting to know that her public strength had helped many others with their own private resolve.

"I'm cognizant that people wonder why so few names are out there," Lisa said. "I've tried from the beginning to say that there were a lot of heroes, that a lot of people did the right thing. Some people have been fighting hard to give Congressional medals to four guys on Flight 93. I don't want to be part of it. My hope is that a couple of people speaking prominently can keep the whole thing in the eyes and ears of America, so amends can be made for what happened and it can be prevented from happening again. And so people will keep three thousand families out there in their hearts and minds."

The hijackers had expected to devastate and paralyze the United States, she said. Instead, they unleashed things they weren't expecting to unleash: Patriotism. People looking beyond their own lives to show concern for others. Perhaps this will change American society for the better, she said.

"The thing holding me together is knowing that the person Todd was on his easy days was the person he was on his hardest day," Lisa said. "One of the hardest things is knowing that he had time to know that he wasn't coming home. Even so, he was able to do the right thing. He was able to maintain the perspective, 'I'll be okay at the end of the day, Lisa will be okay, ultimately, and the kids will be okay.' That's the big picture. My faith and my perspective of eternity are keeping me from losing it. You still have to deal with the little picture. I've really tried to stay focused on the here and now, what I need to do today. I need to give my kids a bath, and get them to bed, not to think about how I'm going to have to do it alone for the next ten years until they can do it themselves. Just that I have to do it tonight. Every day I wake up and say, 'God, help me through today, whatever it brings, because you never know these days what it is going to bring.' Obviously the overriding things are making sure the kids are secure and well taken care of."

Some people lived their whole lives without leaving anything behind, Lisa said shortly after September 11. Her children would always be told that their father was a hero, that he saved lives. It was a great legacy for a father to leave his children. On November 24, which would have been Todd's thirty-third birthday, Lisa and her sons, David and Drew, decided to celebrate. "We can still have cake, right?" asked David, who was three.

"As long as he knows Mommy is here and loves him, and Daddy wishes he was here, that's all he wants to know," Lisa said. "The hard thing is knowing this shadow will keep coming back all the time for them. From an adult perspective, when tragedy strikes, it changes you forever, but you get healed over time. With kids, you get a scab and it gets pulled away at different stages. You never know how this is going to manifest itself at different ages with different children. You say, 'Okay, when it comes up, we'll deal with it in the appropriate way at the appropriate time.' The kids have each other and lots of other kids around. Maybe they'll be able to understand each other."

On January 9, 2002, Lisa Beamer gave birth to a daughter, Morgan Kay Beamer. Morgan was Todd's middle name.

In February, the children's foundation created in Todd's name sought to have "Let's roll" trademarked in an attempt to protect his image and to prevent others from profiteering on his call to action. Another person who had applied for the trademark offered to sell it to the foundation for $50,000, Lisa said. She had also become concerned when "Let's roll" began appearing on militia uniforms.

"We wanted to make sure this was not attached to anything that would be detrimental to who Todd was," Lisa said.

After the 2001–2002 school year was completed, Deena Burnett moved from her gated community in San Ramon, California, to her native Arkansas, so she could raise her three young daughters with the help of relatives. In the months after the crash, her daughters began demanding more attention and did not like being away from their mother, even for the slightest time. When Deena went to the garage, they followed her. When she went to the mailbox, they wondered where she was going and wanted to go with her. There were days when they began crying in school and Deena had to be with them. Some days they played as other kids do. Other days they asked the most heartbreaking of questions:

"Are the bad people in Heaven with Dad? If they're in Heaven, are they going to hurt him again?"

Even though they were only in kindergarten, her twins became vaguely aware of

Osama bin Laden, not of the name or the face really, but of a particular man who told bad people to get on their father's plane. "Have they caught that bad man yet?" Deena's daughter, Madison, began asking. "Have they found him?"

Even when they went to a park, they no longer felt completely safe. "Do you think any bad people are here?" the girls asked Deena. And how was a mother to console a daughter, as she had to console her youngest, three-year-old Anna Clare, who was reminded every time she saw an American flag that her daddy was in Heaven?

"She's probably always going to associate the American flag with her Dad's death," Deena said. "I don't know if that's good or bad. Maybe it's a good thing. I hope it is."

She felt a kind of acceptance in her husband's death, she said, because she had long expected that they would not grow old together. She also felt cast in a role that she was not prepared to play. She would be going forward with her life being known as the widow of Tom Burnett from Flight 93. While her husband was alive, she realized now, she did not speak much because he spoke for both of them. Now, she made phone calls and everyone seemed to know who she was. She walked into a store and people recognized her. They came up to her and hugged her, and she found herself standing there and thinking, *Okay, who are you? They all know about me, but I don't know about them.*

"It gives you an incredible sense of responsibility to live your life better and to be aware of how you can inspire those around you to live a better life," Deena said. "I hope I can handle the responsibility as heroically as my husband did, as honorably."

Yet, it was an awkward role, being despondent over a lost husband and having to remain strong and to support friends and strangers in their own vicarious grief. "In the beginning, everyone asked, 'Aren't you proud of him? Aren't you happy that he's a hero?' " Deena said. "I thought, my goodness, the first thing you have to understand is, I'm just trying to put one foot in front of the other. For my husband to be anyone's hero, I'd much prefer him to be here with me. As selfish as that is, it's the truth. Use Thomas Jefferson as your hero, not my husband."

It seemed hollow now to hear people in other situations say, "If I can have a positive effect on one person, then it will have been worth it."

"Let me tell you, that means nothing to me," Deena said. "I'm not giving my husband up for one person. I'm not giving him up for a thousand people. If it had been my decision to choose between my husband and a thousand people at the White House, my husband would be sitting on this sofa. To affect one person doesn't mean anything. But maybe I can find the strength to let go of the fact that he's gone if I can affect a nation. I hope it's a positive effect that lasts a long time."

Some families believed the passengers had boarded Flight 93, not out of statistical randomness, but for a higher, perhaps more providential, purpose. "I have an inner faith that these people could have been placed on the plane," said Allison Vadhan, the daughter of Kristin White Gould. "God knew we were strong enough, we would be able to handle this. I believe my mother was needed on that plane, along with all the others." Others felt differently. Joan Glick, the mother of Jeremy Glick, said that to ascribe the events of September 11 to fate was to absolve everyone of responsibility. "It's easier to think it was fate," Joan Glick said. "Then everyone is off the hook, the government, the airlines, the security people. If people start to believe it was fate, that means there is no way you could have controlled the destiny of September 11."

One family from Flight 93 anonymously joined a liability lawsuit against United and American airlines and the security companies affiliated with the airports where the doomed flights originated. At least two other families also filed lawsuits in connection with the crash. A number retained lawyers to advise them about the federal Victims' Compensation Fund, which offered $1.6 million per family (many would get much less) but required a forfeiture of the right to sue.

Alice Hoglan, the mother of Mark Bingham, and Sandy Dahl, the wife of Captain Jason Dahl, were both United flight attendants who became airline-safety activists. Sandy Dahl lobbied for more aggressive defense training for flight attendants. "Offering hijackers food and making myself small isn't going to work anymore," she said.

Alice Hoglan decried as insufficient the matching of luggage with each passenger that airlines began in mid-January 2002. Such a measure did not protect against suicide bombers who could place a bomb in their checked bags, she noted. She began lobbying for X-ray inspection of each bag, as well as the use of bomb-sniffing dogs.

"We continue to see the effects of the airlines' emphasis on the bottom line at the expense of safety," she wrote in a newsletter to other families of passengers aboard Flight 93.

Melodie Homer, the wife of First Officer LeRoy Homer Jr., said she and her husband had discussed their concerns about inadequate airport security long before September 11. In the ensuing months, she found herself becoming exasperated by double and triple random searches to which she was frequently subjected when boarding airplanes.

"I'm five foot two, one hundred fifteen pounds; to pull me out of line is ridiculous," Melodie said. "This is too little too late." She added: "Had they done a sliver of that before, my husband would be alive."

A number of families said they took solace in the gallant death of the passengers and crew, in the final phone calls, in the brave resistance and defiant attempt to regain control of the plane. In knowing those aboard the plane made a decision about their destinies. In the bittersweet fortune to have had the deaths of their loved ones noted by the world. They longed for answers to the lingering questions about Flight 93, and not knowing consumed them. But not knowing also freed them to write their own endings, to come to their own heroic conclusions. Lyz Glick saw photographs of the hijackers, and she came to feel strongly that her husband, Jeremy, had killed the one with a mustache, maybe the one who claimed to have a bomb. And if some families came to feel that Flight 93 had been somehow forgotten, or overlooked, in the larger tragedy of September 11, they could also take solace in omission. The jet carrying their loved ones had dived into a bucolic field in Pennsylvania, beyond video's documentary reach. Families would be spared the endless slow-motion replay, the hellish loop, of planes crashing into the World Trade Center. "If Jeremy died in a car accident, I wouldn't have the same peace," Lyz Glick said. "If he had come out of this without his name being known, or without making a phone call to me, telling me he wanted me to live my life, it would have been harder for me going forward."

But, of course, there would be no easy way to patch the holes in these torn lives. Closure was a word almost taunting in its inadequacy, a shibboleth that mollified public guilt, not familial grief. A numbing despair took hold after September 11, heartbreaking incomprehension. Many people could not sleep for weeks. Some became irritated when they saw others happy. Others could not bring themselves to use the past tense. Lyz Glick and her friends called Jeremy's cell phone number, just to hear his recorded voice. They wondered whether they should leave messages. Lorne Lyles sprayed his wife CeeCee's perfume on a teddy bear and placed it next to him as he slept. Feelings of guilt and anger and loss tumbled with the randomness of lottery Ping-Pong balls. *What if I had talked him out of taking the flight? If I had only been there to protect her.* A song on the radio brought people to tears. Holidays and birthdays passed in solemn absence. Phone calls at familiar hours brought a flicker of anticipation, then sad reality.

Families learned to give social answers, not real answers, when people asked how they were doing, expecting them to be on the mend. They waited months to receive and bury the remains of their loved ones, and the repeated mentions of September 11 interrupted the grieving process. There were good days and bad days. Good hours and bad hours. And dreams, frustrating and reassuring. Carole O'Hare dreamed that her mother, Hilda Marcin, received a manicure from Laura Bush. Ryan Brown, a Marine, sensed that his girlfriend, Nicole Miller, was behind him on a plane, and he was choking faceless men who held box cutters in their hands. Ilse Homer said that her son, First Officer LeRoy Homer Jr., came to her in a dream, saying, "Mom, I want you to know exactly what happened in the cockpit." They were standing on the ground, outside of a plane, and LeRoy had a smile on his face and they began to walk up a set of stairs to the cabin. As they were about to climb the first step, Ilse Homer's granddaughter nudged her and she woke up.

Sooner for some, later for others, there came an acceptance of farewell, even a rueful laugh. Lisa Beamer came to think of the hijackers as incompetents, "the Bad News Bears of terrorists." Laura Brough, the daughter of Georgine Corrigan, said, "I heard they found bin Laden. The government sprayed Viagra over Afghanistan and the little prick popped up." David Dosch, a United captain and close friend of Captain Jason Dahl, sent out a holiday card that said, "All I Want For Christmas Is A Taliban." The card showed him in the cockpit of a jet holding a bag of pork rinds and the plane's fire ax.

Paula Jacobs got a Superman tattoo in memory of her brother, Lou Nacke, who had the same tattoo on his left arm. "He was my super-hero," she said. On February 12, 2002, Lou's eighteen-year-old son, Joe Nacke, became a father. He named his son Louis J. Nacke III. "I wish my dad could see him," Joe Nacke said. "The baby looks just like he did. Like a replica."

On January 18, Melodie Homer, the wife of First Officer LeRoy Homer Jr., flew from Newark to San Francisco aboard United, symbolically completing Flight 93 for her husband. "It was difficult," Melodie said. "I was listening to air traffic control and I heard the Cleveland center and I had to stop listening. But once I arrived in San Francisco, I felt I had accomplished something for LeRoy and myself. He would have been very proud that I did that for him."

Lyz Glick and Dorothy Garcia, the wife of Andrew Garcia, participated in the torch relay prior to the Salt Lake City Olympic Games. A week before Christmas, her husband's recovered wedding ring was returned to Dorothy Garcia.

"It was a great comfort," she said. "I gave that to him thirty-two years ago, and he and the Lord gave it back to me. It was as if he was saying, 'I love you dear, and it's going to be okay.' It means so much to me."

Esther Heymann, the stepmother of Honor Elizabeth Wainio, and Alice Hoglan, the mother of Mark Bingham, said they had conflicted feelings about moving forward with their lives. Intellectually, they realized they had to move on, for their own health, for the well-being of their families. Yet, once they moved on, they knew they would lose a certain way of remembering their children. Somehow, they felt, that would be a betrayal.

"I know I have to find a contentment in my life," Alice Hoglan said. "You can't prevent the birds of sorrow from flying over, but you can prevent them from building a nest in your head." Still, she added, "I don't ever want to feel good anymore, really. Much of the time, I feel like I want to be in the ground with my son."

Jack Grandcolas, the husband of Lauren Grandcolas, said that longing felt to him in some ways more painful than the original shock of losing his wife. He had confronted his anxieties, flying into Newark to see Lauren's family, leaving through the same Gate 17 that Lauren departed from on September 11, seeing the American flag waving from the jetway, feeling he had to walk the final steps that his wife had walked. He lost twenty-five pounds and knew that denial caused physical pain. It was not true, he said, that time healed all wounds. Not yet, anyway. He thought of loving memories of his wife, but they made him cry, not laugh, brought him heartache, not joy. It felt, he said, like having the wind knocked out of you, like having a headache so bad that you couldn't see straight, like having legs so wobbly you couldn't stand up. Life was like food that couldn't be tasted. And yet he continued on, each day seeming like a first, his wife's courage and support from family, friends and strangers having buoyed him. He came to associate himself with the tattered flag that had flown over the World Trade Center and later flew defiantly at Yankee Stadium during the World Series, then was movingly carried into the opening ceremonies at the Salt Lake City Olympics: Ripped apart, tattered, burned, torn, still flying proudly. It could be repaired, stitched together, but the scars would always remain. September 11 still seemed surreal to him. Sometimes, he awakened and felt that it was a bad dream. He waited for Lauren to call or walk through the door.

"Lauren's bravery has given me hope, all their bravery has given me hope," Jack Grandcolas said. "Her courage has given me courage. They gave the ultimate sacrifice. They were the ultimate patriots. They did the most democratic thing they could do. They gathered information, they did reconnaissance, they voted to do something. They were ordinary citizens thrown into a combat situation. No one was a general or a dictator. Their first thought was to be selfless. They knew 'There's a ninety-eight-percent chance we're not going to make it, but let's save others.' That's what Americans are about."

The family of Ziad Jarrah, the suspected hijacker pilot, continued to deny that he was a terrorist. The most troubling matter, said his uncle Jamal Jarrah, was that Ziad's passport was reported missing in Germany at the same time in 1999 as Mohamed Atta's. Perhaps someone else had been using his passport. "The question is, where's Ziad?" Jamal Jarrah asked. No one had heard from him since September 11. Perhaps some terrorist group had him killed, his uncle said.

Some of Ziad's relatives, however, began to shed their denial and to consider the possibility that he might have hijacked Flight 93.

"I can't say yes or no," said Walid Jarrah, who identified himself as a nineteen-year-old cousin. "I'm not sure."

Shortly after Christmas, Ryan Brown, a reservist, was activated in the Marine infantry.

On February 9, he began training at Camp Pendleton in San Diego, California. He was a soldier, and yet on September 11 he had been helpless to assist the woman he wanted to marry, Nicole Miller. They had taken separate flights home to the Bay Area. Hers crashed into a field in Pennsylvania, his was diverted to Toronto. He said he was eager to be activated and hoped that he would see duty in the war against terrorism. "I do want revenge," he said. "I will have a lot more purpose for it, if it comes to that." His life had been on hold since September, he said. "My hopes and goals and dreams all involved her," Ryan said. "It's hard when your dreams are taken away. She was my weak point. Anything that happened to her would have been the worst thing to happen to me."

Phil Bradshaw said his feelings toward noncitizens living in the United States began to harden. His wife, Sandy Bradshaw, was one of the flight attendants aboard Flight 93. His young daughter, Alexandria, awakened at night, screaming for her mother. "We should throw everybody out of the country that's not a U.S. citizen and make them prove they ought to get back in," Phil said. A captain for US Airways, he had become angry when he walked into a flight school at a local airport in Florida and encountered three Muslim men training to fly. "I wanted to say something, 'Where are you from?' It made me mad," he said. "They need to crack down on these flight schools and shut them down. I don't mean to put people out of business, but you can't be doing stuff like that."

Jennifer Price, who lost her mother, Jean Hoadley Peterson, and her stepfather, Donald Peterson, said she felt it was time for Americans to look outward, not inward. As the lone superpower, the United States should consider how its actions will affect other people in the world, she said, even if extremists like Osama bin Laden and his Al Qaeda network would not likely alter their views based on small political and cultural alterations made by this country.

"I always felt very strongly, and my parents would disagree, that the U.S. sometimes goes in with a weed-whacker and goes crazy," said Jennifer, who is house master at Lincoln-Sudbury High School in suburban Boston. "We need to think about that, about how our economic system, our culture, affects others. I hope as a nation we have learned that sometimes a gentler hand may go farther than one that disregards other cultures, their beliefs, their way of life. Shouldn't we have learned that back at Wounded Knee?"

Two days after his daughter, Deora Bodley, died aboard Flight 93, Derrill Bodley sat at the piano at his home in Stockton, California. He was a music professor at Sacramento City College. He had written songs before, and usually they did not come easily. This one seemed to emerge from his fingers already finished. "Steps to Peace," he called it. It was almost as if Deora wrote it for him, Derrill said. "It was as close as I could come," he said, "to having my daughter telling me, 'Don't worry, Dad, I'm okay. Just do the right thing.'"

What was the right thing to do?

Derrill Bodley wrestled with this in the abject days after September 11. At one point, stress overcame him and he checked himself into a hospital for a day. It was not serious, but he gave up caffeine. The meaning of everything changed the day his daughter died. At fifty-six, he had built a life to pass on to her — ideas, property, books. Now that would never happen. At the same time, he seemed to have a public license to do other things that could be shared and left behind.

Shortly before Christmas, he learned of a trip to Afghanistan being sponsored by Global Exchange, a human-rights group based in San Francisco. He did not want vengeance or retaliation. He wanted justice, but justice was a complicated issue, and he couldn't say for sure what it was. A trip to Afghanistan might help him learn something about the religious aspects of the terrorist attack against the United States.

Arriving for a four-day visit to Kabul in January, Derrill found a jarring place, the arid beauty of surrounding mountains and the archeology of violence: Dead tanks, mine fields, pavement gouged by bombs, fractured earthen homes, huge tracts of historical devastation, a timeline of rubbled destruction from the Soviet invasion in 1979 through the American reprisal bombing in 2001. He visited five families whose homes had been destroyed in the autumn bombing. Four of the families had lost loved ones. Derrill cried with a man named Abdul Basir, whose five-year-old daughter, Nazilla, had been crushed when an American bomb missed its target. He met children left with no parents and grandparents. He visited a woman who was still living in the skeleton of her crumbled house, now without her twenty-year-old son, the wage earner for the entire family. He visited an orphanage and buildings for displaced persons, where people huddled in concrete squares without electricity. Bread was the only food, and water was available in a tank several hundred yards away. He visited a school for street children that taught woodworking for boys, math for girls and wariness for anyone who would come across a land mine or a grenade or a cluster bomb. He brought music with him and played a song for girls who were making paper flowers. He handed out photographs of his daughter, Deora, in her high school graduation gown. Afghan girls were allowed back in school after the fall of the Taliban, and Derrill urged them to work hard in their studies as his daughter had worked hard in hers.

"What we were trying to do was point out that there were people in Afghanistan who were suffering the loss of innocent relatives, the same as I had lost my daughter," Derrill said.

Until September 11, he was not very familiar with the issues and politics of Afghanistan. He did not have many details about restrictive life there, the way women moved like ghosts, covered and diminished, the way offenders were strung like nets in the goals of the national soccer stadium. While in Afghanistan, he experienced a personal epiphany. He would help to rebuild this broken country, raising money, soliciting volunteers and donations. From his own pocket, he would give a portion of what he received as compensation for the death of his daughter. And he would challenge the American war effort, believing the United States was treating the symptom, not the cause, of terrorism. It will be impossible to provide adequate security in this country, he said, unless the government dug to the root causes of the mayhem of September 11 — alienation, poverty, egregious disparity between rich and poor, the hegemony of Western culture that overwhelmed and threatened the traditions of other cultures.

He distilled the problem to a kind of mantra: There is a lack of respect and love by all human beings for all human beings. There is a lack of peacefulness within each human being, which would lead to peace among all human beings. There is a lack of sharing equitably the resources of the world among all people, all life and the world itself.

"If I could help solve the problems in each of those areas for the rest of my life, I know I would be doing the right thing by my daughter," Derrill said. "I can't say, 'Bring her back by taking someone else's life.' The only thing I can do after something happens is to try to do better. To do what's right."

23

Wallace Miller stood on a mound above the crater at the crash site of Flight 93. It was the second week of December. The air was chill and the sky was dishwater gray. Roses and notes of remembrance had been left from recent visits by families of several passengers. The flowers rested on a hay bale atop the mound. The nearby crater had been filled in with dirt. A layer of topsoil would be added later. Scorched trees in the woods behind the crater had been felled and mulched. A sodden wind whipped the silence of the afternoon. Miller was the coroner of Somerset County, Pennsylvania. When the FBI pulled out two weeks after the crash, the site was turned over to his care. It was then declared a death scene, no longer a crime scene.

Six foot four inches tall, thin in the strict vegetarian manner of a man who allowed himself to eat shrimp only on Christmas Eve or on trips to New Orleans, Miller referred to himself archly as the hick coroner from

Somerset. In his four years as coroner, he had not encountered a death scene with more than two fatalities. Yet, there was a certain gravity about him that was evident even among high-ranking law enforcement officials. He had provided an articulate, compassionate presence from the first hours after the crash. While others seemed flustered in the tumult, he operated with a relaxed and gentlemanly but firm manner. He told reporters and reassured families that he considered the crash area to be hallowed ground, and that the human remains would be treated with the utmost dignity.

"I wanted to make sure everyone was respectful of the site," he said now, three months later. "I didn't want anyone to get the impression that the FBI was just out there to get the black box, or if they were, that somebody was thinking about the people and the survivors."

One hundred fifty FBI agents, walking shoulder to shoulder, crawling on their hands and knees, using handmade sifters of wood and wire screen, spent two weeks searching for evidence, retrieving airplane parts, collecting human remains. Bob Craig, coordinator of the evidence-gathering team and a thirty-year veteran of the bureau, made it a point not to read newspaper accounts of the cases he investigated. It was a defense mechanism to keep the grim work impersonal, to avoid the humanizing details of names and faces.

After the FBI completed its work on September 25, Miller and two hundred fifty firemen swept an area the size of fifty acres, searching for more remains. Climbers were brought in to carefully remove airplane parts and remains lodged in the coniferous trees south of the crater. Miller, who was forty-four, became a kind of spokesman and father-confessor for the families of the passengers and crew members. He provided them with information when they became frustrated by United Airlines or by law enforcement officials. He consoled them in their grief. He looked out for their interests when others wanted to profit from the crash, when proposals were made to build a permanent memorial. He took them to the floor of the crash site if they requested it. He participated in private memorials, taking part in a Buddhist ceremony with the family of Japanese student Toshiya Kuge, raising a glass of port in toast with the wife and best friend of Captain Jason Dahl.

"He treated that place like a neo-natal nursery," said Sandy Dahl, the wife of Captain Dahl.

Esther Heymann, the stepmother of Honor Elizabeth Wainio, said the families were lucky that Flight 93 crashed in Somerset County. Miller, she said, had gone the extra mile, had given the families a sense of empowerment in a situation over which they had little control.

"He took into his hands the lives of forty people and treated them as his own," said Deborah Borza, the mother of Deora Bodley.

Some of the relatives wanted to know in great detail about the remains that were discovered. Others did not. The plane had hit with a great violent force, one hundred fifty feet of jetliner ramming the ground at five hundred seventy-five miles an hour and telescoping thirty-five feet into the ground. Fragmentation had been immense. "Turn the picture of the second plane hitting the World Trade Center on its side, and, for all intents and purposes, the face of the building is the strip mine in Shanksville," said Craig of the FBI's evidence-gathering team. "Look at the fireball in the picture. That's what happened."

The collective weight of the forty-four people aboard the plane was seven thousand five hundred pounds, the coroner said. Only six hundred pounds of remains were recovered, hands and feet and fingers because they were bundled by tendons and ligaments, pieces of skin, joint tissue, bone fragments, a flap of a torso, a mask of a face, scattered teeth. Sixty percent of the recovered remains were unidentifiable. A dozen passengers and crew members were identified by fingerprints or dental records, the remaining twenty-six by matching DNA samples taken from hair brushes and toothbrushes, and blood provided by immediate relatives. DNA profiles for the four hijackers were also established, although they were not identified by name. The cause of death for each person was listed as fragmentation due to blunt-force trauma. The deaths of the seven crew members and thirty-three passengers were ruled as homicides, and the deaths of the four hijackers were ruled suicides.

"I never saw a drop of blood," Miller said. "Not even the first day."

On the morning of September 11, he had worked at his family funeral home in nearby Somerset, population six thousand five hundred, paying monthly bills. His father, Wilbur Miller, previously had served as county coroner for twenty years. Wallace was up for reelection in two months. A woman who cared for his mother told Wallace and his father that a plane had flown into the World Trade Center. They switched on the television and saw the second plane ram the south tower. Wallace turned to his father and said, "How would you like to be the coroner in New York City?"

He would know the feeling soon enough.

About ten-fifteen, a call came from a neighboring county. Other coroners would be available if he needed help with the plane crash. "What are you talking about?" Wallace asked. "A plane crash?"

Had a commuter plane gone down in Johnstown?

A jetliner, he was told.

"You shouldn't be kidding around," he told the secretary on the other end.

"I'm not kidding," she said. "There's a crash."

He tried to call 911 but could not get through. Finally, Miller got on the radio and reached the Somerset emergency center. "You better get out there right away," he was told.

He jumped in his truck, thinking, *If a jetliner went down out here, it can't be good.*

Three months later, Miller stood at the filled-in crater, looking north toward a scrap yard located on a bluff hundreds of feet away. Flight 93 had flown low over the scrap yard, traveling nearly three football fields per second, turtling on its back, and it had burrowed into the ground of this reclaimed mine. Both wings had gouged indentations in the dirt, the right wing digging a more sharply defined trough, perhaps indicating it hit first. A whole plane had burst into rivets and bundles of wire and shattered aluminum. The pungency of unburned jet fuel was so strong that it blistered the lips of investigators. "You couldn't take a step without stepping on some part of that aircraft," said Craig of the FBI.

Even now, two weeks before Christmas, rivets and wires littered the ground as if someone had spilled a plane-building kit. Ninety-five percent of the airplane had been recovered, the FBI said, but thousands of splintered pieces lay about in the field. Miller reached down and picked up a piece of the aluminum skin of the plane. "There were tons of this stuff," he said, pointing to a piece of honeycomb material that was evidently used for sound baffling. Sticks were planted in the ground where the crater had been, marking soil-core tests. A telephone pole, charred by the fireball, stood sentry near the crater, but hundreds of burned trees had been cut down and reduced to a pile of wood chips. Miller reached for a piece of what seemingly had been a seat back and was now just a strip of material, saying, "Think of the devastation. How could you get a piece that small of a seat?"

A crumpled part of the plane, the size of a football, was still visible in a pine tree south of the crater. The tree climbers had not collected everything. A leather pouch holding the credentials, driver's license and credit cards of Richard Guadagno, who had run the Humboldt Bay National Wildlife Refuge in northern California, had fallen from a hemlock pine in the rain and wind of late October. His badge had also been found in nearly perfect condition. Investigators always marveled at this kind of random preservation.

Miller and Dennis Dirkmaat, a forensic anthropologist from Mercyhurst College in Erie, Pennsylvania, had wanted to map the crash area in tight sixty-foot grids. The distribution patterns developed from such precise marking of airplane parts, remains and personal effects might have told them such things as exactly how the airplane struck the ground. Theoretically, by associating the location of particular remains with the location of parts of the airplane, they may have also gained some clues about which passengers had rushed the cockpit.

The FBI overruled them, instead dividing the site into five large sectors. It would be too time-consuming to mark tight grids, and would serve no real investigative purpose, the bureau decided. There was no mystery to solve about the crash. Everyone knew what happened with the plane.

"I can't conceive that anything we found would allow us to say that this person or that person was found near the front of the aircraft," said Craig, who later retired from the FBI. "We all agree that this was a collective act of heroism. Does that mean that a gray-haired, sixty-five-year-old grandmother in 17B was any less of a hero because she didn't charge the cockpit? Come on."

In retrospect, Miller said, even with tight gridding, it might have been impossible to determine who had rushed the cockpit, given the speed of the plane and the explosive, fragmenting nature of the impact. The remains of a number of passengers had been found in all five sectors, he said. In a way, Miller was relieved not to have the answers. It was his job to determine the cause of death, to identify and treat respectfully the remains, not to serve as an arbiter for heroism. This was not an Olympic contest, where some passengers deserved gold and others only silver and bronze.

"Even if we could say, 'These people were associated with the cockpit and these remains went into the hole,' I don't know if we would want to do that," Dirkmaat said. It would not be fair, he said, to imply, "My loved one went up front, so he's a hero, and anyone left in the back was a coward."

"Everybody should be considered the same there," he said.

A Dumpster left behind at the site was half-filled with the jetliner's brutal dismantling, bundles of wire, a piece of fuselage wedged into a tree limb as if hurled during a tornado, circuitry, a tiny wedge of what might have been a wing, a fire extinguisher device for an engine, paper instructions for using or purchasing a cell phone, thousands of broken parts tossed together with the chattering of dinner plates.

Conspiracy theorists continued to assert that the plane was shot down, but evidence indicated otherwise. The F-16 pilots scrambled over Washington said they were given no orders to fire on a civilian airliner, and that they knew nothing about Flight 93 until they had landed back at Langley Air Force Base. A plane, spotted by some witnesses as it circled the crash site, was identified by the FBI as a Falcon 20 corporate jet en route to Johnstown. The jet had been authorized to descend from thirty-seven thousand feet in an attempt to locate Flight 93. The only military plane in the area, the FBI said, was a C-130 cargo aircraft that was flying at twenty-four thousand feet, seventeen miles from the crash site.

Not a single piece of debris was found in the path the plane traveled before it crashed, said Craig of the FBI. If the plane was hit by a missile, or crippled by an explosion from a hijacker's bomb, it likely would have come apart. Parts of the plane, even parts of bodies, could have been expected to fall in open fields, in people's yards. Debris was found as far as eight miles from the crash of Flight 93, in a southeast direction, but this airborne material had traveled from the crater in the direction of the prevailing wind. No evidence of explosives was found, the FBI said. Numerous eyewitnesses reported the plane intact in its final moments. The fact that indentations from both wings could be seen on either side of the crater, along with a gouge from the inverted tail, was "proof positive" the airplane was intact when it crashed, Craig said.

An early news report indicated that a passenger had called from the bathroom of the plane to a 911 dispatcher in Westmoreland County, Pennsylvania, saying that the plane "was going down" and that he had heard an explosion and had seen white smoke coming from the plane. A male passenger, Edward Felt, did call from the bathroom of the plane, but never mentioned an explosion or puff of smoke, said John Shaw, the dispatcher who took the call. "Didn't happen," he said. Felt's wife, Sandra, who heard a tape of the call, corroborated Shaw's story.

"The plane was not shot down," said Wells Morrison, the deputy on-scene commander for the FBI. "It did not explode. It flew into the ground." If the plane had been hit with a missile, he said, "The debris field would have been much larger. If that plane had been shot down, no way that would have been kept a secret."

Wallace Miller, the coroner, said he also believed Flight 93 was not shot down "unless there is some new technology we don't know about." The Bush administration said the plane would have been shot down if it threatened Washington, Miller noted. So the administration likely would have admitted a missile attack if one had occurred, he believed.

"There would have to have been debris before here," Miller said, standing near the crater where Flight 93 had crashed. "And there would have to have been ten thousand FBI agents collecting all that stuff the first day so no one else would find it. This is hunting heaven out here. Small-game season was a month later. Hunters would have picked up one of these pieces and it would have been big news. All the debris was in the direction of the prevailing wind that day. The fuel didn't burn in a wider area. There were no bigger pieces found," as there were when TWA 800 crashed in New York in 1996, and when Pam Am 103 was brought down by terrorists in 1988 over Lockerbie, Scotland.

Prior to September 11, Miller's job had been much quieter. He handled two hundred fifty cases a year, most of them natural deaths, performing thirty-five to forty autopsies and coordinating about eighty-five funerals. There was plenty of time to help coach the freshman basketball team at Somerset High, where he had once played, to serve as public-address announcer for the high school games, to coach jumpers on the school track-and-field team. He did not much like flying. In fact, he feared it. Now he was handling forty-four airplane deaths at one time. He spent so many hours searching for remains, picking up airplane parts, that he found his eyes instinctively wandering down to the carpet even when he was at home.

Each morning, Miller said a prayer before he entered the crash area. He considered himself a transcendentalist, like Thoreau, and he had an interest in Eastern religions. "Move on," he told the souls of the passengers. "There's nothing left here. There are good things waiting on the other side. We all know that. Look for the loved ones you admire."

An area of about eight acres was fenced off to keep trespassers from entering the crash site. "I don't want to see any of this stuff for sale on eBay," Miller said. In late winter, he coordinated a gathering of Flight 93 families, who were longing for information about the crash, about relief funds, about federal compensation, about plans for a permanent memorial. After the spring thaw, Miller made another sweep through the crash site, searching for remains that had been overlooked in the fall.

He was something of a Civil War buff, and at the Gettysburg battlefield, he said he felt "the incoherence of history." At the crash site of Flight 93, Miller said he did not feel the same violence. Perhaps it was because he encountered so few remains. It was as if, he said again on this afternoon, the passengers had been let off somewhere else. In the days after the crash, Miller was often the last one to leave the site in the evening. On that first day, smoke was everywhere, and melting plastic kept falling from the trees, sizzling at his feet. Later, when he worked alone in the woods behind the crater, as he did on this day, the wind blowing through the pine trees, everything quiet but the distant thrum of the interstate, he said he felt tranquility, not turmoil. It was as if the resolve to take control of the plane had given some passengers a sense of peace, he said, an acknowledgment "that you're going to go, your place is ready, get it done, here we come."

He thought of the site as a cemetery and hoped it would be preserved as one.

"These were citizen soldiers," Miller said. "When can you think of, other than the Revolution or the Civil War or Pearl Harbor, where American citizens died defending their home ground? These people were not victims. They were soldiers. One of the FBI guys said to me once as we were walking down here, 'We're part of history. This is Ground Zero of World War III.' I guess he was right."

A day later, on December 11, the sky was as blue and clear as it had been on September 11. Visitors to a temporary memorial for Flight 93 stood quietly reading testimonials to courage and sacrifice that had been placed along a tall fence. The hillside was quiet but for the clanging of a flagpole. OUR PRAYERS ARE WITH YOU was painted on a piece of plywood adorned with one red-white-and-blue ribbon for each of the forty passengers and crew members. A Japanese flag had been left in honor of Toshiya Kuge. The sisters of LeRoy Homer Jr. had left a prayer card in his name. There was a photograph brought by the family of Tom Burnett. Ceramic angels, crosses and American flags decorated the memorial. Rain-streaked remembrances said that no one would forget the bravery and heroism, the purposeful uniting in the face of fear, the sacrificing of their own lives to protect the lives of others.

One of the missives left was a Native American prayer.

> *Do not stand at my grave and weep,*
> *I am not there, I do not sleep.*
> *I am a thousand winds that blow,*
> *I am the diamond glints on snow.*
> *I am the sunlight on ripened grain,*
> *I am the gentle autumn rain.*
> *When you awaken in the morning hush,*
> *I am the swift, uplifting rush*
> *Of quiet birds in circled flight.*
> *I am the stars that shine at night.*
> *Do not stand at my grave and cry,*
> *I am not there, I did not die.*

EPILOGUE

On April 18, 2002, about seventy family members gathered to hear the cockpit voice recorder from Flight 93 at a hotel in Princeton, New Jersey. The FBI initially declined to play the tape, saying it was too disturbing, and it was evidence that might be used in criminal prosecutions related to the attacks of September 11. Some families kept applying pressure, and the government relented, citing "the extraordinary nature of these events."

Federal prosecutors planned to introduce the tape in the fall of 2002 at the trial of Zacarias Moussaoui, a Frenchman accused of conspiring with Osama bin Laden and his Al Qaeda terrorist network and of being the intended twentieth hijacker on September 11. Moussaoui was jailed in Minnesota a month before the attacks, on an immigration charge. The government intended to seek the death penalty against him, in part by citing the impact that the tragedy of Flight 93 had on victims' families. Many agonized for days about whether they wanted to hear the voice recorder. Cathy Stefani, the mother of Nicole Miller, had never flown before. She took half a Valium upon boarding her cross-country flight from northern California. "My son cried, my husband was upset," she said, "but I felt I needed to go."

Sandra Felt, the wife of Ed Felt, wanted to hear the tape so that she would not be blindsided by a public airing during the trial. It would be stressful, sure, but nothing could match the horror of September 11, when she picked her two daughters up at school and told them that their father had been killed.

"I am here to honor my daughter's last moments and to be as close to her as I could be," said Derrill Bodley, the father of Deora Bodley.

Other family members chose not to hear the tape.

"I have enough grief and sadness every day," said Jack Grandcolas, the husband of Lauren Grandcolas. "I don't believe this audio will cheer me up or bring me closure. Quite the contrary, it could very well add to the horror of the image of that day, one I am constantly reminded of when hearing the date nine-eleven."

Before they could listen to the voice recorder, family members had to sign a waiver, agreeing to not sue the government over any issue regarding the airing of the tape. They were also forbidden from recording the tape, or from taking notes. Prosecutors later allowed note taking, but urged the families not to reveal the contents of the tape to reporters, saying it might compromise the prosecution of Moussaoui.

Security was tight in the hotel ballroom. Family members walked through a metal detector and placed cell phones, pagers and purses on a table, which was covered by a tarp to prevent any unauthorized recording of the tape. Headphones were provided, and a transcript of the voice recorder was projected onto a screen. Alice Hoglan, the mother of Mark Bingham, described the tape as "powerful, muffled, confused, violent." The noise of wind and alarms further muddled the sounds. Actions seemed disconnected, incoherent. Without a transcript, listeners said they would have been able to distinguish few words. Some later said that the tape raised more questions than it answered.

Yet, family members also heard David Novak, an assistant United States attorney and a lead prosecutor in the Moussaoui case, theorize that the passengers had advanced into the cockpit, using a food cart as a shield. Two government officials also said that Novak had expressed his theory to them. In the final minutes of the flight, the voice recorder picked up a desperate commotion, a feral struggle, rustling and scuffling, grunting, a groan, shouts in English and Arabic, the sound of crashing dishes and breaking glass. The crashing sounds could have come as passengers hurled plates and glasses, or as the dishes fell from a meal cart when the plane's wings began rocking, officials said. At nine fifty-eight, the final battle for control of the plane began. The passengers were coming, trying to get into the cockpit, the hijackers said, admonishing each other to hold the door. "In the cockpit, the cockpit," was shouted in English. A thumping sound could be heard. A male voice screamed, perhaps as one of the hijackers was overtaken. "Hold!" was screamed in English. To some, it sounded as if the passengers were saying this in unison. "Stop him," someone shouted. "Let's get them," one of the passengers yelled. "Cockpit!" was yelled again in English. If they didn't do this, one passenger said in garbled words, "We'll die."

The hijackers could be heard praying: "God is great." Desperate, one of the terrorists urged that the oxygen supply to the cabin be turned off. This would have had little or no effect on passengers below ten thousand feet, aviation officials said. One of the hijackers spoke about finishing off the flight, though the transcript suggested he could have been referring to the woman who had pleaded earlier for her life. Not yet, another terrorist cautioned.

Near the end of the tape, muted voices seemed to grow louder, closer. The scuffling continued. "I'm injured," someone said in English. More shouting: "roll it" and "pull it up" or "lift it up" or "turn up." A final rushing sound could be heard and, about three minutes after ten, the tape went silent. It is not known what the final shouts referred to. Families interpreted them as an effort to retake the controls from the hijackers or to stabilize the plane after overcoming the terrorists. Some thought they heard the voices of particular passengers, but the voices could not be positively identified. "I can't discuss evidence," said Novak, who declined to say anything about the voice recorder.

Many families were emotionally frayed after hearing the voice recorder. Preconceived ideas and the power of suggestion complicated the actual distressing sounds and words on the tape. "You are cueing into particular sounds," Sandra Felt said. "You don't know if it is fitting into a dream. The whole thing was so surreal. It bordered on the bizarre."

Daniel Belardinelli, the nephew of William Cashman, returned to his New Jersey home and drew a disturbing picture of United Flight 93. He sketched the plane in black and white and wrote the words of the hijackers, as he remembered them, in nail polish the color of blood: "This is your captain speaking. We have a bomb onboard and are returning to the airport to meet our demands. Everyone remain seated and be quiet and everything will be okay."

"I was so freaked out by the callousness of what they were saying and what had actually happened," said Belardinelli, an attorney and an artist. "He just killed someone and he was talking matter-of-factly, like, 'Can you get me a soda?'"

Elsa Strong, the sister of Linda Gronlund, said she felt a sense of calm in the corroboration that passengers had put up a gallant struggle. "Things like this become legend and you begin to wonder what's real and what isn't," Strong said. "It's nice to hear that confirmed."

Kenny Nacke, the brother of Lou Nacke and a police officer in Baltimore County, Maryland, was struck by the group effort and the resolve of shouted voices, which contained "no fear, all pure anger." "I don't think they thought they would lose," he said.

Phil Bradshaw, the husband of flight attendant Sandra Bradshaw and a US Airways captain, said it seemed clear to him that some passengers and perhaps crew members reached the cockpit. "A few more minutes and maybe things would have turned out different," he said. "They just didn't have enough altitude to mess around with what was going on. I believe they were trying to go more for the controls than taking out the hijackers. You could hear male voices so clearly. It seemed like they were trying to fight for control rather than fight for space. They just didn't have enough time."

The tape brought no closure to Alice Hoglan, nor did she want any. "I want to go to my death tormented by the events of September 11," she said. "I want the news of my son's death, and the deaths of nearly three thousand other people, to be a raw bit of news in my mind and have it drive me to act, and the commercial airline industry to act, to make sure it doesn't happen again."

Hamilton Peterson, whose father and stepmother, Donald A. Peterson and Jean Hoadley Peterson, were on Flight 93, spoke of the noble sadness of the voice recorder. It was bittersweet to hear the tape. The enormity of the tragedy was evident, yet he felt proud as well. "These were clearly people who were informed of the unthinkable, digested it and acted upon it in no time at all," he said. Their actions reminded him of the selfless heroism of Normandy, and sent a message about the vitality of the American spirit.

In the end, what happened remained more murky than clear. The details had to be confirmed by the character of the passengers and crew, beyond the validation of voices on a tape or words on a transcript. Even if they didn't reach the cockpit, or reached it too late to gain control of the plane, their bravery was not diminished. It is uncertain how far they got, but it is clear they got as far as they could. They set out that morning as businessmen and businesswomen, students, vacationers eagerly leaving the congested city for open spaces, a mourning stepfather going to retrieve the remains of his stepson. In the final desperate minutes, they were all trying to get home safely to their families. Their personal courage became a wider heroism. Their accomplishment lay in the bold effort. They were scared, but they did not let fear overwhelm them. They knew the odds were slim, but they retaliated with headlong valor and prevented the terrorists from reaching their target. At a time of grieving, confused, enraged vulnerability, when the United States appeared defenseless against an unfamiliar foe, the passengers and crew of Flight 93 provided the solace of defiance. They fought back, bringing a measure of victory to unthinkable defeat.

SOURCES

My primary sources for this book were personal interviews I conducted with family members, friends and coworkers of the passengers and crew, government and aviation officials, and eyewitnesses.

A number of ambitious journalistic efforts were made in the coverage of Flight 93 that I found helpful. Among them were a special section reported by Tom Gibb, Steve Karlinchak, Cindi Lash, Steve Levin, Dennis B. Roddy and Jonathan D. Silver in *The Pittsburgh Post-Gazette* on Oct. 28, 2001; an article by Karen Breslau, Eleanor Clift and Evan Thomas in the Dec. 3, 2001 issue of *Newsweek*; an article by Bryan Burrough in the December 2001 issue of *Vanity Fair*; a report by Brian Ross broadcast on ABC's *PrimeTime* on Nov. 15, 2001; the Oct. 10, 2001 broadcast of *The Fifth Estate*, anchored by Linden MacIntyre, on the Canadian Broadcasting Corporation; a report by Jane Pauley broadcast on NBC's *Dateline* on Oct. 2, 2001; and an article by Scott McCartney and

Susan Carey on Oct. 15, 2001 in *The Wall Street Journal.*

Newspapers such as the Ft. Lauderdale *Sun-Sentinel* and the *Palm Beach Post* also were helpful in their reporting of the activities of the hijacker Ziad Jarrah in South Florida. The foreign desks of *The New York Times, The Washington Post, The Los Angeles Times, The Boston Globe, The Vancouver Sun* and *The Sunday Times* of London also provided valuable insight into Jarrah's life in Germany and his native Lebanon.

Foreword: FBI Director Robert S. Mueller III's remarks about Flight 93 were made at a news conference on September 20, 2001. President Bush's remarks about sacrifice appeared in excerpts from an interview that appeared in *The Washington Post* on Feb. 3, 2002. Ed Figura's remarks about the Flight 93 passengers were told to the Associated Press on Oct. 11, 2001.

One: Interviews. Information concerning United's pre-flight preparations and instructions for hijackings came from interviews with pilots and flight attendants. The book *Airliners in Flight* by Nicholas A. Veronico and George Hall was also useful in detailing pre-flight activities. Technical information about jetliners is explained in an accessible way by Stanley Stewart in his book *Flying the*

Big Jets. Information regarding the Boeing 757 came from Boeing and United as well as from the book *A Field Guide to Airplanes of North America* by M. R. Montgomery and Gerald Foster. Bryan Burrough's article in the December 2001 issue of *Vanity Fair* magazine also was helpful in explaining preflight activities of the pilots, flight attendants and passengers.

Two: Interviews. A special section in *The Pittsburgh Post-Gazette*, published on Oct. 28, 2001, contained biographies of Flight 93's forty passengers and crew members, which I found very useful throughout the book, both in my reporting and in contacting family members.

Three: Interviews.

Four: Interviews. The pre-departure sequence was based on standard call-and-response conversations as provided by United pilots. The description of American Flight 11 being hijacked was reported by Matt Wald in *The New York Times* on Oct. 16, 2001. A translation of the hijackers' last-night preparation letter appeared in *The New York Times* on Sept. 29, 2001. The FBI's awareness that Osama bin Laden's terrorist network might attempt to use a hijacked plane on a suicide mission into a federal building was reported by Philip Shenon in *The New York Times* on May 18, 2002. On the same date, Bob Woodward and Dan Eggen reported in *The Washington Post* a warning made in 1999 that bin Laden's network might hijack a plane and fly it into the Pentagon, White House or CIA headquarters. President Bush's remarks regarding an Aug. 6, 2001 briefing were made on May 17, 2002. Argenbright's security missteps were reported by David Firestone in *The New York Times* on Nov. 10, 2001. An investigation into security loopholes at American airports was reported in *The Los Angeles Times* on Sept. 23, 2001 by Michael A. Hiltzik, David Williams, Alan C. Miller, Eric Malnic, Peter Pae, Ralph Frammolino and Russell Carollo.

Five: Interviews.

Six: Interviews. The message sent from United to Flight 93 was first reported by Matt Wald in *The New York Times* on Oct. 16, 2001. The air traffic control tape depicting the takeover of Flight 93 was obtained by Brian Ross of ABC News and broadcast on *PrimeTime* on Nov. 15, 2001.

Seven: Interviews. Remarks from the F-16 pilots scrambled from Langley Air Force Base and information on American air defense preparedness were first reported by

Kevin Sack of *The New York Times* on Nov. 15, 2001. Eulogies given by Brian Binn and Joe Maksimczyk, friends of LeRoy Homer Jr., were first reported by the *Courier Post* of Camden, New Jersey, on Sept. 29, 2001. The changes in altitude and speed on Flight 93 were tracked by Flight Explorer, a software firm that uses data provided by the Federal Aviation Administration. The path of Flight 93 can be viewed online at *www.aviation now.- com/media/images/news/wtc/ual93final.gif.*

Eight: Personal interviews.

An Al Qaeda training manual, found by the police in Manchester, England, was translated and placed on the Justice Department Web site at *www.usdoj.gov/ag/trainingmanual.htm.*

Information regarding Jarrah's activities in Florida and foreign travel were included in the indictment of Zacarias Moussaoui on Dec. 11, 2001. At a news conference, on Oct. 23, 2001, Attorney General John Ashcroft said that Ziad Jarrah had lived with Mohamed Atta in Hamburg. Later, government officials said that Jarrah had been a frequent visitor, according to an article by Doug Frantz in *The New York Times* on May 1, 2002. At a news conference on Dec. 11, 2001, Ashcroft said that all nineteen hijackers on September 11 had trained in Afghanistan.

That Ziad Jarrah and Mohamed Atta received Florida driver's licenses on May 2,

2001, was reported on Sept. 28, 2001, in the Ft. Lauderdale *Sun-Sentinel.*

Interviews with Michael Gotzmann and Thorsten Biermann were provided by Steven Erlanger, Berlin Bureau Chief of *The New York Times.*

The MSNBC interview with cleric Abdul Rahman al-Makhadi was shown on March 16, 2001.

Jarrah's journal entry was reported by *The Sunday Times* of London on Jan. 13, 2002 in an article by Stephen Grey and other reporters.

Interviews with Jarrah's landlady, Rosemarie Canel, and the cleric al-Makhadi were shown on the CBC on Oct. 10, 2001.

Jarrah's arrival in the United States on June 27, 2000, was first reported by Alfonso Chardy of *The Miami Herald* on Oct. 1, 2001.

Jarrah's dropping off a suit to be tailored was reported by the *Sun-Sentinel* on Oct. 7, 2001.

The dearth of information in Germany about Jarrah's connection to Atta was reported by Carol J. Williams of *The Los Angeles Times* on Oct. 23, 2001.

Reports about Jarrah's life in Lebanon were written by Elizabeth Neuffer of *The Boston Globe* on Sept. 25, 2001, and by Marina Jimenez of *The Vancouver Sun* on Sept. 28, 2001.

The anthrax connection to Ahmed Alhaznawi was first reported by William J. Broad and David Johnston in *The New York Times* on March 23, 2002.

The news conference by the FBI and the Maryland State Police, detailing the traffic stop of Ziad Jarrah, was held on Jan. 7, 2002.

The stop in Customs of Jarrah by officials in the United Arab Emirates was reported on Dec. 13, 2001, by John Crewdson of *The Chicago Tribune* and by the Associated Press.

The letter Jarrah wrote to his girlfriend before he boarded Flight 93 was first reported by the German magazine *Der Spiegel* on Nov. 17, 2001.

The Cleveland air traffic center tape was broadcast by ABC on Nov. 15, 2001.

Nine: Interviews. Deena Burnett played for me a copy of the 911 call she made to authorities to report that her husband Tom's flight had been hijacked. Tom's boss, Keith Grossman, provided a copy of the speech that Burnett made to Thoratec employees.

Ten: Interviews. Jack Grandcolas played for me a tape of the call that his wife Lauren made from Flight 93. Remarks by Jeff Trichon were made in a eulogy provided to me by the wife of Lou Nacke.

Eleven: Interviews. Alice Hoglan played for me a tape of the calls that she made to her son Mark Bingham's cell phone. His father, Jerry Bingham, also gave me permission to reprint his call to Mark's cell phone. Comments by Mark Wilhelm were written as a tribute on the Web site *www.markbingham.org.*

Twelve: Interviews.

Thirteen: Interviews.

Fourteen: Interviews.

Fifteen: Interviews. Remarks by Rick Vercellotti were made in a eulogy provided by Elizabeth Wainio's family.

Sixteen: Interviews. A tape of CeeCee Lyles's call to her husband from the plane was played for me by her mother.

Seventeen: Interviews. Remarks by Leonard Greene, Dan Merrick and Elie Hirschfeld were contained in eulogies provided to me by the family of Donald F. Greene. Remarks by Louis S. Lombardi were made in a eulogy provided to me by the family of Andrew Garcia.

Eighteen: Interviews. The discussions between President Bush and Vice President

Cheney regarding Flight 93 approaching Washington were reported by *The Washington Post* by Dan Balz and Bob Woodward on Jan. 27, 2002.

Nineteen: Interviews with eyewitnesses, as well as with government officials and family members who heard the voice recorder and read a transcript. Detail about the cockpit voice recorder was first reported in *Newsweek* on Dec. 3, 2001. Condoleezza Rice's remarks about Flight 93 were reported in a *Washington Post* story by Dan Balz and Bob Woodward on Jan. 27, 2002. *The Wall Street Journal*, in an article by Scott McCartney and Susan Carey, reported on Oct. 15, 2001 that a flight attendant called United to report that a hijacker was holding a knife on the crew.

Twenty: Interviews.

Twenty-one: Interviews. Remarks by Frances Borden were made in a eulogy provided to me by friends of Kristin White Gould. The conversation between Ramzi Yousef and an FBI agent were broadcast on NBC's *Dateline* on September 23, 2001.

Twenty-two: Interviews. An account of Derrill Bodley's trip to Afghanistan was first reported by Valerie Reitman in *The Los Angeles Times* on January 22, 2002.

Twenty-three: Interviews. A profile of Somerset County Coroner Wallace Miller, written by Sara Rimer, appeared in *The New York Times* on Sept. 22, 2001.

Epilogue: Information about the final minutes of Flight 93, captured on the cockpit voice recorder, was gathered primarily by recollections and notes of family members who heard the tape and saw a transcript. Some information was provided by government officials. Detail about the hijackers threatening to finish off the flight and to shut off the oxygen in the cabin was first reported in the Dec. 3, 2001, issue of *Newsweek*.

The employees of Thorndike Press hope you have enjoyed this Large Print book. All our Thorndike and Wheeler Large Print titles are designed for easy reading, and all our books are made to last. Other Thorndike Press Large Print books are available at your library, through selected bookstores, or directly from us.

For information about titles, please call:

(800) 223-1244

or visit our Web site at:

www.gale.com/thorndike
www.gale.com/wheeler

To share your comments, please write:

Publisher
Thorndike Press
295 Kennedy Memorial Drive
Waterville, ME   04901